D1526678

SPECTERS OF CONQUEST

SPECTERS OF CONQUEST

Indigenous Absence in Transatlantic Literatures

ADAM LIFSHEY

Fordham University Press

NEW YORK   2010

© 2010 Fordham University Press

Fordham University Press has no responsibility for the persistence or accuracy of URLs for external or third-party Internet websites referred to in this publication and does not guarantee that any content on such websites is, or will remain, accurate or appropriate.

Library of Congress Cataloging-in-Publication Data

Lifshey, Adam.
    Specters of conquest : indigenous absence in transatlantic literatures / Adam Lifshey.—1st ed.
        p.   cm. — (American literatures initiative)
    Includes bibliographical references and index.
    ISBN 978-0-8232-3238-3 (cloth : alk. paper)
    ISBN 978-0-8232-3240-6 (eBook : alk. paper)
        1. Literature—History and criticism—Theory, etc.   2. America—
In literature.   3. Western Hemisphere—In literature.   4. Comparative
literature—Theory, etc.   5. America—Civilization   I. Title.
PN441.L445   2010
809'.933587—dc22

                                                                2010008940

Printed in the United States of America

12 11 10   5 4 3 2 1

First edition

THE
AMERICAN
LITERATURES
INITIATIVE

A book in the American Literatures Initiative (ALI), a collaborative publishing project of NYU Press, Fordham University Press, Rutgers University Press, Temple University Press, and the University of Virginia Press. The Initiative is supported by The Andrew W. Mellon Foundation. For more information, please visit www.americanliteratures.org.

For my grandparents

Contents

Acknowledgments

Throughout the years of this project, I have been bolstered by support from many people. My thanks go out to all of them.

In the early stages, I was aided greatly by the advice of faculty and staff at the University of California, Berkeley, particularly José Rabasa and Gwen Kirkpatrick. I benefited as well from ongoing conversations with Dru Dougherty, José David Saldívar, Michael Iarocci, and Verónica López. I also was helped uniquely by Brian Stiegler and by many librarians on campus and elsewhere, most of whom I never knew personally but who kindly lent their time and expertise to my searches.

Of particular importance to the second chapter of this book was the time I spent studying K'iche' in Quetzaltenango (Xela), Guatemala, and living with a Mayan family. I would like to thank my K'iche' teachers there and all the friends I made in Xela. Wherever you are now, may you be on paths of peace and happiness. My own dreams remain where the quetzal flies.

While teaching at the University at Albany (SUNY), I gained much from discussions with colleagues such as Lotfi Sayahi, David Wills, and Branka Arsić. I thank David especially for his suggestion that I contact Fordham University Press about publishing the manuscript.

At Georgetown University, I have been fortunate to have supportive colleagues in the Department of Spanish and Portuguese and elsewhere.

Two chapters of this book have been published in earlier forms as articles. A version of Chapter 4 appeared as "'No podemos soñar': A Hispanophone African Literary Displacement of the Spanish-American War of 1898," *Hispanic Journal* 27, no. 1 (Spring 2006): 119–34. A version of Chapter 5 appeared as "Bordering the Subjunctive in Thomas Pynchon's *Mason & Dixon*," *Journal x* 9, no. 1 (Autumn 2004): 1–15. I appreciate the support that *Hispanic Journal* and *Journal x* thereby gave to my work.

I would like to thank Helen Tartar of Fordham University Press for placing my manuscript under review and for supporting it through publication. I appreciate as well the assistance of Thomas C. Lay, Tim Roberts, Katie Sweeney, and all others at the American Literatures Initiative and Fordham University Press who have guided me through this process. I thank, too, the reviewers who read the manuscript closely and recommended its publication. I am grateful for their generous commentary.

In my graduate studies and as a teacher, I have been aided at different moments by funding sources that have freed up time so that I could pursue this project. My thanks go out to all of them at Berkeley, Albany, and Georgetown. I am appreciative particularly of The Andrew W. Mellon Foundation for its grant to the American Literatures Initiative, under whose auspices this book is published.

During the itinerant process of constructing this book, I was assisted at diverse junctures by a broad range of individuals on library and administrative staffs, many of whom I never even met. All their work helped me greatly along the way and I thank them profoundly for it. I also thank all those fellow students and teachers who discussed the project with me informally in sundry corridors and cafés.

I thank, too, all my students who engaged themselves in the questions of this manuscript in disparate classrooms. You taught me much.

Although I finished the early version of this book before I was fortunate enough to have research assistants, I appreciate very much the work of those who did aid me directly or indirectly during subsequent revisions. My thanks therefore also go out to Ayako Urao, Christina Marzello, Scott Noble, Susanne Stover, Nina Gleiberman, Anne Micheau Calderón, and Ha Na Park. May all of your roads be good ones.

I would like to thank all those singer-songwriters whose work helped sustain me along the way, especially Bruce Springsteen, Bob Dylan, Leonard Cohen, and Neil Young. I would like to thank Hugo Arroyo and everyone at Los Cenzontles Mexican Arts Center for teaching me much more than the music I came to learn. And I would like to thank all those who ever listened to whatever folk music I have been able to offer the world in my own small way.

In the ups and downs of life, my family has always stood by me with love. This book reveals that. Thank you, Mom, Dad, Joanna, David, Katarina, Joshua, Elliot, and Sigmund, for everything.

In the last stages of revising this manuscript, I met my wife, Jennifer, twenty years after we graduated from high school together. Jen, thank you for your wonderful support and savvy editing of these pages. Your love and insight have made this project stronger. I feel most fortunate, Joan, Raymond, Kirby, Sue, Megan, Connor, and Pookie, to join you as family. Thank you for all your smiles and support.

This book is dedicated to my grandparents, real and symbolic. May they all rest in peace. Thank you, Mom-Mom, Pop-Pop, Cookie, Nanny, Papa, and Aunt Sylvia. I know you would be kvelling.

K'o nab'e uwujil, ojer tz'ib'am puch, xa k'u'tal chuwäch ilol re, b'isol re, nim upetik, utzijoxik puch.

—*POPOL WUJ* (EDITION OF THE ACADEMIA DE LAS LENGUAS MAYAS DE GUATEMALA, 1998)

Introduction

America was forged by an ongoing production of absence: the lives that disappeared, the societies and ecologies that vanished, the dynamics of disembodiment that were constituent of the Conquest in all its variegated forms. These disembodiments are haunting and transatlantic in nature. They are haunting because, from a position of absence, they contest all our foundational narratives of material environments and flesh-and-blood peoples. They are transatlantic because they emerge from five centuries of oceanic crossings and conflicts among Amerindians, Africans, and Europeans. All humanity today is a product of these wakes. All of us are inheritors of the Conquest. Whether conscious of it or not, we are all therefore haunted by its dead. This is to say that we are all, inescapably and tragically, Americans.

This book posits "America" as not a particular country or continent or hemisphere but as a reiterating foundational narrative in which a conqueror arrives at a shore determined to overwrite local versions of humanity, culture, ecology and landscape with inscriptions of his own design. This imposition of foreign textualities—with "textualities" a shorthand for the totality of verbal and nonverbal codes (and their implicit hierarchies) of any society—however dominant and complete it may appear, is never fully successful at the multiple exterminations both explicit and implicit in the conquering project. This is because even in the cases of the most thorough omnicides, the absences of the disappeared still linger in persisting ways. These absences are therefore present. And it is that apparent paradox that provides for an America whose Conquest is always partial and whose conquered are always contestatory.

The question is not whether indigenous peoples and cultures survive today, for of course they do. Nor is the question whether they resisted their obliteration through a wealth of strategies and tactics, for of course they did and do. This book instead examines how the disjunctions and ruptures that took place on the shores of the Atlantic upon the arrival of Europeans became insinuated as recurring and resistant absences in the texts of the conquistadors and their heirs. These absences are presences, again, precisely because they exist. They can take many forms: an indigene who abandons a village just before the conquerors arrive; a language that seemingly disappears as a translation seeks to overwrite it; a footprint in the sand that suggests a distant body of flesh and blood; a death that never is as finite or as permanent as might initially appear. There are as many variations of such absences as there are of presences. The latter, by virtue of their visibility, are what nearly always compel attention. Yet in the invisibilities of imperialism lie the most overlooked resistances to the Conquest. No power can suppress that which escapes it, however weak the exile may be. In a context of imposed foreign presence, the very suggestion of absence by the indigenous and colonized calls into question the completion of the conquering performance itself.

This book refers to the Conquest as a performance in order to highlight the iterative nature of the dynamics of absenting at hand, regardless of century or continent. The Conquest on its own terms, certainly, is not a single entity or act but a fluctuating, polyphonic, grotesque, and macabre experience of genocide and ecocide that began with the first voyage of Columbus and has continued, in forms only sometimes mitigated, through our present day. Each manifestation of the Conquest is characterized by different details of who is attempting to inscribe whom, and where and how that takes place, and under which terms. But each microcosmic America that appears is not so much an inscription as a re-inscription, which is to say a performance, one endlessly repeated, each staging a restaging, each production of presence a reproduction of absence. And though featured may be a particular cast, crew, backdrop, score, array of props, and arrangement of lights, there are also critical and diverse players who escape all the above to an uncircumscribed off-stage. The enactment of scripted presence in these performances of America is matched by a corollary enactment of unscripted absence. The Conquest is a show that always goes on, but also a show whose most compelling counter-narratives are often unperceived by its playwrights and their audiences.

Readers of Diana Taylor's *The Archive and the Repertoire*, a major recent contribution to performance studies in the Americas, may remark some overlapping terminology amid this emphasis on iteration, absence, and haunting in the hemisphere. Her argument that genealogies of performance can be identified and analyzed commences from the tensions between "the *archive* of supposedly enduring materials (i.e., texts, documents, buildings, bones) and the so-called ephemeral *repertoire* of embodied practice/knowledge (i.e., spoken language, dance, sports, ritual)."[1] Western scholars, notes Taylor, have focused historically on the archive and its matrices of written traditions and influences while relegating the repertoire as short-lived performances of one sort or another that, in their transience, do not constitute "an important system of knowing and transmitting knowledge."[2] Nonetheless, traditions of performances do exist and do endure and can be traced over time in their evolving iterations. Taylor proposes that a way to study the repertoire, and thereby reconfigure conventional understandings of the Americas, is by discerning a repetition of what she terms "scenarios." These are the stagings of certain dramatic scenes, such as that of Columbus arriving at the New World, planting a flag before gathered indigenous people, and proclaiming territorial ownership. Performances of this dramatic sequence have played out in many places and media since 1492. All scenarios are marked by "once-againness" but they are not necessarily mimetic.[3] On the contrary, writes Taylor, they "are formulaic structures that predispose certain outcomes and yet allow for reversal, parody, and change."[4] Her objective in *The Archive and the Repertoire* is to "make visible" the hitherto invisible transmissions of cultural memory through scenarios as "embodied," iterated, and adaptable performances.[5] A chief accomplishment of her work is its fostering of new potential cartographies for scholarship of the Americas that could bring to the surface unseen cultural and political interconnections of the Western hemisphere.

The present book pursues an objective that is complementary to Taylor's by registering the invisible and disembodied but paradoxically leaving them as such. The goal is not to incorporate the unincorporated but to examine the contestatory and diverse possibilities of their bodilessness in the first place. If a foreign narrator scripts bodies as present only in order to manifest their subjection, as with the indigenes in the flag-planting scenario, their roles, as Taylor observes, tend to be mute.[6] If those same bodies, however, voluntarily withdraw from the scenario—if they find a way to leave the stage on their own terms, refusing to stay in the blocking accorded them by a determined stage director—then a very different sort of performance at hand. There is a divergence between the conscripted silence of secondary characters visible to an audience and the unheard communications that the actors who play them may assert to each other in the wings, behind the backdrop, in the pathways behind the theater, on their roads home, wherever and whatever home may be for them. The present book does not attempt to capture those voices, merely to acknowledge their disembodied presence and thus the alternative stories they insinuate. Since the focus in this book will remain steadily on material from the archive rather than the repertoire, an ongoing implication is that the theatrics of absence can be perceived as reenacting even within the confines of written texts.

To the extent that such texts can be envisioned not as fixed arrangements of words composed by individual writers but as openly dynamic interactions among multiple co-authors, then scenarios may be perceived to unfurl in the perduring space of aging books as well as in the ephemeral time of live performance. This approach thereby diverges somewhat from Taylor's premise of oppositionality when she writes, "Scenarios, like narrative, grab the body and insert it into a frame. The body in the scenario, however, has space to maneuver because it is not scripted."[7] Taylor does grant repeatedly that an absolute binary distinction between the archive and the repertoire is impossible and that they often interact with each other, such as in flag-planting performances. Her principal aim, however, is to prove that the repertoire, underprivileged and overlooked by scholars as a source of cultural transmission, is marked by diverse communicative strengths and potential as much as the archive. This is true, but the archive itself is not as static as might seem. Read for openness and movement, bodies have "space to maneuver" in written texts, too. This is demonstrated by their movement out of foreign scriptings on their own terms, indeed, out of embodiment itself.

The presumption in the present book that America and the Conquest amount to an iterating foundational drama may seem to run the risk of homogenizing incongruent sources. Yet the premise is meant to be anything but restrictive, anything but simplifying. The principal texts to be examined are rarely if ever read together by scholars because of their discrete provenances in time and place. Shared implications, however, are revealed if the indigenous absentings of the diary of Columbus's first voyage across the Atlantic are studied alongside those in a Thomas Pynchon novel that, though written five centuries later, is likewise haunted by aboriginal ghosts born of an originary and westward mapping. New oceanic imaginaries are also made possible if Daniel Defoe's *Robinson Crusoe* is interpreted with the inaugural African novel in Spanish, Leoncio Evita's *When the Combes Fought*, as twin engagements with New World imperialism.[8] Evita's novel subverts the transatlantic project upheld in the Caribbean story of Defoe while transposing it onto facing continental shores. And within the tensions of another new New World order, indigenous peoples can be perceived as strategizing absence through their ambiguous bracketings of an ancient narrative, the *Popol Vuh*. These five source texts all present foundational stories of America because, however differently, they imagine its transatlantic commencement as inseparable from the production of absence as resistance. Reading them together does not deprive any of its individuality, does not foreclose their respective uniquenesses through overdetermination and resolution. The juxtapositions herein, rather than reducing inherent heterogeneity, open spaces for additional diversity by offering comparative frames beyond the conventional scaffoldings of disciplines and academic departments.

Some of these texts have centuries of criticism constructed around them. Others have received far less scholarship to date. Regardless, when all are abstracted from their customary coordinates and read with each other, certain elements stand out in common. These commonalities are absent and invisible while being present and visible. And in the pages ahead, inquiries into such paradoxes are meant to interrogate, not to prescribe or proscribe. Such irresolution befits the subject. Taylor, as part of her critical achievement, reveals a variety of performance genealogies of the Americas that previously were unrecognized. The textual concurrences of the present book, however, do not emerge from an untangling or unearthing of direct links and provable lines of inheritance. The effort is not to make visible the invisible but to meet the invisible as such. In contrast to Taylor's focus on how performances "participate in acts of transfer, transmitting memories and social identity," few lineages will be sought or established among the spectralities that will appear in the pages to come.[9] That does not make their interconnections any less real. The remapping of America, tantamount to the rereading of America, gains from the aggregate diversity of approaches and interpretations. None of them should be taken as exclusive. There are many ways to query absence beyond those in this book, many other ways to perceive hauntings, many other texts, infinite other texts, to select as foundational for one reason or another. This irreducible multiplicity is particularly just to specters.

Absent presences constitute hauntings, which is to say, manifestations of a ghostly sort. When a ghost appears, it forces a revisioning of its environment by indicating that something in the scene at hand has been unaccounted for, that something in a staging—a performance of reality as perceived and accepted—has been rendered absent. In other words, a ghost is an absence that compels its witnesses to question a present, current, and assumed narrative by revealing it to be other than complete. Yet supplying the absented thing simply by adding it to the staging and filling in the gap will not make a partial representation whole because the recognizing of a ghost forces a complete reframing of the scene in the first place. Such reframing of the *presence* of the scene is accompanied by a reframing of its *present* because the absent something always arises from the past. A spectral appearance automatically contests from a position of historicity a prevailing account of the state of things. Some way of seeing the world in the here and now has been revealed, by the ghost, to carry hidden within it some account left pending and repressed. That account is therefore at once an alternative narrative, an inheritance, and a demand: a haunting.

With regard to the demand, witnesses to a ghost find their understanding suddenly and irrevocably altered, not just because a new phenomenon has evinced itself but because that phenomenon exhorts to action. This action entails both recognition of the presence of the ghost and a subsequent attempt by the witnesses to meet the injunction that its pending account be satisfied. All hauntings, therefore, take place as quests for justice, the deliverance of which may be impossible but which is nonetheless an obligatory task set upon the witnesses. Consequently, those who see an apparition are never quite the same thereafter. The ghost forces its witnesses to question an accepted narrative and performance of how the world is and came to be, and to find it wanting, and, in the end, to do something about it. This holds true even if nothing can be done to make amends for a foundational wrong except to acknowledge and communicate that that wrong occurred in the first place.

Paradoxically, a ghost makes itself present to indicate its absence. It is scarcely discernible and yet entirely exigent. The revenant, via haunting, keeps coming back, keeps claiming presence in the present despite having (been) disappeared once upon a time. All ghosts are therefore iterative. And all, in their repeated appearances, alter qualitatively their witnesses forever. There are no unaffected or disinterested witnesses to a specter, for the latter, again, transforms the former by setting upon them a search. Spectral interrelations therefore develop among phenomena of absence and presence, loss and transformation, historical destruction and historical recollection, disappearance and the remembrance thereof, originary wrongs and quests to right them. At stake in all ghost stories are such quests. That is why Jacques Derrida, whose reading of *Hamlet* in *Specters of Marx* inspired much of the above discussion of haunting, speaks of scholarship about and with ghosts as a conjuration in the name of justice.[10] And Avery Gordon, writing after Derrida, concurs that "the ghost is alive, so to speak. We are in relation to it and it has designs on us such that we must reckon with it graciously, attempting to offer it a hospitable memory *out of a concern for justice*."[11] Justice, then, would involve welcoming back the spectral, accepting that there are unbalanced accounts that must be acknowledged. It may not be possible to set those accounts right, but at least their imbalance can be recognized as such. This is not akin to justice, yet it is not opposite it either. As heirs of the transatlantic holocaust that is America, as therefore Americans ourselves, it is the least we should ask ourselves to do.

Accepting apparitions is a labor undertaken by the living in the name of the dead. It is a duty for the inheritors of the disappeared, whose absent presences are myriad and unresolvable whether they are of the indigenous peoples whose near-annihilation Columbus inaugurated or of individuals and societies singled out by more recent endeavors of extermination. All alive on the planet today are heirs of the Conquest. And as heirs, like it or not, conscious of it or not, of the tragic consequences of five centuries and more, of the deaths of countless people and flora and fauna, all humankind is set the task of our inheritance. To not recognize this inheritance is to participate, however inadvertently and unwillingly, in its repression. In *The Columbian Exchange*, a landmark attempt to narrate the biocultural destructions pursuant to 1492, Alfred Crosby concludes that "Man kills faster than the pace of evolution: there has been no million years since Columbus for evolution to devise a replacement for the passenger pigeon. . . . The Columbian exchange has left us with not a richer but a more impoverished genetic pool. We, all of the life on this planet, are the less for Columbus, and the impoverishment will increase."[12] Crosby is right in his recognition of the apocalyptic results of the Conquest—many indigenous human and ecological worlds really did come to an end, whether through eradication or fundamental alteration—and particularly on target in the mournful use of the first person plural. We are all inheritors of the omnicide and we are all far the worse for it. We cannot resurrect the passenger pigeon nor, of course, the human dead bequeathed to us by Columbus and his successors. We must at least, however, mourn them and keep their memory alive. And we must learn from the dead what we can in hopes of forging a less fatal future. That endeavor may very well fail. The destructions of the Conquest proceed apace today. Yet even if we learn nothing from our ghosts, we do them only further injustice if we meet them not on their terms or, with the violence of ignorance, not at all.

None of the forthcoming arguments in this book is intended to ignore the very real indigenous peoples and ecologies that have continued to exist from 1492 through the present. The focus on aboriginal absent presences within both aboriginal and non-aboriginal texts is meant only to complement more traditional recognitions of indigenous presences on all Atlantic shores. Hopefully, the considerations of spectral resistance will add to the many studies of armed aboriginal responses to European invasions and of cultural expressions, both historical and ongoing, of indigenous peoples across the planet. Such expressions can be found in sculpted glyphs, web sites, codices, film, oral traditions, pictorial art, radio broadcasts, novels, live performances and other media. The absences annotated in this book aim to broaden the overall effort, in which many individuals have been involved, of imagining America in the sundry spirits of justice.

The strategy herein is to query the transatlantic via specific readings of texts that, though separated widely in time and place, together reveal a diversity of absences: silences, vanishings, emptied lands, banished bodies, exiled communities, suppressed languages, withdrawn literatures, and disappearances of innumerable sort. The central goal is to interrogate what happens when a character leaves the page or when a people does, or a tradition, or an ecosystem, or a document, or a matrix of codes of any type. Given the primacy of the individual but interlaced interpretations, this book juxtaposes the disparate in a spirit evocative of, but not reducible to, more familiar paths of spectral inquiry in which some readers might surmise themselves located. For example, although derivations of Derridean ideas inform much in this book, there is neither an attempt at an explicit exegesis of poststructuralist philosophies nor an invocation of the canonized terminologies of literary theory. A methodical development or concretization of aspects of deconstruction might satisfy certain expectations in certain quarters but also would enclose these pages within unnecessary walls. And there is something to be said for keeping informal and itinerant the idiosyncrasies inspired by the invisible. Derrida, hopefully, would have agreed.

This book also does not attempt to develop formally or apply systematically the Freudian concepts of the uncanny and of mourning and melancholia that may often seem relevant to readers already conversant with them. Many other scholarly texts expound well upon those ideas. Rehearsing them and their psychoanalytic sources here would entail a performance of little novelty. Again, the hope of this book is to foreground absences that remain relatively unacknowledged to date, not to (re)present corpora that long have been visible to those who desire to look. For such reasons, too, this book does not interact directly with most of the fine scholarship on specters that has grown out of Freud and surged particularly since Derrida's *Specters of Marx* appeared in French and then English in the 1990s. A basic keyword search in any research library database would yield many germane titles that, in their collectivity, attempt to build vocabularies and methodologies and subjects for a broad and open field of spectrology that does not currently exist in any institutionalized academic form. The bibliographic and topical choices of the present book constitute an effort not to repeat those studies but instead to enter stage left with the eccentricities proper to all ghosts: meandering where unexpected, hovering and pulling back, making rounds and exiting at an unforeseen point, and reemerging again somewhere else.

At a less abstruse level than the above, the pages ahead do not interrogate literary representations of ghosts. Texts, famous or otherwise, that feature phantoms as characters and explicitly haunted environments are not at all the focus. That is why there is no analysis of any number of renowned prose works that might be expected to appear in a study of ghosts and the Americas: *Beloved* by Toni Morrison, *The Woman Warrior* by Maxine Hong Kingston, *One Hundred Years of Solitude* by Gabriel García Márquez, *The House of the Spirits* by Isabel Allende, and so on.[13] Similarly not the subject is the Gothic as a genre overtly dedicated to the ghostly, nor the scholarship of the Gothic composed in response. This book instead is a conjuration of foundational fragments in disparate writers from many sides of the Atlantic that imply the transoceanic ghostings of five centuries and counting. Even the epilogue on Mary Shelley's *Frankenstein* does not concentrate on the novel as an exemplar of Gothic literature but on its subtler hauntings in a few particular and unexpectedly spectral passages.

There is nothing sacred in the choice or quantity of the texts studied in this book, nor in the splices surmised among them. Other literatures of America might have been interwoven differently and, as a result, yielded different senses of absent presences. Notwithstanding the genealogical structures anticipated of most analytical endeavors, the idiosyncratic nature of the selection of sources is a strength in that it wards off the charge of attempts at the programmatic and paradigmatic. America and the Atlantic ought to remain open texts, not closed ones. In contrast, the linearity of even innovative genealogies tends toward teleology. A case in point is *In the American Grain* by William Carlos Williams, a profoundly Atlanticized writer. Williams frequently is perceived as a New Jersey poet situated within an expansive national tradition extending from Walt Whitman beforehand through Allen Ginsberg afterward. In *In the American Grain*, he seeks to evoke the United States as not a nation-state so much as a narrative outcome of a polyphonous New World and the ocean crossings that led to it. Published in 1925, the text offers creative essays on such figures of Atlantic history as Hernán Cortés, Juan Ponce de León, Hernando de Soto, Samuel de Champlain, Cotton Mather, George Washington, Benjamin Franklin, John Paul Jones, Edgar Allan Poe, and Abraham Lincoln. The chapters merge colorful and dramatic prose by Williams with excerpts translated or paraphrased from the subjects' original documents. The section on Columbus, for example, interlaces Williams's own vibrant musings with passages revised from the writings of the explorer. Given this sinuous interplay of commentary and source, Williams's entwinings of conquistadors generally assigned to Latin American history alongside prominent figures from the early United States seems to suggest a lithe and fluid imagining of the Atlantic world.

Yet while *In the American Grain* deserves to be foregrounded in any listing of major transoceanic texts, its Atlantic vision is more fixed and programmatic than might initially appear. Williams's implicit genealogy takes a noticeably sharp turn northward when reaching postcolonial ages. Although he constructs a lineage that links his United States subjects to more southerly conquistadors, thereby transcending distinctions in language and national origin, Williams bypasses their modern Latin American counterparts. For instance, there is no chapter on Simón Bolívar, the great liberator of South America, to parallel that on George Washington, nor one on Benito Juárez, the great Mexican president, to match that on Abraham Lincoln, his contemporary. Columbus, Cortés, Ponce de León and de Soto turn out to be the transatlantic forefathers of a New World ultimately defined by the United States. Such is the sense of the titular "American" that prevails. Although a sequel to *In the American Grain* was planned to include a chapter on Pancho Villa, the Mexican revolutionary hero, the successor volume never came to be.[14] In short, *In the American Grain* at first appears to be radically idiosyncratic because its temporal and geographic and stylistic juxtapositions are unusual. But behind the vivid and seemingly eccentric selection of Atlantic subjects is a mostly unidirectional set of vectors that lead readers toward a decidedly national narrative. A more plural and open approach to the Atlantic would not so markedly coalesce into recognizable form and orientation.

The principal sources in the pages ahead conjoin into various asterisms more than a single constellation. This seems apt to absent presences. Asterisms, like ghosts, are textualized but uncodified, connected but unsanctioned, more subjective than subject. The diary of Columbus's first voyage remains in a very real sense the foundational text of the transatlantic itself. The *Popol Vuh* narrates the birth and life of an indigenous society but one that can no longer be envisioned outside the fact of European arrival. Daniel Defoe's *Robinson Crusoe* imagines a microcosmic America that emerges from his protagonist's twinned Atlantic voyages: Crusoe travels westward across the waves and then back eastward, only to be shipwrecked onto a ghosted island. Leoncio Evita's *When the Combes Fought* features a Spanish military man who arrives on African shores determined to colonize the locals with an imperial gusto that recently had failed him on the other side of the ocean. Thomas Pynchon's *Mason & Dixon* follows two Englishmen who journey via South Africa to the United States in order to write a line upon a supposedly uncharted land that they find to be not a blank slate after all. These five texts, though originating in differentiated centuries and dissimilar polities, all emanate from ongoing foundational moments that are inconceivable without the transatlantic. Literal and figurative movements across the ocean in every direction are inseparable from the America that comes into being as a result. Allegories and extended metaphors blend into each other: Europeans become Americans; Americans become Africans; Africans become Europeans. Islands turn into continents and vice versa; fiction turns into fact and vice versa as well. Nothing is left unopen to change. The patterns formed are protean yet persistent, the asterisms present or absent depending on what ocean-bound travelers allow themselves to see.

The malleability and metamorphoses of the transatlantic remain to be recognized in many manifestations, particularly those that involve southern oceanic regions. As a scholarly endeavor, contemporary transatlantic studies emerged in large part upon the proposal by Paul Gilroy that "cultural historians could take the Atlantic as one single, complex unit of analysis in their discussions of the modern world and use it to produce an explicitly transnational and intercultural perspective."[15] Writing in 1993, Gilroy worked to realize his own suggestion by analyzing African-American writers and singers whose cultural productions traveled across the ocean and, in western Europe and particularly Great Britain, underwent striking permutations and hybridizations. His emphasis on the transatlantic as a "pattern of movement, transformation, and relocation" has influenced a generation of scholars, mostly in English and American Studies departments, to strive beyond the national boundaries that delimit traditional university and publishing architectures.[16] Yet equally significant was his North Atlantic area of interest. Gilroy in *The Black Atlantic*, like later prominent transatlanticists such as Paul Giles in *Transatlantic Insurrections: British Culture and the Formation of American Literature, 1730–1860* of 2001 and *Virtual Americas: Transnational Fictions and the Transatlantic Imaginary* of 2002, did not engage with the transatlantic worlds of Latin America.

The work of specialists in the histories and literatures of the Spanish and Portuguese empires has long been innately transatlanticist due to its subject matter. The fundamental significance of Columbus's diary, after all, is that it is an oceanic production. To this day, however, there has been relatively little attempt to interact with the efforts in North Atlantic transatlantic studies that have developed and proliferated since Gilroy. In contrast to recent scholarship on the anglophone Atlantic, texts rarely emerge from Spanish departments that bill themselves as transatlantic. When they do, they tend to stay within Iberia and Latin America. A salient example is Julio Ortega's *Transatlantic Translations: Dialogues in Latin American Literature* of 2006, perhaps the most known such book. As its subtitle suggests, the study does not range broadly over the ocean so much as concentrate on texts from the southwestern Atlantic. Moreover, the authors whom Ortega highlights tend to be among the most esteemed Latin American writers of all time. A prominent scholar for decades, Ortega seems to see the transatlantic as primarily a way to read anew well-established texts from Latin America rather than to reimagine the Atlantic world per se. He thus opens his "Conclusions" by summarizing his project as follows: "We have reconstructed the cultural history of the Spanish American subject by looking at some of the mechanisms that confer its identity."[17] Ortega does reference western European writings throughout *Transatlantic Translations* but the most prominent of these is William Shakespeare's *The Tempest*, a drama whose influence on twentieth-century Latin American literature is so great that for all intents and purposes it has been a virtual part of that canon for over a hundred years anyway. With the studies by Gilroy and Ortega as prominent examples of scholarship of the anglophone and hispanophone transatlantic, the present book is unusual in its juxtapositions of an African novel in Spanish, an indigenous metanarrative in a Mayan language, novels from England and the United States, and a Genovese travelogue in Spanish. This geography of texts is somewhat off the maps established for the transatlantic by different surveyors to date. Consequently, the implicit lines of latitude and longitude may no longer seem familiar. Cartographies, however, can be compelling when they leave known coordinates behind. It is one way of finding new paths.

Scholars of the transatlantic often act on the premise that new analyses of ocean crossings will result in the revelation of previously invisible circulations of people, texts, concepts, and goods. Gilroy, for his part, famously "settled on the image of ships in motion across the spaces between Europe, America, Africa, and the Caribbean as a central organising symbol. . . . Ships immediately focus attention on the middle passage, on the various projects for redemptive return to an African homeland, on the circulation of ideas and activists as well as the movement of key cultural and political artifacts: tracts, books, gramophone records, and choirs."[18] His tracing of the hybridization of African American music in its transatlantic travels leads to his powerful arguments against uncomplicated essentialist or anti-essentialist notions of ethnic identity. Documenting and theorizing unrecognized transatlantic genealogies, however, is not the principal aim of the present study. On factual grounds, certainly, there is no reason to assume that Evita, author of the African novel, read *Robinson Crusoe* and sought to rewrite it in some fashion. And Defoe was unaware of the *Popol Vuh*, and so on.

There will be plenty of ships that crisscross the Atlantic in the following pages but this does not mean that unnoticed but directly intertwined itineraries will be unveiled. Many of the vessels to come travel routes unanticipated by their own sailors. Often, the ships do not reach intended destinations or establish the lines of contact that their navigators seek. Columbus finds himself in a somewhere that is not the Orient that he desires. Crusoe washes up onto an island unknown to him while trying to reach Africa from Brazil. Mason and Dixon, in Pynchon's novel, sail to Pennsylvania via South Africa and St. Helena and yet, in Mark Knopfler's song about Pynchon's novel, never quite land in the New World. Frankenstein's monster longs to voyage to South America but does so only in his dreams. The Maya who produced the *Popol Vuh* frame their story within the transatlantic though they themselves never leave Central America. Rigoberta Menchú, one of their descendants, departs from her K'iche' home for a resistance movement and, via routes unimaginable when she started, ends up as an interviewee in Paris and a Nobel Peace Prize winner in Oslo. A West African indigene in *When the Combes Fought* achieves a paradoxical regional victory over forces whose wakes wend all the way from Spain and the United States and Cuba. The transatlantic that appears in these texts emerges out of an oceanic world reducible to neither North nor South, minority or majority rhetorical spaces, travels easterly or westerly, inheritances invisible or otherwise.

Boundaries are artificial more often than not. Their significance thus lies primarily in their trespassing. Architectures, whether of institutions or canons or nations, are always a mix of assumption and assimilation. For such reasons, this book does not make sharp distinctions between history and literature, solid ground and fluid water, genealogies real and imagined, putative causalities and possible casuistries. Such a strategy elusive of limits, self-imposed or otherwise, is appropriate to the absent presences of the transatlantic. None of the texts under consideration will prove more or less bordered than any of the others, nor more or less veridical. At stake are imaginaries and the discourses that compose them, not categories and the truth claims that allegedly justify them. All these texts, as imaginaries, have an equal claim on the real. The Atlantic is not a space of division of one world from another. It is a space of trespass.

A taxonomy that distinguishes historical from fictional texts is not important here because evocations of America are at play, not truthful accounts, whatever those may be, should they be granted to exist. For the purposes of this study—and *it is but one possible study*, an open one, not meant to be exclusive or colonizing of other approaches—these texts, some of them quite old and famous, others relatively new and unstudied, form together an arrangement of absence and the Atlantic. Perhaps even the most familiar of these texts will appear differently when viewed in this way. That is often the advantage of unexpected configurations and cartographies. And hopefully, this study manifests a will to quest rather than conquest, if such a distinction can be made at all. As a gesture toward that hope, while all forthcoming citations in Spanish and French are approximated by English translations in order to maximize the accessibility of their contents, the single quote in an indigenous language—the epigraph in K'iche' that forms part of a larger citation in Chapter 2—is left untouched. Its illegibility to the reader and the author is haunting. In its unreadable metatextuality, it offers the argument that connects all the pages to come.

A reader who has Columbus in hand or the *Popol Vuh* or Defoe or Evita or Pynchon may not realize that the authors of America themselves lack a certain substance in a different sense: all these texts, one way or another, are produced by ghostwriters. All incorporate other scribes, thereby becoming, paradoxically, deincorporated. The diary of Columbus that survived to posterity is a version profoundly edited by the Dominican priest Bartolomé de las Casas, while Evita's novel was amended acutely by a Spanish colonizer, Carlos González Echegaray. The *Popol Vuh*, virtually inaccessible for assorted reasons in K'iche', its original language, is the product of centuries of unknown Mayan poets contributing to a multimedia tradition, as well as of known, nonindigenous translators and transcribers of the lone, extant, written version. The narrative of the life of Rigoberta Menchú—a successor text to the *Popol Vuh* in some senses— has been the subject of the most polemical case of contested authorship in Latin America in recent times. Its early editions in Spanish, in fact, name the anthropologist Elizabeth Burgos and not Menchú as the writer of the putative autobiography. Defoe and Pynchon appear to conform more closely to conventional ideas of the author as a solo figure who uniquely produces and controls a text, but they, too, in basing their protagonists on historical figures, lean on earlier accounts composed by voices distant and distinct from their own. Any approach to the ghostings of the literatures of America must seek to be as fluid as the absences inherent in these texts. They are the products of pens often unseen and of actors often invisible whose lines cannot always be identified.

In the principal sources of this book, different foundational parameters successively may seem to appear for a transatlantic imaginary. Yet the Conquest, whatever its variegated and asymmetrical manifestations, ultimately abstracts to the impositions of foreign narratives on local ones. These impositions never prove totalizing because the suppressed textualities hover all around the newly dominant ones, disrupting the latter's colonizing presence by indicating their grounding on the former's incomplete erasure. This disembodied shadowing of imperial embodiment is therefore inherently contestatory: it is absence as resistance. Since this resistance grows out of an original crime of intended but failed erasure, it constitutes a *ghostly* resistance, absent but present all the same and bound ever to return. The only way to exorcise this specter and complete the colonizing project would be to conjure it forth in an attempt to incarnate it and chain it down. Bodies can be inscribed into an imperial narrative but spirits cannot. To gather with ghosts without seeking to dispel them—to sit at a common table and acknowledge them, envision them, listen to them—would be a conjuration in the name of opening and sharing space, not conquering it. That is the hope of this endeavor.

Setting sail in this fashion amounts to a search for the transatlantic hauntings of America. Ultimately, there is no right or wrong answer as to whether a truly transatlantic literature exists or what its nature might be. There are only subjective, partial, qualified readings of an enormous array of texts. And yet amid all the currents that flow, there is something to be said for trying to bear witness to an America emergent among the disembodied presences in that elusive corpus. The hope is not to channel them but to be open to their channels. All humanity is bereft of the absented of the Conquest. Regardless of the many distinct historical trajectories in motion, we all sit aboard the same ship that is the common human past. We are all haunted by those who five centuries ago began becoming ghosts. The least that can be done is to leave them a seat at the table and, as the waves swell, listen to their stories from beyond.

A search for hauntings is always propelled by questions that the quest itself produces without end. Why do so many texts, for example, begin by invoking something that is not there? How many writers are engaged, one way or another, in channeling the dead? How many are mediums? How many are exorcists? Are not all writings works of mourning? But for whom? And in the name of what? How many absent worlds are there to conjure? How many promised lands? Are not all writings works of conjuration? Can an ocean be a conjuration? Is the Atlantic? Is America? Is absence? What kinds of apparitions walk upon water and through walls, slip over borders, cross frontiers? What phantoms still float unperceived? How many footprints in the sand are we yet to see? How many are we never to see? What specters may haunt us without our knowing it? Questions, like ghosts, gesture that we follow.

Chapter 1, "Columbus the Haunted," considers the absences present in the diary of the first voyage. The journal begins by invoking an Iberia disembodied in part by the historic expulsions of Moors and Jews in 1492. When Columbus traverses the ocean, he finds additional bodies disappearing before him, those of indigenes who remove themselves from his reach. The diary, though usually read as a story of European arrival, is here interpreted as one of aboriginal departure insofar as local people repeatedly leave the textualities into which Columbus attempts to inscribe them. By contrast, William Carlos Williams in *In the American Grain* edits the diary entry of October 12, 1492 in ways that emphasize the persistent presence of indigenes within the physical and narrative space of Columbus. Williams's censorship of the account of the inaugural transatlantic day allows almost no space for aboriginal absence and virtually none, therefore, for its accompanying potential for resistance.

Chapter 2, "Indigenous Atextualizations," focuses on how indigenous authors can be envisioned as strategizing absence within written descriptions of their own culture. The source texts here are the *Popol Vuh*, a Mayan narrative of the history of the K'iche' people, and the much later testimonial *I, Rigoberta Menchú: An Indian Woman in Guatemala*, which was likewise produced within the ongoing context of the Conquest.[19] The chapter offers close readings of various translations of the opening and closing moments of the *Popol Vuh* in which the anonymous authors haunt Spanish hegemony by framing their stories from an unarticulated or "atextualized" space. A similar strategy of silencing appears in Menchú's text.

Chapter 3, "Castaway Colonialism," gauges *Robinson Crusoe* as an account of invested transatlantic imperialism rather than as a tale of a man stranded in unfamiliar coordinates. Successive colonizing performances by Crusoe imply that his world is coherent to him only when populated by servant bodies. His need for indigenous attendants, which melds discrete presences from both sides of the Atlantic, is fundamentally challenged by the incorporeality of a footprint in the sand that shadows him. Daniel Defoe's narrative, like that of the Spanish explorer Álvar Núñez Cabeza de Vaca, concerns a transatlantic figure struggling to incorporate uncolonized bodies and thereby divest them of the resistances inherent in their absence.

Chapter 4, "Apparitions of Africa," reads Leoncio Evita's *When the Combes Fought* as an allegorical reenactment of the 1898 war between Spain and the United States that resituates the conflict to lands that now are part of the West African country of Equatorial Guinea. The plot offers a counterhistorical inversion of the war, in which this time the United States cedes power to Spain and in which a Spanish empire is won, not lost. This literary compensation for historical reality is haunted by indigenes who, from positions of apparent absence, successfully manipulate the characters from both imperial nations. The aboriginal revenants, by reappearing frequently in a text that seemingly celebrates empire, unnerve it until its climactic homage to Spain seems but a fantasy. The explicit and implicit assertions of local subjectivity amid the persistence of colonial power recall those in the essay "Our America" by the Cuban revolutionary José Martí, a historical contemporary of the characters in the novel.

Chapter 5, "Subjunctive America," examines Thomas Pynchon's novel *Mason & Dixon*, in which two British surveyors, as they gradually inscribe a line of latitude westward across North America, find themselves overwriting the traces of indigenous societies that disappear just prior to their arrival. The actions of Mason and Dixon are palimpsestic, for the line of latitude they are composing is a script in the earth that exists by virtue of a simultaneous suppression of the plural peoples and phenomena that Pynchon refers to collectively as "subjunctive America." To the extent this superinscription fails to altogether erase diverse indigenous textualities, the absences remain as presences that disjoint Mason and Dixon and their cartographic endeavor. Passages in Gabriel García Márquez's *Love in the Time of Cholera* that describe two river journeys taken many years apart likewise reveal an apparent erasure, this time of indigenous flora and fauna, that is belied in a ghostly way by the elusive and enduring narratives of the disappeared.

The Epilogue, "The Elision Fields," suggests that Mary Shelley's *Frankenstein* is the great American novel.

The Postscripts offer four final thoughts.

All translations in this book are original save for those credited otherwise. All translated passages are available in the endnotes. The page numbers given for the standard editions of Columbus and Cabeza de Vaca, both of which are bilingual, encompass both the Spanish and English texts.

Terms such as specter, ghost, apparition, and phantom are used more or less synonymously to avoid undue lexical repetition of any of them. From time to time, nonetheless, the phrasings may echo differently, with "specter" more evocative of Marx and Derrida, "apparition" more emphatic regarding an appearance per se, and so on. In other moments, the rationale is more stylistic in nature.

Metaphoric rather than literal images are often used for richer symbolic import. In this book, a ghost is never draped in a white sheet and a corpus always implies multiple meanings of body and text. Haunting is a multilayered phenomenon that cannot necessarily be reduced to other words. Spanish, in fact, has no verb that means "to haunt." The most commonly used in spectral situations is *perseguir*, which can signify "to pursue" and "to persecute," but a haunting surely is not resolvable to either English translation nor comprehensible as simply the two put together.

The temporal starting point of this book is 1492. America, whatever it is, commences in that year, for America can be defined as such only in the wake of the first transatlantic voyage whose effects proved perduring. This is not to say that the history of humans in the Western hemisphere begins in 1492, nor that the calendrics of the conquerors must always dictate chronological frameworks. It is also not to say that imperialism and colonization were inventions solely of Europeans. Inordinate amounts of violent territorial expansion and bloodshed and enslavement mark many intra-indigenous conflicts prior to any transatlantic contacts. These histories are the subject of many accomplished studies. Isolated from transoceanic phenomena, however, they are outside the purview of this book. Pre-Columbian voyages across the Atlantic by Leif Ericsson and others lie equally beyond this inquiry into the more influential legacy of 1492.

In the pages ahead, America, like a ghost, appears and disappears in places where it is not expected to be seen. Fictional and historical characters mingle, as do the living and the dead, as do centuries and genres and hopes. Whether this is sleight of hand or the weight of history is for the reader to decide. The main of this study begins on the western shores of Europe and ends on the western shores of Africa. It never once leaves America.

Perhaps more than any other poet, Walt Whitman has stood as the central imaginer of one type of "America" whose boundaries were inchoate and inclusive. His support of the 1846–48 war by the United States against Mexico and his verses proclaiming a nation destined for a vast, even hemispheric identity, attempt to incorporate much of the New World into a single body. Within that corpus, despite the democratic moves often associated with Whitman, not all disparate elements are joined equally. As Kirsten Silva Gruesz notes of "Our Old Feuillage"—a poem that imagines a United States of continental breadth—Whitman "insists on linking the southern, eastern, and western seas as compass points conceived and valued through their common and presumably subordinate relation to the exemplary North. The Latin race contributions thus have to do with the reunification of the divided continents of the hemisphere into a single nation."[20] This fusion of discrete territories and peoples of the New World reveals an inclusionary vision of an America marked not by egalitarian and enduring relationships among the included but by the subsumation of some group identities to a dominant one. Yet Whitman's attempt at incorporating those who exist beyond boundaries cannot take place even on asymmetrical terms if a phenomenon of absenting makes such bodily convocation impossible. In such a case, absence constitutes a particular and powerful oppositionality.

For example, in "Starting from Paumanok," a paean to the United States' expansive present and expanding future, Whitman writes,

> On my way a moment I pause,
> Here for you! and here for America!
> Still the present I raise aloft, still the future of the States I harbinge glad and sublime,
> And for the past I pronounce what the air holds of the red aborigines.
>
> The red aborigines,
> Leaving natural breaths, sounds of rain and winds, calls as of birds and animals in the woods, syllabled to us for names,
> Okonee, Koosa, Ottawa, Monongahela, Sauk, Natchez, Chatta-hoochee, Kaqueta, Oronoco
> Wabash, Miami, Saginaw, Chippewa, Oshkosh, Walla-Walla,
> Leaving such to the States they melt, they depart, charging the water and the land with names.[21]

In this canto, Whitman pauses in time and space to recall those societies ostensibly disappearing before the advancement of the United States. Notwithstanding his salutation of this manifest destiny, he remains conscious that indigenous absences yet retain a certain presence: "what the air holds of the red aborigines." His cataloguing of allegedly bygone peoples is meant to confirm the success of the colonial performance that is westward expansion. Still, his very evocation of those peoples shows that the performance is not totalizing. Though the indigenes may "melt" and "depart," they remain present and potent: their stories are not erased in full. Their "charging the water and the land with names" also charges the water and the land with deincarnated alterities, implicit counter-histories and counter-narratives that offer a textual affront to complete imperial overwriting. The incanted indigenous names form a dissonant and contrapuntal collectivity to Whitman's hemispheric hymn.

The absent presence of indigenes in "Starting from Paumanok" is spectral because it is a disembodiment that haunts the forces that pretend to conjure it away. And this transformation of the aboriginal into the ghostly is not necessarily as passive as Whitman implies. It does not take place only on the terms of the conquistadors. Confronted with imperial scripts, indigenes become ghostwriters of their own conditions.

Through their enduring and contestatory absences, they act as coauthors with all those who seek to insert them into foreign texts and fail. When absence cannot be converted into presence, when absence cannot be controlled via incarnation, spectral challenges to colonizing narratives abound. This happens far more often than is perceived and in far more diverse fashions and moments. Even the barest traces of such author-ship—aboriginal footprints in the sands—imply anteriority, autonomy, and persistent power. And the absent presence of the suggested body is, by its nature, resistance. This is America; this, the ongoing dynamics of the transatlantic.

1 / Columbus the Haunted: The Diary of the First Voyage and William Carlos Williams's "The Discovery of the Indies"

The diary of the first transatlantic voyage by Columbus is the inaugural ghost story of America. Initial word of his experiences circulated in Europe primarily via his February 1493 letter to Luis de Santangel, which appeared in various Latin and vernacular editions by the end of the following year. Since the nineteenth century, however, the diary has been the most widely read and referenced account of the events of the 1492–93 crossing. It has been canonized despite the issues of unreliability that result in part from the changes introduced by its editor from early colonial times, the Dominican priest Bartolomé de las Casas. The version by Las Casas, produced some four decades or more after Columbus wrote the original diary, is the basis of all modern editions. The manuscript by Columbus and a contemporary copy did not survive into posterity. The Las Casas document itself was lost until the end of the eighteenth century and remained unpublished until 1825.[1] It alternates between Columbus's first-person narrative in allegedly verbatim citations and Las Casas's third-person paraphrasings of the explorer's entries. Given the composite nature of the extant text, Peter Hulme characterizes it as but "a transcription of an abstract of a copy of a lost original."[2] Margaret Zamora adds that it is "impossible to determine with absolute certainty which portions of these texts are Columbus's 'very words,' . . . the very signature 'Columbus' must be seen as an aggregate, a corporate author as it were."[3] Yet despite the opacity of authorship and sundry other problematics, the diary stands as the seminal representation of the transatlantic in its paradoxically reiterating foundational moment.

Traditionally, the journal is read as an account of arrival. First, the three ships led by Columbus sail westward from Iberia and eventually encounter a series of islands in an uncharted space. There they meet indigenous peoples and explore and survey the terrains. Then they return home to report on the lands they have found. Regardless of how Columbus is portrayed in this narrative sequence (as conqueror, saint, genius, liar, hero, antihero, etc.), its fundamental tale of his becoming-present is almost always retained. In other words, the analytical approach tends to concentrate on how Columbus arrived at the unfamiliar archipelagos, what he saw and perceived there, and what he did there: in effect, how he made himself present. But his diary can be read also as a narration of indigenous people who become absent. The key moments are not only those in which flags are brought forth and conquests proclaimed. There are equally important disappearances from the storyline, episodes of vanishing from imperial textualities into uncircumscribed otherworlds.

Any sustained consideration of such absentings must question why they happen, how they function, and what their relationship is to Columbus's many inscriptions. Modern scholars have labored to complement Columbus's account of his first voyage by searching out indigenous people's experiences and viewpoints during the initial encounters. The task is challenging, in part due to the lack of aboriginal records from those inaugural months of 1492 and 1493. Yet there are ways of interpreting imperial texts for the very indigenous counter-narratives they seek to overwrite. Such resistances can include the performance of absence. Columbus's diary, read in this manner, depicts a constant struggle between colonizing inscription and aboriginal withdrawal from the same. It does not offer only a narrative of arrival, presence, and departure, nor a story crafted only in a conqueror's voice. And those who disappear in the diary haunt not only Columbus's particular voyage but also the transatlantic America that was created in its wake.

The first absence in the diary, however, is of Moors and not indigenes. Successive Moorish societies ruled over territories in what today is Spain for well over seven hundred years. This epoch ended with the fall of the realm of Granada in 1492. Columbus hails the victory of King Ferdinand and Queen Isabella of Spain in the prologue to his journal as follows:

> This present year of 1492, after Your Highnesses had brought to an end the war with the Moors who ruled in Europe and had concluded the war in the very great city of Granada . . . I saw the Moorish King come out to the gates of the city and kiss the Royal Hands of

> Your Highnesses . . . you thought of sending me, Christóbal Colón [Christopher Columbus], to the said regions of India to see the said princes and the peoples and the lands and the characteristics of the lands and of everything.[4]

This announcement of the ejection of the Moorish king from power and, by symbolic extension, of an autonomous Moorish presence in Spain that had lasted for centuries, is the frame of Columbus's journal and thus of his whole enterprise, textual and imperial alike. The Moorish absence initiates the Columbian presence. The import of this initiation is as much metaphoric as literal, for individual Moors continued to live in Spain, or at least bore traces of their Spanish heritage, long after the fall of the kingdom of Granada. In fact, Xury, a character in *Robinson Crusoe*, a novel written more than two centuries later, is of Moorish-Spanish descent. Nonetheless, the resonance of the prologue to the diary is clear: the disappearance of Moorish rule from Spain is replaced by the appearance of Columbus as a national standard-bearer.

Subsequently in the opening passage, Columbus advances a similar apposition when he links the expulsion of the Jews from Spain, also in 1492, with his quest across the waters: "after having expelled all the Jews from all your Kingdoms and Dominions, in the same month of January Your Highnesses commanded me to go, with a suitable fleet, to the said regions of India."[5] Here again are absence and presence juxtaposed. Iberia is emptied metaphorically and to a significant extent literally of its Jews as well as its Moors, while Columbus writes as the witness of this past and the performer of its future. Many Jews remained in Spain after 1492, as did many Moors. The persistence of the Inquisition, paired with the continuing fervors over blood purity, testifies partially to that. The power of Columbus's rhetoric therefore resides not in its factual accuracy ("all the Jews" did not leave Spain in 1492) but in its highlighting of absence at the very commencement of his journal. All narratives begin within frames, if only by virtue of all texts starting somewhere, and even when those frames seemingly disappear, they most surely have not. They are, after all, the frames of the text ahead and so condition its parameters, no matter whether they are explicitly referenced again. On the first page of the foundational text of America, Moors and Jews vanish. They do not return to the text as themselves but rather in sublimated or, viewed otherwise, ectoplasmic forms. They provide a ghostly structure for the indigenous disappearances to come.

As Zamora observes, the opening by Columbus acquires a "metatextual role as reader's guide and interpretive paradigm for the *Diario*."[6] Neither Moors nor Jews are featured as subjects again in the rest of the diary, and yet their absence from it and from Spain remains constantly palpable. For example, when Columbus later writes from the Caribbean, "And I say that Your Highnesses ought not to consent that any foreigner set foot or trade here except Catholic Christians, since the beginning and end of the enterprise was the increase and glory of the Christian Religion," he is effectively exorcising once again the Moors and Jews who were conjured out of Spain at the foundation of his narrative.[7] He invokes their invisible presence in order to dispel them anew. Yet the decision to channel their spirits in this way suggests that he has never put those ghosts entirely behind him. He does not feel free of their shadows. Their absences haunt him still, else he would not call them forth anew in an attempt to demonstrate his ongoing control over them.

The qualities and quantity of the numerous absences in the diary are compelling. The New World is often not so much coming into being before Columbus as vanishing before he can get there. Read this way, the diary is notable more for what slips away from his ken than for what emerges into it. In this sense, the primary issue concerns not what and how Columbus perceives (e.g., with what prejudices or degrees of comprehension) but all those who withdraw themselves from his perception in the first place. *Indigenous individuals are constantly leaving the textualities into which he is attempting to write them.* This pattern commences just a few days after Columbus initially steps onto the western shores of the Atlantic and declares them his. In recounting the events of the inaugural day of the transatlantic, October 12, 1492, Columbus notes that he plans to capture six indigenes and take them to the king and queen of Spain.[8] By October 14 he has realized this plan by seizing seven individuals from an island he dubs San Salvador and putting them in his flotilla.[9] Almost immediately, however, he experiences the first of many indigenous removals from his intended script of conquest:

> a large dugout was alongside the caravel *Niña*. And one of the men from the island of San Salvador who was in the *Niña* threw himself into the sea and went away in the dugout. And the night before, at midnight, the other man had thrown himself into the sea and fled. Men of my company went after the dugout, which fled [so speedily] that there was never ship's launch that could overtake it even if we had a big head start. However, the dugout made land, the natives

left the dugout, and some of the men of my company went ashore after them; and they all fled like chickens.[10]

Columbus's master pen has suddenly and unexpectedly been inverted. An eraser has rubbed out the latest line. A contestatory authorial hand has inserted itself into this narrative in that the "San Salvador" men have successfully withdrawn themselves from the storyline composed by Columbus. The indigenes have rendered themselves invisible to the explorer and to his unfolding scripting of his voyage. This becoming-absent, though seen as unmanly by Columbus ("all fled like chickens"), is actually a mark of resistance. At least one of the escapes was conspiratorial, involving as it did a dugout brought to the *Niña* by indigenous sailors. They worked in concert with at least one of the kidnapped men so that he could leave the role that Columbus had assigned him.

The journal is ambiguous on whether there were one or two escapes by indigenes from San Salvador, though the latter seems probable. For syntactical clarity and uniformity, this chapter will assume that the initial description is correct in referring to two flights. In any case, the importance lies not in the number of men or escapes but in this inaugural acknowledgment of indigenous disappearance per se. The narrative of conquest that Columbus intends to develop involves his capturing of locals as part of its plot. The individuals who escape him, however, provide a plot twist on their own terms. Rather than serve as extras in a dramatic sequence directed by someone else, they extemporize as leading actors in their own script. Suddenly, there are two authorial forces at work in the diary, pitted against each other and productive of opposing renditions of the transatlantic encounter. The diary becomes a dynamic space in which the visible voiceover by Columbus is disputed by the invisible and inaudible communications among the indigenes in the dugout and the island locales where they seek refuge.

As the foreign crew returns to the *Niña* from the unsuccessful attempt at recapturing the man who escaped in the dugout, "from another cape came another small dugout with one man who came to trade a ball of cotton; and some sailors jumped into the sea because the man did not want to enter the caravel and they laid hold of him."[11] The sailors, in effect, attempt to regain control of the drama by substituting a new player for those who unexpectedly have left the stage. Yet Columbus gives him some glass beads and other presents and notes, "I ordered his dugout, which I also had in the ship's launch, returned to him and sent him to land. And then I set sail to go to the other large island that I had in view to the west."[12] After the flight of two men, the decision to not imprison an available third indigene seems surprising. Columbus justifies his action with the explanation that he hopes to ingratiate himself with the local population for the sake of subsequent voyagers from Spain.[13] This rationale makes little sense, however, given that desires for future warm receptions did not enter into his decision to seize the seven indigenes from San Salvador in the first place. Moreover, after deciding not to take prisoner the man who came to trade the ball of cotton, Columbus prepares to sail onward to "the other large island." He does not sustain any attempt to curry further favor with the people on the nearby island to which the escapees have fled and where, presumably, they are spreading unfavorable news about the foreigners who had kidnapped them.

Columbus does not compensate for the disappearance of two prisoners although a third body is available for abduction. As a transaction of scriptural and spectral economy, the substitution would have made sense. An incorporation would have been exchanged for a deincorporation. Yet scripting the third indigene to assume the role of the first two also sets up the possibility of a reiteration of flight. In the event of another escape, those whom Columbus seeks to inscribe in a unilateral narration of conquest would be responding again with counter-narrations composed of their own invisible ink. Columbus cannot risk that. Unsettled by the inaugural absentings of the San Salvador indigenes, he tries to discredit them by presenting gifts to the third man so that he would conclude "that we were good people and that the other man [i.e., presumably, the man who escaped in the dugout] who had fled had done us some harm."[14] The gift-giving can be read as an effort to propitiate a revenant in the hope it will not return, which is to say in the hope that it will not go away again. Columbus is satisfied that he has righted his ship here through the lie that the escaped indigene(s) had done him "harm." The interruption in his imperial plottings, however, remains potent in its uncontrollable immateriality. The moment the replacement indigene is bribed, Columbus decides to "set sail," as if to escape the escapees and the contestations to his presence that their disappearances imply. The space of the indigenes who have vanished from his script is now haunted, so Columbus turns his eyes quickly to another island. Unlike the Moors and Jews he invokes in the prologue, the indigenes who leave his narration do so of their own volition and so Columbus, perturbed by the improvisations of his expected extras, tries to turn the page and move on. Ultimately, this cannot be. He is no longer the lone author of his own pages. And those who are haunted can never truly move on.

The escapes recorded in the diary entry of October 15 are only the first occasions in which indigenous people withdraw from Columbus. As he wends through the Caribbean, although many individuals appear before him to greet and parley, many disappear before him, too. There is a constant outflow as well as inflow of aboriginal presences. The latter, with the scenes of boat landings and petty commerce, receive most scholarly and popular attention. Yet the traces of absenting locals in the diary are abundant and align within three subsets: (1) escapes from capture, (2) flights before the foreigners arrive at particular homes and villages, and (3) retreats after unsuccessful military showdowns. The second type of absence is the most numerous and constitutes the bulk of the disappearances in the middle of the diary. The first such event is recorded on October 21, when Columbus notes, "after having eaten I went ashore, where here there was no other settlement than one house. In it I found no one, for I believe that they had fled with fear, because in it was all their household gear."[15] Fewer than ten days after stepping on dry land and claiming its resources and people for Spain and Christianity, and less than a week after the escapes by indigenous captives in response to such inscription, Columbus is confronted by the first haunted house of America. Its inhabitants do not wait to be captured by his quill. They decide to disappear before it.

Columbus prohibits his men from pillaging the house.[16] The reason is surely the same as when he resisted their attempt to substitute the escaped prisoners with a replacement aboriginal body: provoking ghosts can only lead to more hauntings. Columbus realizes that he has little choice but to live with the absences of the house for now. Since his endeavor opens in a Spain replete with intended erasures, those of its Moorish and Jewish narratives, Columbus is experienced with palimpsestic phenomena and believes that he can script them in a controlled fashion. This explains why he accepts with relative aplomb the initial disappearances of indigenes before him, both those of the San Salvador men whom he kidnapped and those of the abandoned house. But here reemerge the spectral tensions in his diary: Columbus aims to author solely his voyage and yet he does not. As these absentings amount en masse to successive and substantive resistances to his own presence, the ghostings will unnerve him profoundly. That is when Columbus will advise that his men take up arms against the very aboriginal apparitions he constantly describes as having none.

The flights of island inhabitants mount. Later on October 21, writes Columbus, "we went to a nearby village, half a league from the place where I am anchored; and the people of it, when they heard us, took to flight and left the houses and hid their clothes and what they had in the bush."[17] On October 28, according to one of the many passages that Las Casas edited and put into the third person, Columbus "went ashore and reached two houses which he thought belonged to fisherman who had fled in fear."[18] On October 29, when the foreigners approached another indigenous locality, "All the men and women and children fled from them, abandoning the houses with everything that they had."[19] On November 1, Columbus sent his men ashore and "they found that all the people had fled."[20] As the weeks pass, these accumulated disappearances form a catalog of deliberately vanishing presences. On November 15, "There were a few people and they fled."[21] On November 17, the inaugural indigenous escapes reiterate when "of the six youths that he took captive at the *Río de Mares* and ordered to go in the caravel *Niña*, the two eldest fled."[22] On November 28, the sailors "found large settlements and the houses empty because everyone had fled."[24] On November 29, "Some of the Christians went as far as another nearby settlement to the northwest and found nothing and no one in the houses."[25] On November 30, "They reached many houses and found nothing and nobody, for all had fled. They saw four youths who were digging in their plots of land. As soon as they saw the Christians they took to flight, and the Christians could not catch them."[26]

These iterations take on the rhythm of an incantation, gathering an uncanny strength that dislodges Columbus's presumption of authorship and authority. The continual absentings by indigenes imply that he is neither the only playwright of this drama nor the only stage director of this theater. In *The Archive and the Repertoire*, however, when analyzing Columbus's report of his inaugural act of flag-planting before assembled locals, Diana Taylor stresses how "The mute acquisition of naked, defenseless native peoples is forever plotted into the sequence."[27] That is, in the myriad reenactments of this scenario since 1492, aboriginal bodies are convoked forth repeatedly to bear passive witness to the appropriation of their lands by conquistadors. This leaves the indigenes as scripted things, not as scriptwriting humans. As Taylor puts it, "The Amerindians, though physically present, are acknowledged only to be disappeared in this act. They, like the animals Columbus says they resemble, become part of the landscape, found objects to be transferred (like servants and slaves), not subjects or landowners."[28]

This is true enough in the countless restagings in visual arts and written literature of the flag-planting scenario, given the archetypal role of voiceless acquiescents that is almost always allotted to the massed indigenes who surround the speechifying conquistador. But it does not account for the deliberate reiteration of absence that pervades the whole of Columbus's diary. The repeated performances of disembodiment by indigenes, their strategic withdrawals from many additional flag-planting scenarios, reveal them to be actors of spectrality whose improvisations cannot be controlled by a director desirous of placing them in a set he has designed for them. Taylor suggests that "performance makes visible (for an instant, live, now) that which is always already there: the ghosts, the tropes, the scenarios that structure our individual and collective life."[29] In the assertive indigenous absences of Columbus's diary, however, ghosts do not incarnate to stand there archetypically and assimilate into the narrations of others. Instead, they appear as invisible individuals who do not accede to directions to materialize in flesh and blood. In so doing, they turn Columbus and his readers into helpless witnesses of indigenous absence rather than policers of aboriginal presence. Such is the power of their haunting.

On December 3, as if to reassure himself more than his readers, Columbus writes that "ten men make ten thousand flee, they are so cowardly and fearful, for they carry no arms except wooden javelins."[30] As in the case of the indigenes who fled earlier "like chickens," Columbus attributes these disembodiments to pusillanimity.[31] Yet it is clear that he is disconcerted by the apparently concerted attempts to disappear before him. Some sort of word of mouth among the indigenes is preceding his arrival, for their villages are abandoned prior to any direct encounter with him and his men. And Columbus begins to see the indigenous withdrawals as an untenable situation, for the multiple absentings imply a conspiracy of resistance to his own presence. These concerns seem borne out, for example, on November 27, when the largest indigenous population encountered to date shows a threatening front, yelling and bearing javelins.[32] They disperse when Columbus's men approach their shore:

> The Indians made gestures threatening to resist them and not to let them land . . . three Christians got out, saying in their language not to be afraid . . . but finally all took to flight and neither grown-ups nor little ones remained. The three Christians went to the houses, which are of straw, made the same way as the others they had seen; and they did not find anyone or anything in any of them.[33]

Although Columbus attributes such flights to fear and therefore can pretend to accept them calmly and sail on, it is evident that these varied and continual vanishings (escapes from incarceration, deserted homes, tactical retreats) collectively begin to worry him. Flight by indigenes before the foreigners is proving not the antithesis of manly resistance but rather resistance by other means.

Indigenes continue to disappear. On December 6, "All the Indians fled and kept on fleeing when they saw the ships."[34] Evidently, local people do not plan to let Columbus author their lives. They will, at the very least, set themselves up as co-authors who compromise as much as possible his codes and intended codifications. And so the aboriginal vanishings keep reiterating. On December 7, the foreigners "saw five men, but they did not want to wait for the Spaniards but [wanted] to flee."[35] On December 12, three of Columbus's men "heard a large band of people, all naked like those seen previously, to whom they called, and they chased after them. But the Indians took to flight. Finally they captured one woman—for they could catch no more."[36] On December 13, Columbus's men "went to the village, which was four and a half leagues to the southeast, and which they found in a very great valley. [It was] empty because, when they heard the Christians coming, all of the Indians fled inland leaving everything that they had."[37] On December 15, Columbus "also saw people at the entrance to the river, but all took to flight."[38] On January 12, 1493, Columbus "sent the launch ashore for water and to see if they could talk to the natives; but the people all fled."[39] The absentings in this inaugural transatlantic text seem endless. And they always connote resistance to one kind of capture or another.

These absentings are discursively distinct from those depicted by Las Casas in a text he wrote entirely himself, *A Very Short Account of the Destruction of the Indies*, in which he emphasizes the eradication of indigenous peoples at the hands of conquistadors.[40] For example, he writes of one archipelago, "there were more than five hundred thousand souls; there is today not a single baby. They [the Spaniards] killed all of them by bringing them to the island of Hispaniola, after seeing how that island's own indigenes were dying out."[41] Regarding Puerto Rico and Jamaica, Las Casas writes that the Spaniards tortured and killed indigenes "until destroying and finishing off all of those unhappy innocents: there had been in the said two islands more than six hundred thousand souls . . . and today there is not in each one two hundred people, all having perished without faith and without sacraments."[42] In this environment of genocide, Las Casas awards little agency to indigenes. He characterizes them instead as "very docile lambs" and "docile sheep" who are led to slaughter.[43] In this tropology, absence really is absence: bodies vanish and they do not return. The dead stay dead. There is no aboriginal haunting here, no spectral resistance of any kind, just a Spanish juggernaut whose Conquest cannot be undermined or thwarted by helpless victims.

Columbus, however, senses more than lambs and sheep in the towns that depopulate before him. With his projected imperial extras exiting the stage instead of stepping forward to serve in their scripted role, he now prepares for a drama with those he cannot see. On December 26, he writes that he is commanding his men to erect a stronghold: "Now I have ordered them to build a tower and a fort, all very well constructed, and a big moat, not that I believe it to be necessary because of these Indians for it is obvious that with these men that I bring I could subdue all of this island, which I believe is larger than Portugal and double or more in [number of] people, since they are naked and without arms and cowardly beyond remedy."[44] This passage is entirely unconvincing. A tower, a fort, and a moat are major endeavors, not undertaken at a whim. Against what antagonist does Columbus defend? He knows that there are no competing European powers in the area. And if the local inhabitants really are unclothed and unarmed and "cowardly beyond remedy," they are improbable attackers and certainly not effective ones, fort or no fort. The boasting by Columbus is empty. He claims that he could readily subdue, without constructing any garrison, a population at least twice that of Portugal on a landmass of greater size, but then why build it? He asserts of the stronghold, "not that I believe it to be necessary," but obviously he does believe it to be necessary. Something on the island opposes him and must be confronted aggressively.

Columbus, aware that his reasoning is weak, explains to his royal audience, "But it is right that this tower be made and that it be as it should be (being so far from your Highnesses) in order that the Indians may become acquainted with the skills of Your Highnesses' people and what they can do, so that with love and fear they will obey them."[45] This justification is feeble. The indigenes are already made aware on a daily basis of the technological advantages of the foreigners. And Columbus has claimed from the beginning that local individuals are already extremely fearful. He writes of those he meets on the first day of his arrival, October 12, 1492, that "They should be good and intelligent servants, for I see that they say very quickly everything that is said to them; and I believe that they would become Christians very easily."[46] Writing these people into colonial codes will be unproblematic, he suggests, because they will present themselves readily to be inscribed upon. But then, why the tower and fort and moat? Vengeful ghosts, perhaps, could challenge him and his men, but hardly a population that flees before a handful of sailors "like chickens."[47]

As scholars often have noted, the tenor of Columbus's diary toward indigenous people becomes more and more tense as he travels through the Caribbean. Columbus does distinguish among various aboriginal individuals and societies, in part by assigning increasingly hostile characters to them. Those who retreat from him in the early days of his arrival at the islands are not those who retreat from him at the end. Columbus knows that. The heterogeneity of these people and events notwithstanding, the cumulative phenomenon of flight amounts to a repeated appearance of absence. And these absences in the aggregate obnubilate the real or perceived distinctions of the successive peoples whom Columbus encounters. The hauntings, as they follow upon each other, link all the islanders in a spectrum of shadowings that progressively darken Columbus's confidence in his control, scriptural as well as military, of his transoceanic performance.

A performance of America by a much later author of the Atlantic seaboard, William Carlos Williams, complements Columbus's account of the first voyage and its dramatic tensions of indigenous absence and imperial presence. Williams's *In the American Grain* of 1925 includes a chapter, "The Discovery of the Indies," in which he rewrites passages from various texts by Columbus, juxtaposes them out of chronological sequence, and mixes them with his own creative musings. The Columbus who emerges from this collage is a heroic but tragic figure whose "miraculous" and "pure" first voyage was subsequently spoiled by others from Europe with maleficent powers and intents.[48] The dismal fate of Columbus, who is brought low by those antagonists, is depicted as unjust. Williams climaxes the chapter, however, not with the despair of an aging and wronged pathfinder but with the flush of initial promise presumed to be felt by Columbus on the day of the inaugural encounter:

On Friday, the twelfth of October, we anchored before the land and made ready to go on shore. Presently we saw naked people on the beach. I went ashore in the armed boat and took the royal standard, and Martin Alonzo and Vincent Yañez, his brother, who was captain of the *Niña*. And we saw the trees very green, and much water and fruits of divers [sic] kinds. Presently many of the inhabitants assembled. I gave to some red caps and glass beads to put round their necks, and many other things of little value. They came to the ships' boats afterward, where we were, swimming and bringing us parrots, cotton threads in skeins, darts—what they had, with good will. As naked as their mothers bore them.[49]

This passage is an abridgement of the corresponding section of the version of Columbus's diary that Williams relied upon in his research, an English translation offered in the 1906 tome *The Northmen Columbus and Cabot* by editors Julius E. Olson and Edward Gaylord Bourne. The Olson and Bourne text is a reprint with very slight alterations (e.g., minor changes in punctuation and amended footnotes) of a translation by Clements R. Markham that was published in 1893. Williams rephrases some of the Olson and Bourne sentences, such as by converting the above citation from the third-person description of Las Casas to the first-person voice of Columbus—he changes "The Admiral went on shore in the armed boat" in Olson and Bourne to "I went ashore in the armed boat"—but also maintains much of their vocabulary and syntax.[50] In this sense, he stays fairly faithful to a professional translation of the diary. He thus would appear to be immune from any charge of deliberately misrepresenting Columbus. At hand seems to be essentially a reproduction.

The implicit logic of the passage in Williams, however, is structured by several pairings of corporealizations. First, foreign bodies arrive and anchor; in response, "naked people on the beach" appear. Next, Columbus and his two companions go ashore; consequently, "many of the inhabitants assembled." Finally, the sailors return to their boats, whereupon nude indigenes "came to the ships' boats" and readily give their possessions away. The drama is uncomplicated. The appearance of Columbus is matched each time by the becoming-present of local bodies. These bodies, unclothed and unresisting, avail themselves as submissive to the space of the foreigners. There is no hint of indigenous absence and no hint, beyond the flagged and armed boat, of any anticipation by Columbus that he will struggle to incorporate the islanders into his narrative of conquest. He does not have to, it seems, for they decide of their own accord to present themselves as scripted subjects.

Such is Williams's version of the Olson and Bourne reprint of Markham's translation of Las Casas's account of the diary. A reader of Williams would have no clue that the passage has been edited heavily in the process. The Olson and Bourne reproduction, following Las Casas, contains many descriptions of October 12 that are eliminated altogether in "The Discovery of the Indies." Williams's key changes to his source translation are his wholesale exclusions, not his light amendments. In his rendition he does not mention, for example, what the three foreign mariners actually do with "the royal standard" once they get ashore. In Olson and Bourne, Columbus "said that they should bear faithful testimony that he, in presence of all, had taken, as he now took, possession of the said island for the King and for the Queen his Lords, making the declarations that are required, as is now largely set forth in the testimonies which were then made in writing."[51] Williams also leaves out, once the indigenes assemble on the beach, Columbus's explanation of why he gave them the "red caps and glass beads." According to Olson and Bourne, it is "that we might form great friendship, for I knew that they were a people who could be more easily freed and converted to our holy faith by love than by force, [so I] gave to some of them red caps, and glass beads."[52] And when the indigenes swim out to the boats, Williams excises the statement by Columbus that they "appeared to me to be a race of people very poor in everything."[53] Finally, the description of the rest of October 12 by Williams does not include the comments by Columbus, translated from Las Casas by Markham and relayed in Olson and Bourne, that the indigenes "should be good servants and intelligent . . . I believe that they would easily be made Christians . . . I, our Lord being pleased, will take hence, at the time of my departure, six natives for your Highnesses, that they may learn to speak."[54]

Read against this litany of heavily charged exclusions, "The Discovery of the Indies" seems not a neutral reenactment of October 12 but an extraordinarily forced account designed to convoke indigenous bodies into unproblematized presence. Williams is not faithful to any source text. This is because the censored sentences, in their bald-faced assertions of colonizing power, contain within them the potential for resistance in the form of absence. Perhaps, for example, the indigenes will try to escape from their kidnappers. Or perhaps they will not prove such ready converts. Perhaps "the testimonies which were then made in writing" will not contain or contextualize individuals as willing to be scripted as the foreigners desire. The oppositionalities of indigenous absence are not allowed for in Williams's description of the first encounter. His performance of the original transatlantic moment repeatedly denies entry to ghosts.

Bryce Conrad comments that "in his rendition of Columbus' entry for Friday, October 12, Williams cuts the original text by half . . . trimming statements such as" those about the "'very poor'" race who "'would easily be made Christians.'"[55] Conrad thereby only partially describes the excisions made by Williams and he does not interrogate their significance; in fact, he consigns his observation to an endnote. Molly Metherd, by comparison, foregrounds some of the missing text upon suggesting that Williams "does not change any of the explicit facts, he includes the armed boat, the royal standard, and the characters; however, he excludes the description of the banners. That exclusion can be understood on aesthetic grounds: the detailed description would slow down the speed of the narrative and is in contrast to his style of paring down images."[56] Surely, though, "aesthetic grounds" are only a minor impetus to the deletions. The missing "description of the banners" in Williams, for example, seems far less important than the missing depiction that succeeds it of the act of taking possession of the island. The elimination by Williams of such moves by Columbus is primarily ideological in nature, not aesthetic. Metherd herself seems to agree with this conclusion to some extent, writing that "Arguably, however, Williams also alters Columbus's language in his description of the arrival of the Europeans to downplay the antagonistic nature of this first expedition."[57] Still, though, the main issue is not the altering of language but the deliberate purging of entire lines. Metherd notes this directly when pointing out that Williams "omits mention of conversion present in the source material" prior to Columbus's giving the indigenes the red caps and glass beads.[58]

Vera M. Kutzinski, whose *Against the American Grain* of 1987 remains an important contribution to hemispheric literary studies, proposes that "The Discovery of the Indies" in its bricolage of texts has "very little to do with the actual discovery of America, that is, with the moment of contact. . . . The account of the actual discovery follows almost like an afterthought."[59] Yet Williams's narrative of October 12 is the climax of the chapter; the denouement concludes quickly with Columbus's marvel at the beauty of local flora and fauna and then a brief prayer in Latin. Given the highlighted positioning of the day of encounter and the sharp edits by Williams to its recounting, Kutzinski's conclusion is difficult to sustain. The decisions made by Williams are clearly foundational to his vision of the transatlantic commencement of America. This is not to say, however, that Williams and *In the American Grain* move in lockstep with the Conquest. On the contrary, there is far more concern with indigenous subjects and subjectivities throughout the text than in, say, "Starting from Paumanok" by Whitman, in which the poet suspends for a stanza his celebration of the United States in order to wave goodbye to indigenes supposedly exiting history. But Williams's particular version of October 12 does reinforce what Columbus came to know, that the incarnating of indigenous bodies empowers imperial script and that divergences from the same translate to spaces of spectrality and all its persistent oppositionality.

Williams sensed himself to be an heir of the New World interweavings that began that day in 1492 and that are reducible to neither conquistadors nor indigenes. He knew his own life to be rooted in diverse cultural flows of the transatlantic. Throughout his childhood, his Puerto Rican mother spoke Spanish with his father who, though born in England, was raised in Caribbean environments where Spanish was prevalent. As Julio Marzán notes, Williams's father translated various Latin American authors into English and even collaborated with his son on the translation of a Guatemalan short story.[60] The younger Williams's links to Columbus and to Caribbean islands are not straightforward, regardless of his bowdlerizing of the narrative of October 12, 1492. Conrad points out that Williams's work on "The Discovery of the Indies" went "through as many as ten different versions before it reached its final form," a complex process of revision that at a minimum suggests an unsettled relationship between the author and his historical subject.[61] And Williams recalls in his autobiography that he carried with him "the first chapters of *In the American Grain* to do over" when traveling by ship from the East Coast to Europe in 1924.[62] In other words, he began constructing "The Discovery of the Indies" on one side of the ocean and sailed with it in the reverse direction of Columbus while reforming it yet again. In his person and his text, Williams crisscrossed the Atlantic and the Americas; he fits no simple category. To align him in general with Columbus, based upon his excisions and rewritings of the events of October 12, 1492, would be facile. Nevertheless, the two men's accounts of that day are complementary in their implicit openings and closings to foundational spectralities and their inherent potentials for resistance.

The tattooing of corpora cannot take place if bodies disappear, if they unavail themselves in absence. And that is exactly what happens in Columbus's diary. The indigenes whom he intends to write into his codes vanish before him, one after another, quite unlike the rendering in Williams. At first, Columbus accepts these disembodiments as not all that unusual. He personally has witnessed a ghosted peninsula, so a ghosted archipelago lies within a reality he probably figures he can circumscribe. And he continues to claim that the absenting aborigines do not present a substantive subversion of his narrative. Thus, on December 16, 1492, he writes,

> I with the people that I bring with me, who are not many, go about in all these islands without danger; for I have already seen three of these sailors go ashore where there was a crowd of these Indians,

and all would flee without the Spaniards wanting to do harm. They do not have arms and they are all naked, and of no skill in arms, and so very cowardly that a thousand would not stand against three. And so they are fit to be ordered about and made to work, plant, and do everything else that may be needed, and build towns and be taught our customs, and to go about clothed.[63]

Such authorial confidence would seem convincing save that, mere days later, on December 26, Columbus orders the construction of the fort and tower and moat against unnamed and unseen enemies.[64] Evidently, despite his hubris, Columbus has been spooked by all the disappearing bodies. He has come to realize that there is something to be afraid of after all, something of a phantasmal nature that will counter his presence despite his insistent claims to the contrary.

There have been far too many flights, far too many disappearances, far too many ghost writings for him to remain confident in his conquering script. That is why he builds the fort and tower and moat with no apparent enemies in sight: something unnerves him into mounting an aggressive defense. A skirmish on January 13, 1493, reveals further that Columbus never believed his own portrayals of a cast of passive extras on his island sets. On that day, his men trade with a few local people on a beach and manage to get one of them to go aboard a caravel and talk directly to him. After this conversation, Columbus sends the man back to shore, where over fifty armed indigenes are waiting behind trees. The warriors put down their weapons and proceed to trade with some of the foreigners, but after a few commercial exchanges "they prepared to attack the Christians and capture them. They went running to get their bows and arrows where they had left them and returned with cords in their hands, he says, in order to tie up the Christians."[65] The Europeans, however, are prepared for such a confrontation because Columbus "was always counseling them about this."[66] Their military superiority quickly wins the day. But in the context of the diary, Columbus's forewarning makes no sense. Hitherto he has trumpeted the cowardice of the aboriginal peoples. Yet his claims of their docility are belied by his advice to his men that they be ready for any assault. Clearly, Columbus allotted local peoples more potential for resistance than he let on when he dismissed them as chicken. And when the January 13 clash turns against the indigenes, they "having seen by this that they were able to achieve little . . . took to flight so that none remained."[67] Their absenting from the scene of conflict is a logical decision given the overwhelming nature of the forces that face them. The withdrawal has been foreshadowed by the flights of the San Salvador men from imprisonment three months earlier and by all the disappearances before the foreigners thereafter. From the initial escapes in October to the retreat from battle in January, indigenes have removed themselves time and again in order to act freely outside Columbus's theater rather than to be directed within it. Columbus, guessing himself ghosted all along, thus had warned his men to be aware of resistance regardless of his many words about submissive indigenous bodies. He was preparing for the spectral to return in one form or another. The repressed always do, eventually.

Columbus knows that the revenants of the islands will be back, those of January 13 and earlier. For the moment, they have retreated into absence. From there they will haunt him. That is why he concludes the January 13 entry by noting "that he would like to capture some of them. He says they were making many smoke signals."[68] Once again, only the forcible conversion of indigenous absence into embodied presence will allow Columbus to regain autonomous authorship of the drama. Meanwhile, the people who withdrew from the battlefield are busy communicating among each other in ways legible to them but illegible to the foreigners. Their aboriginal texts are written in graynesses that float in the air. The spectral narratives of the smoke signals infuse and shadow the story scribbled in the diary, co-authoring it with scriptings beyond Columbus's ken and counter to his own presumption of colonial control. Once again, indigenes are organizing themselves in visible invisibility, in a ghostliness that interrogates and contests his project. And though fresh off the military victory on the beach, Columbus finds himself intolerably haunted anew. On January 14 and 15 he writes of returning to Iberia, and on January 16 he turns tail and heads eastward across the ocean at last. The first voyage of the transatlantic draws to an end. Its hauntings persist to this day.

Throughout the diary, Columbus tries to write of indigenes becoming present before him. In reality, he finds them becoming absent. The Moors and Jews who vanish on the opening pages never stop haunting it. They never return to it. They never leave it either. Frames may be trespassed but their structures do not disappear. At first, with apparent calm, Columbus speaks of naked indigenous bodies ready to be inscribed within a new master narrative, that of imperial and Christian Spain. Yet apparitions that he cannot contextualize keep appearing before him, which is to say, they keep disappearing before him. His narrative cannot comprise completely the aborigines he encounters. Their footprints in the sands remain in his text as hints of bodies unincorporated into a script of colonization. Such absence stands as a counter-story of resistance. That alternative narrative, illegible but apparent to the foreigners who seek to overwrite it, is evident in the inaugural text of the transatlantic, the diary of the inaugural conquistador. And an autochthonous foundational narrative, the *Popol Vuh*, reveals that indigenous peoples can haunt the literatures of America in written texts of their own composition as well.

2 / Indigenous Atextualizations: The *Popol Vuh* and *I, Rigoberta Menchú: An Indian Woman in Guatemala*

The *Popol Vuh* is a sweeping narrative of the Maya-K'iche' people, inhabitants of present-day Guatemala, that commences with the creation of the cosmos and ends with the state of the Conquest in the mid-sixteenth century. No other foundational text in the world comprises such a temporal span. The *Popol Vuh* is an immensely complicated account of origins and social life whose details of, for instance, the multiple attempts at creating humans and the adventures of heroic twins, signify information about Mayan agriculture, astronomy, calendrics, ecosystems, religious practices, and numerous other domains. The focus on absence and translation in the pages ahead is intended to complement the many accomplished studies of the narrative content of the *Popol Vuh*, which this chapter does not address directly. Translation issues are key to the *Popol Vuh* because all of its modern written versions are based on a sole surviving manuscript, a copy made at the start of the eighteenth century by the Spanish priest Francisco Ximénez of a text he saw that many decades earlier had been composed in K'iche' transliterated into Latin characters (i.e., the narrative was conveyed via a Romanized representation of K'iche' words and sounds). The document that Ximénez encountered has been lost. Only his transcription of it remains, along with his translation of it into Spanish. This bilingual version was taken out of Guatemala in the nineteenth century and carried to France. Early in the twentieth century, the manuscript became permanently housed at the Newberry Library in Chicago.

The challenges of understanding the *Popol Vuh* in any conclusive sense are multiple. The issues include the linguistic difficulty of interpreting a text several centuries old that is written in a language with few surviving contemporaneous documents against which to cross-reference particular words. Spanish colonizers made a point of destroying virtually every indigenous text they came across. Another challenge is the intricate symbolism and overall complexity of the narrative itself. Up until the sixteenth century, the K'iche' composed within an epistemological tradition that was utterly unrelated to those of Ximénez and other Western translators who later would try to relay the *Popol Vuh* to foreign audiences. And as with any text, familiar or not, a single meaning cannot be fixed permanently. None of these factors, however, has prevented some translators from claiming to offer an ultimate rendering. Dennis Tedlock, author of the most widely read versions of the *Popol Vuh* in English, subtitles both his original and revised editions as "The Definitive Edition of the Mayan Book of the Dawn of Life and the Glories of Gods and Kings." The contradiction of two distinct "Definitive" versions, each offered moreover by the same translator, suggests both a desire to determine absolutely the text and the impossibility of doing so. The forthcoming discussion of various translations of the *Popol Vuh* attempts to arrive at interpretations of its bookending absences with the full recognition that any conclusions must remain tentative and, at the end of the day, ever deferred.

The vanishing of aborigines from particular landscapes is a common trope in literatures of the Americas, as is the stereotypical association of indigenes with different types of silence. Yet even when compelled by the advancement of conquering forces, movements into communicative invisibility and inaudibility can take place on the terms of those forced to disappear. Though produced amid injustice, specters usually have the last word. And they often pronounce it in absence. Narratives such as the *Popol Vuh* and the much later K'iche' testimonial *I, Rigoberta Menchú: An Indian Woman in Guatemala* perform indigenous resistance via unarticulated textualities whose contestatory stories, like the traces left by indigenes in Columbus's diary, lie beyond the reach of foreign incorporation.[1] Such strategic absenting destabilizes any presumption that spectralization signals defeat. Deliberate indigenous absences, oppositional by virtue of evidently existing, suggest instead what may be envisioned as a discourse of atextuality. Such discourse is explicitly framed and permeated with what is not there. Atextualizing authors openly recognize their own absenting in progress. Their removals to an unexpressed but no less real textuality is haunting because it is manifestly illegible to the reader. The absent script with its unstated codes is at once present and not; it is a bodiless corpus. It is phantasmal and purposefully anticolonial. It is visible invisibility as resistance.

Absence marks explicitly the first and last passages of the *Popol Vuh*, both of which declare that the narrative existing between them of the history of the world and of the K'iche' constitutes a performance set forth within an imperial theater. According to Tedlock, the text's collective narrative voice opens by declaring,

> Here we shall inscribe, we shall implant the Ancient Word, the potential and source for everything done in the citadel of Quiché, in the nation of Quiché people. And here we shall take up the demonstration, revelation, and account of how things were put in shadow and brought to light. . . . We shall write about this now amid the preaching of God, in Christendom now. We shall bring it out because there is no longer a place to see it, a Council Book, a place to see "The Light That Came from Across the Sea," / the account of "Our Place in the Shadows," / a place to see "The Dawn of Life," / as it is called. There is the original book and ancient writing, but he who reads and ponders it hides his face. It takes a long performance and account to complete the emergence of all the sky-earth.[2]

This passage opens itself to a fissured reading. On one hand, the narrative voice declares that the text that follows will "inscribe . . . implant . . . the potential and source for everything" that concerns the K'iche'. On the other hand, that same voice emphasizes that this inscription is but a version of a predecessor text whose principal characteristic is its atextuality: "there is no longer a place to see" it. The aterritoriality of this vanished text is emphasized by the triple repetition of the lack of "a place to see" it. It is not that this anterior text does not exist but rather that it exists beyond the context of this particular *Popol Vuh*, which is produced in a colonized space-time amid "Christendom now." The "original book and ancient writing," by contrast, remains unarticulated and possibly unable to be articulated within a context of Conquest. The lack of articulation seems deliberate, for "he who reads and ponders it hides his face." Present here, therefore, is an absent *Popol Vuh* and its faceless performer, a text and textualizer that are effectively spectral in their entirely apparent disappearance. The act of announcing this act of absenting constitutes a direct challenge to any reader desirous of assimilating the whole of the K'iche' narrative. As Doris Sommer suggests about Rigoberta Menchú,

"The gesture precisely is not silence but a rather flamboyant refusal of information."[3]

References herein and in the *Popol Vuh* to an "original book and ancient writing" and synonymous concepts do not imply that one specific "Council Book" (this phrase is one translation of "Popol Vuh") has vanished. Terms of singular number like "book" or "text" should be read as signifying a collectivity of versions of the *Popol Vuh* that, prior to the Spanish arrival, existed in different forms and among various societies. The narrative tradition of the *Popol Vuh* included not only written but oral, musical, and visual components as well. It comprised performances of many kinds. Therefore, no particular material representation of the *Popol Vuh* could be said to be the definitive version, either before or after the K'iche' encounter with Spanish forces. Notably, the revised edition of Tedlock's translation, published a decade after the first, subtly softens the agency of the atextualizer in the opening passage. Instead of "There is the original book and ancient writing, but he who reads and ponders it hides his face," Tedlock substitutes "There is the original book and ancient writing, but the one who reads and assesses it has a hidden identity."[4] The differences between "has a hidden identity" and "hides his face" suggest the unavoidable fact that any translation, and especially any written codification of any oral text, fixes in time and space a certain arrangement of signs that appears authoritative and rooted in essentialized certainty due to its concretization as a literary artifact. Relatively few readers are likely to conceive of a *Popol Vuh* that is in their hands and proclaimed to be definitive as actually a subjective and particular verbal framing of a fluid and protean source. Yet Tedlock's two translations alone reveal this to be the case. Any reference in the forthcoming pages to a sole antecedent version of the K'iche' narrative functions only as a shorthand for the plural traditions of pre-Conquest *Popol Vuh*s to which its opening passage refers.

Reading and comprehending the Ximénez rendition of the *Popol Vuh* in Guatemala today is complicated by a number of factors, including the illiteracy in K'iche' of many, perhaps most, of its speakers. This illiteracy is owed in significant part to the brutal suppression of the language and its speakers by the Guatemalan government during the civil war of the last third of the twentieth century. Another issue is the innate semiotic instability of the lone surviving manuscript of the *Popol Vuh*. Most K'iche' scholars assume that Ximénez consciously and unconsciously introduced numerous elements, linguistic and ideological and otherwise, into his transcription of the document that he saw. Consequently, these indigenous intellectuals make attempts to offer versions of the *Popol Vuh* that they see as necessary corrections to the faulty copy inherited by posterity from Ximénez. The mutability of the Ximénez manuscript is a story of how even a tangible text is rife with the intangible, how even the seemingly objective physicality of a script can prove subjective in its visible representations.

For example, the important nineteenth-century edition of the *Popol Vuh*, in which L'abbé Brasseur de Bourbourg provides a French translation alongside, ostensibly, the K'iche' version by Ximénez, turns out to be something other than a transcription of a transcription. According to Adrián Recinos, "Comparing the original text transcribed by Ximénez with the text published by Brasseur de Bourbourg, I noticed some differences, important omissions, and other changes which affect the interpretation of the Quiché document."[5] The Brasseur de Bourbourg representation of Ximénez's transcription in K'iche' also contrasts notably with the monolingual K'iche' edition of 1998 by the Academy of the Mayan Languages of Guatemala.[6] This text, entitled *Popol Wuj: pa K'iche' Chi' ch'ab'al*, updates Ximénez's spelling, changes his syntax, and adds in words that are presumed to be missing. Its version of the opening passage cited above in Tedlock is as follows:

> Waral xchiqatz'ib'aj wi, xchiqatikib'a wi ojer tzij, utikarib'al, uxe'nab'al puch ronojel xb'an pa tinamit **K'iche'**, ramaq' k'iche' winaq. Are k'ut xchiqak'am wi uk'utunsaxik, uq'alajsaxik, utzijoxik puch ewaxib'al, saqirib'al. . . . Wa' xchiqatz'ib'aj chupam chik kaxlan tz'ib', pa kristiyan uq'ijil chik xchiqelesaj rumal maja' wi chik ri ilb'al re **Popol Wuj**, ilb'al saq petinaq ch'aqa pölow, utzijoxik qamu'jib'al, ilb'al saqak'aslem. Xe'uchaxik. K'o nab'e uwujil, ojer tz'ib'am puch, xa k'u'tal chuwäch ilol re, b'isol re, nim upetik, utzijoxik puch. Are taq xchik'ïs tz'uk ronojel kaj ulew.[7]

A comprehensible translation of this passage even by most native K'iche' speakers, other than those scholars who actually crafted it, would be extremely challenging. The relatively few individuals who are literate in K'iche' would be stymied by many of its words and phrasings, a number of them archaic or otherwise uncommon. And even if the passage were to be read and interpreted at a certain working level, issues would remain regarding the adjustments it makes to the Ximénez text on which it is based. In addition, of course, the *Popol Vuh* was never a fixed text in the first place, nor was writing/reading its principal means of communication. The narrative known today as the *Popol Vuh* grew out of a plural tradition that was and remains oral, visual and performative as well as written. Any substantive declaration of the superior accuracy of a particular written representation of the *Popol Vuh* over others would need to take into account this historical malleability.

In recent decades, K'iche' scholars have offered various versions of the *Popol Vuh*. The most prominent of these is by Adrián Inés Chávez, a groundbreaking intellectual of Quetzaltenango (familiarly known as Xela), the principal city of the K'iche'-speaking region. Throughout the twentieth century, Chávez published a range of texts on K'iche' culture, history, and language. Jean Loup Herbert, a prologuist to one of those studies, describes Chávez as the "Founder and soul of the Academy of the Maya-K'iche' Language . . . he provides the basis for a science: K'iche'ology, which breaks the silence imposed by the Colony and gives voice anew to the autochthonous society of America."[8] In order to overcome the persistent problem of romanizing K'iche', Chávez created an additional set of characters to signify Mayan sounds that have no equivalents in Spanish. The most comprehensive result of his efforts is an edition of the *Popol Vuh* entitled the *Pop Wuj (Book of Time or of Events)* that offers the narrative in four parallel columns. The first column is a literal copy of Ximénez's transcription in K'iche'; the second is Chávez's transformation of that transcription using the supplemental alphabet he created; the third is Chávez's literal translation of the narrative into Spanish; and the fourth is his idiomatic translation into Spanish.[9]

At the start of the 2000s in Xela, the most widely available written version of the *Popol Vuh* in any language was Chávez's two-columned *Pop Wuj: Mythohistorical K'iche' Poem*.[10] On the left is his representation of the Ximénez transcription in K'iche' using the new supplemental alphabet. On the right is Chávez's idiomatic translation into Spanish. This *Popol Vuh* renders the opening passage as follows:

> And here we write (already in Castilian letters), here we fix the ancient word; the beginning, that is to say, the base of all that has happened in the town of Los Magueyes, but of the great K'iche' people. Thus here we will take up the task of teaching it, of revealing it, that is to say, of relating it. . . . And if here we write already in Castilian letters, already within Christendom, in this form we will divulge it because no longer can be seen anything of the Popol Vuh, the knowledge that came from the other side of the sea and which is the story of our origin, the knowledge of existence as was said. The first book (the Popol Vuh) exists, that is to say, the ancient writing.

This is only to mourn it, reread it, meditate upon it. It is very extensive because it tells of ever since the making of the heavens and earth was finished.[11]

As always with the *Popol Vuh*, the semiotic ambiguity of the text allows ample room for diverse translations. Chávez avails himself of considerable leeway in concretizing and clarifying what he perceives to be implicit in Ximénez's manuscript. In contrast to Tedlock, he inserts the interpretation "in Castilian letters" (i.e., Spanish) on two occasions, a move that underlines that the anonymous K'iche' authors are writing under imperial duress. Chávez also gives a different name for the place, "Los Magueyes," mentioned in the opening line. And twice, unlike Tedlock, Chávez refers to the Popol Vuh as *ciencia*, a loaded word that, in either of its meanings as "knowledge" or "science," suggests a particularly striking conceptualization of the nature of the narrative to follow. Notable, too, is Chávez's emphasis on the extant *Popol Vuh* as a product of grief: "This is only to mourn it, reread it, meditate upon it." The sense of melancholy for a lost world is largely missing in the dispassionate tone and remarkably distinct vocabulary of Tedlock's original rendition of the same line: "he who reads and ponders it hides his face." The two translations do coincide in the passive voice of their statement about the absence of the antecedent text. That is, Tedlock's "there is no longer a place to see it, a Council Book" shares the tenor of Chávez's "no longer can be seen anything of the Popol Vuh." Chávez, however, generally frames the opening passage of the *Popol Vuh* as more directly and explicitly charged with issues of colonialism (the authors writing in Castilian) and haunting (the lamentation for what cannot be seen) than does Tedlock.

The most influential and enduring translation of the *Popol Vuh* is that of Adrián Recinos into Spanish in 1947. It has dominated the global market so thoroughly and for so long that its own 1950 translation into English by Delia Goetz and Sylvanus G. Morley also has become a standard text, despite being twice removed from the Ximénez manuscript in K'iche'. As of 2007, the Newberry Library in Chicago, home of that document, continued to feature the Goetz and Morley translation of Recinos in its own bookstore. Recinos's text has served as the basis for translations of the *Popol Vuh* into Italian and Japanese as well and probably various other languages.[12] The importance of his translation to the global awareness of Guatemalan culture was evident fairly early on, so much so that a local poet wrote upon the death of Recinos in 1962, "The Popol Vuh has immortalized him:/the world knows us through him."[13]

Immortality proper aside, the assessment seems accurate. Until the testimonial of K'iche' activist Rigoberta Menchú became an international sensation and controversy in the 1990s, the Recinos version of the *Popol Vuh* probably stood as the most widely circulated Guatemalan text of any sort in history.

How Recinos came to produce his translation is an itinerant story in its own right. Had the political history of Guatemala worked out differently, the *Popol Vuh* might have remained overlooked in the Newberry Library archives for quite some time. Recinos was born in 1886 into a wealthy Guatemalan family with a lineage of participation in elite national life. His privileged education and connections led him to early involvement in the foreign affairs of the nation. By 1908, barely in his twenties, he worked for a Guatemalan governmental delegation in El Salvador. Various significant political posts followed, including stints as Minister of Foreign Relations and as a diplomat in western Europe. From 1928 to 1944, he served as a diplomat in Washington, D.C., including as the Guatemalan ambassador.[14] This time span comprises not only the Depression and World War II years in the United States but also, in Guatemala, the right-wing dictatorship of Jorge Ubico that lasted from 1930 to 1944. Recinos seems to have spent much of the Hoover and Roosevelt administrations hobnobbing with Washington elites while representing the interests of Ubico, an ally of the United States. In the summer of 1941, with sufficient time and opportunities to pursue scholarly interests, Recinos was sifting through the archives of the Newberry Library and came across the *Popol Vuh* text by Ximénez. This amounted to a rediscovery of the manuscript, for as Recinos recounts in a preface to the Goetz and Morley translation, it was attached to the end of another document by the priest and was neither indexed in its own right nor known, apparently, to librarians at the institution.[15] Recinos, though not indigenous, did know K'iche' and other Mayan languages to different degrees and was able to recognize the translating decisions made by Ximénez and where perhaps they might be altered. Undoubtedly, he was one of the very few individuals then in the United States with the linguistic skills and educational background to realize what he had found. According to the introduction of his *Popol Vuh*, he began working on his translation that very year.[16]

When Ubico withdrew from power three summers later in the face of massive discontent across all levels of Guatemalan society, Recinos decided to return to the country and run for the presidency in the democratic elections to be held in December 1944. He represented whatever remained of the right-wing coalition that the dictator had mustered during his lengthy regime. Virtually the entirety of the Guatemalan population, however, felt a change was due, as more than eight out of ten voters chose the left-wing Juan José Arévalo Bermejo. When Arévalo assumed the presidency some months later, Recinos and two other losing candidates "were implicated in a plot to overthrow the government and were exiled. With them went the hopes of the reactionary oligarchs."[17] The advantage of expatriation turned out to be enough free time to finish translating the *Popol Vuh* and publish it in Mexico. Thereafter, Recinos dedicated himself to other scholarly efforts while remaining in the background as an exiled but always-potential shadow candidate for a right-wing retaking of power in Guatemala. The United States, via the Central Intelligence Agency, helped organize a military coup d'état against the democratically elected government in 1954 and thereby imposed a new dictatorship on the country. That year, Recinos resumed his diplomatic work for Guatemala as a representative to the United Nations. And just before his death, he served for a couple of years as the ambassador to Spain.[18]

Such is the story of the man who rediscovered the *Popol Vuh* and launched the text into the international orbits in which it continues to circulate. How his political views may have colored his translation decisions is not entirely clear. That Recinos represented reactionary ideals in his life may connect to his interest in the retrieval of an ancient narrative and its transmission to future generations, but this does not necessarily imply anything about his choices on how to render particular phrases of the *Popol Vuh* transcription by Ximénez. And though there is a familiar phenomenon throughout Latin America of nationalists being interested in crafting social identities on the basis of indigenous populations perceived to be dead rather than on those actually living, here, too, any direct relationship to the wordings of the 1947 translation is uncertain. The fact that Recinos concluded his diplomatic career as the Guatemalan ambassador to the same country that colonized the K'iche' people whose traditions he translated is darkly poetic. Still, any analysis of his *Popol Vuh* must rest ultimately on a close reading of the text rather than on extraliterary assumptions.

Recinos renders the opening passage of the Mayan narrative as follows:

Here we will write and commence the ancient stories, the beginning and origin of all that was done in the city of K'iche' by the tribes of the K'iche' nation. And here we will bring forth the manifestation, the publication and the narration of that which was hidden. . . . This we will write already inside the law of God, within Christendom; we will bring it out into the light because the *Popol Vuh*, as it is called, is no longer seen, wherein the coming from the other side of the sea, our obscured narration, was seen clearly and wherein life was seen clearly. The original book existed, written long ago, but its vision is hidden to the investigator and the thinker. Great was the description and the telling of how the heavens and earth just had been formed.[19]

Unlike both versions by Tedlock, this translation does not emphasize the specific agency that hides the original text. Recinos employs the passive voice of "its vision is hidden." The implication, though, is effectively the same in that the *Popol Vuh* in hand appears as a simulacrum of atextualized antecedents. It is a restaging of predecessor *Popol Vuh*s but one performed in a vastly different theater. The program may seem the same but the props have been replaced, the lights substituted and the backdrop rearranged. Moreover, the actors no longer can improvise with anything approaching their previous freedom. And all of this cannot help but unsettle the new performance at hand. This disjuncture is what creates the paradoxical reading that is required when the text claims to tell "the beginning and origin of all that was done in the city of K'iche'" while simultaneously noting that it lacks the totalizing narrative that it promises. The unseen text or collectivity of texts remains "hidden to the investigator and the thinker."

Two early French translations of the same opening passage also confirm a strategic discourse of absenting. The first is that of L'abbé Brasseur de Bourbourg, whose 1861 version of the *Popol Vuh* was preceded in Europe only by the Spanish translation of Ximénez, published four years earlier.[20] The second is by Georges Raynaud from 1925 that was later translated, from French to Spanish, by his student, Miguel Ángel Asturias. A future winner of the Nobel Prize in Literature, Asturias ultimately would reimagine passages of the *Popol Vuh* in his novels *Men of Maize* and *Mulata*.[21] The following is a translation of the rendition by Brasseur de Bourbourg:

Here we will write and begin the history of bygone times, the beginning and the origin of all that was done in the city of the K'iche', in the tribes of the K'iche' nation: here thus we will bring forth the manifestation, the uncovering, and the bursting forth of that which was in obscurity. . . . Here is that which we will write since (the promulgation of) the word of *God*, and inside Christianity; we will reproduce it, because the national Book is no longer seen, where the coming from the other side of the sea was seen clearly. . . . There is the first book, written in ancient times; but its view is hidden to he who sees and thinks.[22]

And here is a translation of the version by Raynaud:

Here we will write, we will begin the ancient account of the beginning, of the origin and all that was made in the K'iche' city by the men of the K'iche' tribe. Here we will gather the declaration, the manifestation, the clearing of that which was hidden. . . . We will depict (that which was) before the Word of God, before Christianity; we will reproduce it because there is not (any longer) a visibility of the Council Book, a visibility of the dawn, of the arrival from overseas. . . . There was the first Book, painted long ago, but its face is hidden (today) to the viewer, the thinker.[23]

Subtle distinctions separate the versions by the two French scholars. For instance, Brasseur de Bourbourg recognizes that the Conquest literally circumscribes this *Popol Vuh* when he translates the K'iche' copied by Ximénez as "Here is that which we will write since (the promulgation of) the word of *God*, and inside Christianity." Raynaud arranges the same phrase as "We will depict (that which was) before the Word of God, before Christianity" and thus situates the production of the text not "inside" the context of the Conquest but "before" the colonization and its accompanying suppressions of indigenous peoples and cultures. This difference suggests an aggregate vacillation by the translators regarding how to represent the oppositionality of an indigenous voice that insists on the existence of a "national Book" or "Council Book" that preceded the arrival of conquering forces.

Brasseur de Bourbourg and Raynaud do not coincide in how to handle a collective K'iche' authorial voice that speaks of indigenous textualities alienated from the frame of Christianity. Brasseur de Bourbourg states at first that the forthcoming narrative of the *Popol Vuh* has been hitherto "in obscurity," a rather passive characterization. Only belatedly does he lend more agency to the absence of the "first Book" whose "view is hidden." Raynaud accepts immediately that the atextual text has been "hidden," but his suggestion that the present version arose "before Christianity" and not "inside" it vacates the anticolonial implications of announcing the absence of a precolonial *Popol Vuh*. The joint flummoxing of Brasseur de Bourbourg and Raynaud before the full implications of the K'iche' assertion of atextuality—of the existence of a topography that will remain always terra incognita for the conquistadors and their heirs—is demonstrated by the instability of their translations. Literally, they cannot contextualize a performance of the *Popol Vuh* that is "hidden to he who sees and thinks" (Brasseur de Bourbourg) or "hidden (today) to the viewer, the thinker" (Raynaud). That is an impossible colonization because the objects of their cartography, as in Columbus's diary, have absented themselves evidently to an unreachable and haunting space.

The end of the *Popol Vuh*, like the beginning, puts forth a declaration of atextuality. Here, too, emerges a vocal self-absenting that indicates that an uncolonized K'iche' scripturality exists beyond the frontiers of a narrative that purportedly explains a whole world. According to Tedlock in both his editions, the authors conclude the *Popol Vuh* by telling the reader that "This is enough about the being of Quiché, given that there is no longer a place to see it. There is the original book and ancient writing owned by the lords, now lost, but even so, everything has been completed here concerning Quiché, which is now named Santa Cruz."[24] The same passage, according to Recinos, translates as "And this was the existence of the K'iche' because the [*Popol Vuh book*] can no longer be seen, that which the kings had in ancient times, for it has disappeared. And thus have been terminated all those of K'iche', called *Santa Cruz*."[25] The version by Recinos is a powerful example of a scriptural production of indigenous absence by a foreign pen. Whereas Tedlock in his final line only indicates that the K'iche' narrative that is the *Popol Vuh* is hereby finished, Recinos implies that local K'iche' have been finished off. Today, notably, over a million K'iche' are still very much in existence, including Rigoberta Menchú.

The inequivalency and cumulative instability of the translations by Tedlock and Recinos are apparent. The "original book and ancient writing" wavers between "lost" and "disappeared." This raises the question of who lost it or who made it disappear, plus the corresponding issue of how it became absent. There seems to be another world indeterminable and therefore unmappable by the Conquest, a space where imperial overwriting of aboriginal textualities cannot take place because the colonizers' narrations cannot unfurl that far. Only by positing such a space can the following statements be explained: "This is enough about the being of Quiché, given that there is no longer a place to see it" and "this was the existence of the K'iche' because the [*Popol Vuh book*] can no longer be seen." In other words, all has been narrated that could be narrated within the context of the Conquest. Beyond that context, however, there is a narration that remains unseen and unarticulated.

Adrián Inés Chávez, the local K'iche' scholar whose bilingual K'iche'/ Spanish edition is probably the most disseminated in the Guatemalan highlands today, concludes his version of the *Popol Vuh* with phrasings that closely resemble those of Recinos up until the final line: "This was the existence of the K'iche'. No longer is there a place in which to see it. There was an ancient document of the lords but it has disappeared. Here ends what today is called Santa Cruz of the K'iche'."[26] Like Recinos, Chávez prefers "disappeared" instead of Tedlock's "lost" to describe what happened to the previous text. The nature of that script, however, is communicated with different nuances in the three translations. Tedlock calls it "the original book and ancient writing," thereby emphasizing that the text in hand is derivative and supplemental. Chávez designates it as "an ancient document" without a qualifier like "original." And Recinos refers to the *Popol Vuh* as "that which the kings had in ancient times" and so brackets the text within a royal context that apparently since has been terminated. The era of K'iche' power is "ancient" in Recinos; only the "writing" or "document" is "ancient" in Tedlock and Chávez.

In the final sentence of the translations, the distinctions grow even stronger around the question of what and who is ending. Chávez represents that line as "Here ends what today is called Santa Cruz of the K'iche'," which implies that a narrative of rather limited frontiers has concluded. The phrasing implies that other narratives exist beyond the pale of Santa Cruz of the K'iche'. Tedlock, by contrast, is emphatic that although the "original book" is "lost," there is not a problem of present incompleteness, for "even so, everything has been completed here concerning Quiché, which is now named Santa Cruz." There is a noticeable difference between Chávez's "ends" and Tedlock's "even so, everything has been completed." It is as if the anteriority of the "original book" that Tedlock stresses earlier does not equate to the allowance of a space where that atextualized *Popol Vuh* still exists. There is a foreclosure of textual slippage in the Tedlock phrasing. This foreclosure is totalizing, however, in the sweeping implications of the Recinos version: "And thus have been terminated all those of K'iche', called *Santa Cruz*." This translation admits no space for the continuing existence of local K'iche' people, much less for an atextualized K'iche' manuscript. Recinos's rendition, additionally, stands in sharp contrast to a curious moment in Chávez's version when the penultimate sentence, which ends with "has disappeared," is followed by a reference to an endnote, number 108, that does not appear in the cross-referenced appendix of citations. There, only the first 107 footnotes are given. In other words, upon declaring that the ancient *Popol Vuh* "has disappeared," Chávez provides the documentation of a nonarticulated endnote. The point of reference itself is atextual and therefore haunting. It exists and does not exist at the same time, lingering in the realm of the reader but forever emanating from an unspoken and thus contestatory otherworld. The absence of a text corresponding to endnote 108 may or may not be a printing error; regardless, it gestures at an atextual space in a way that Recinos and, to a lesser extent, Tedlock, manifestly do not.

The aforementioned French translators of the *Popol Vuh* do echo the différance between the articulated text in hand and the nonarticulated one they can neither possess nor circumscribe. Brasseur de Bourbourg, for example, translates the ending passage as "And there you have all (that remains) of the existence of the K'iche'; because there is no longer a means of seeing the (book), where in bygone times the kings (read everything). Since then it has disappeared. In this way thus ended all those of K'iche', which is called *Santa-Cruz*."[27] The same passage, according to Raynaud, reads "Such was the existence of the K'iche', because there is no longer, it is lost, that which rendered visible those who long ago were the first chiefs. In this way therefore is the end of all of K'iche', called Santa Cruz."[28] As in the case of Tedlock and Recinos, there is disagreement here as to whether the book "has disappeared" (Brasseur de Bourbourg) or "is lost" (Raynaud). The only certainty is that the present manuscript is bookended by affirmations that its production is conditioned and encircled by the colonization represented by "Christendom" at its beginning and "Santa Cruz" (literally, "Holy Cross") at its end. The greatest extant narration of indigenous life prior to the arrival of Europeans is thus transatlanticized within a framing of anticolonial absence. The location of Santa Cruz of the K'iche' adds to the sense of that absence, for according to Allen J. Christenson, the town was "founded by the Spanish conquerors near the ruins of Cumarcah/Utatlan, the ancient capital of the Quichés."[29] Where once the K'iche' had their capital, Holy Cross now rises.

The absenting bookends of the *Popol Vuh* are the principal but not lone moments of atextualization in the K'iche' narrative. Two other passages refer to an illegible antecedent. The clearer reads, according to Tedlock, "They were great lords, they were people of genius.... Whether there would be death, or whether there would be famine, or whether quarrels would occur, they knew it for certain, since there was a place to see it, there was a book. Council Book was their name for it."[30] Recinos translates the last part of that passage as "They knew well that there was a place where they could see it, that there existed a book by them called the *Popol Vuh*."[31] Chávez renders this phrase as "there was a book to know it called the 'Book of Time.'"[32] These three translations are all similar in their agreement that the absent book was indivisible from precolonial K'iche' epistemology. The importance of stating so resides not primarily in the particular information contained in the atextualized narrative but in the acknowledgment of an entire alternative way of interpreting and understanding the world. Operational was an autonomous and autochthonous system of knowing, not just a local familiarity with local things unknown to Europeans but knowable within European epistemes. In this assertion of the absence of what no longer avails itself in the present lies not only loss but also profound resistance. Due to the fact of colonialism, access to the old epistemology may be now unreachable by all parties, yet the K'iche' still collectively remember that there were ways of taking the measure of the world that were absolutely independent of the context of the Conquest. The colonizers are not privy to that memory. The announcement that there existed a tradition of knowledge and knowing reserves an absent space, however barricaded now its entrance by Spanish presence, where precolonial indigenes were epistemologically autonomous and where postcolonial indigenes, through their remembrance and evocation of the same, remain independent and sovereign regardless of the foreign textualities that have sought to circumscribe them since the Conquest began.

The second moment of atextualization in between the opening and closing frames of the *Popol Vuh* does so more apparently in the revised edition of Tedlock than in Recinos. In this instance, Tedlock translates a passage as "As they put it in the ancient text, 'The visible sun is not the real one.'"[33] Recinos, in comparison, renders it as "It definitely was not the same sun that we see, they say in their accounts."[34] Chávez offers alternatively, "[the sun] only showed itself when it was created; then only the reflection remained, it was no longer the same Sun that shone, thus says tradition."[35] The explicit suggestion by Tedlock of an "ancient text" would seem to be an overly concretizing insertion. The choice of "accounts" by Recinos and "tradition" by Chávez is probably closer to the sense that the anterior *Popol Vuh* was not a unique physical text but a gamut of textualities that were written, spoken, painted, carved, sung, danced, and so on, and which signified meaning for precolonial K'iche' via the individuals who interpreted the world through those code systems. In any case, all three translations emphasize that now the K'iche' live in an extended historical moment of second order: the sun is not the original sun but a successor to it. The light of current time is but a simulacrum, perhaps one, as inferred by Chávez, less substantive than its predecessor. And the absence of the ur-sun, like that of the ur-book, should not be read simply as loss. In the enduring memory of a previous age and its guiding lights resides a challenge to the powers of a contemporary age whose forces seek to impose different guides, different lights. The announcement of the first-order sun, the first-order book, puts forth an absent presence that haunts the projects of empire.

The references to earlier traditions and earlier suns that are positioned in textual moments less obvious than those that open and close the *Popol Vuh* reinforce the atextualities of the alpha and omega passages. The spaces of the absent indigenous narrative are again those to which the conquistadors and their inheritors cannot stake claim. The reach of the Conquest extends to the space now rewritten as Holy Cross but not to that unknown to foreigners but still known or at least remembered by locals. In other words, the imposed context of Christendom signaled at the beginning and end of the Ximénez manuscript serves as notice that everything narrated in between is situated within the frame of the Conquest. The stating of this imperial context functions as an inverse bookmark by informing readers not where they are but where they are not. Tedlock, Recinos, Chávez, Brasseur de Bourbourg, and Raynaud do not arrive at a consensus about the exact nature of this process of absenting but instead are uncertain in the aggregate before it. The flux in their interpretive metatext of the *Popol Vuh* indicates the success of the authorial strategy itself. Faced with suppression, the K'iche' arrived at a way of absenting themselves into narratological autonomy.

Ghosts come from spaces of scriptural absence. These spaces exist despite not existing; they have presence despite being intangible; they have textuality despite being illegible. Such spectrality haunts the embodied scriptings of conquistadors. The extant *Popol Vuh* was produced in a K'iche' topography now rewritten as "Holy Cross" but this place name has not erased altogether its indigenous antecedent. The textualities of its predecessor hover disembodied and defiant in the air. And centuries later, in a related haunting, Rigoberta Menchú concluded her own narrative of the K'iche' by saying, "I still keep hiding my identity as an indigene. I keep hiding that which I consider nobody knows. Not even an anthropologist, not an intellectual, regardless of how many books he might have, knows how to discern all of our secrets."[36] Here again appears a contestatory K'iche' discourse of aboriginal absence.

Vociferous debates from the mid-1990s onward about the authenticity of *I, Rigoberta Menchú: An Indian Woman in Guatemala* have focused on the disputed factuality of particular statements in it. Volumes such as *The Rigoberta Menchú Controversy*, an ideologically riven collection of essays edited by the Guatemalan scholar Arturo Arias, have emerged around these polemics. At issue is whether Menchú inaccurately represents indigenous experiences in Guatemala and, with regard to the underlying theoretical questions, what it means to represent anything accurately in the first place. Menchú, however, did not offer the interviews that form the basis of the text with the aim of providing Western scholars an anthropological case study, although the individual who taped and rearranged and edited those interviews, Elizabeth Burgos, was indeed an anthropologist. Menchú relayed her life story instead to garner recognition and support for her political cause against a repressive military state, the same for which Adrián Recinos had served as a diplomat and which the United States had helped establish through its support of the 1954 coup. And when Menchú received the 1992 Nobel Peace Prize for her struggles as portrayed in the book, she stood as a living symbol of not only the particular resistance movement to which she belonged but also of the five centuries of indigenous suffering marked by the quincentenary that year of the transatlantic voyage recorded by Columbus in his diary.

Although Menchú offers in her testimonial a wealth of information (some of it now contested) about contemporary K'iche' history, she maintains for herself a space of absent subjectivity. That is, the aboriginal textualities she presents are matched by unarticulated ones that she explicitly does not. She proclaims frequently the existence of an indigenous otherworld whose cartography she will not delineate. As Doris Sommer notes, that declaration of secrecy seems "the most noteworthy and instructive feature of her book, however one judges the validity of the information or the authenticity of the informant. Why should she make so much of keeping secrets, I wondered, secrets that don't have any apparent military or strategic value?"[37] Sommer concludes tentatively that Menchú asserts a possession of secrets in order to refer to a sociocultural space beyond the discernment and control of her presumably Western reader. This would constitute a strategy of forestalling what Sommer describes as "evaporations of difference" between the reader and the narrator.[38] The goal would be to retain a realm of indigenous subjectivity beyond the contextualization of a nonindigenous reader even though the ostensible purpose of producing a testimonial is the exact opposite.

According to Alberto Moreiras, "Rigoberta Menchú's word is founded on the continuous insistence on a secret that will not be revealed."[39] He adds that "she forecloses the content of the secret, thereby opening a fold that becomes not only the site of identity, but precisely the site of abjected identity, as well as the site of a certain resistance to abjection . . . the secret, in Menchú's text, stands for whatever cannot and should not be reabsorbed into the literary-representational system."[40] Such authorial references to what will not be articulated recall those in the written *Popol Vuh*. Both the Ximénez manuscript and Menchú's testimonial conceptualize a K'iche' space alienated from and therefore contrarian to colonization. In academic analyses it has become almost commonplace to focus on Menchú's proclamations of secrecy as asserting a kind of fundamental alterity from which non-K'iche' or nonindigenes in general must stand at a respectful distance. Yet her atextualizations do not separate herself and her society from various colonizations so much as haunt them in a persistently and performatively spectral mode.

Focusing on specific secrets in *I, Rigoberta Menchú* tends to yield equally specific critical misreadings. John Beverley, for instance, writes that there is at least one obvious reason for Menchú's unwillingness to reveal everything about the K'iche': "Menchú, worrying, correctly, that there are some ways in which her account could be used against herself or her people (for example, by academic specialists advising counterinsurgency programs such as the one the CIA set up in Guatemala), notes that there are certain things—her Nahuatl name, for example—she will *not* speak of: for example, 'I'm still keeping my Indian identity a secret. I'm still keeping secret what I think no-one should know.'"[41] But there is no proof in the text that Menchú chooses that stratagem as a tactical maneuver against spy agencies. These do not seem to be the spooks at which she hints. More significant than the particular content of her secrets or their supposed anthropological or political value is her overall rhetoric of atextualization. Her discursive strategy creates a recognizably spectral contestation, an unstated and hauntingly absent textuality, that complements a fully present political and cultural oppositionality. Rather than being withdrawn in a wholesale sense, this phantasmal scriptural resistance hovers everywhere the reader turns. Menchú serves as a guide of the ghostly sort, a guide who gestures at what she will not express directly, who speaks of foundational crimes, whose presence signals her absence. Such spectral performances destabilize those of stage directors like Columbus who would prescribe lines and indicate blockings without any autonomous input from the actors.

Menchú foregrounds absenting, for example, when she describes a rite of passage of a K'iche' child: "the parents have to teach the child . . . [sic]—more than anything else the ancestors are referred to—that he learn to guard all the secrets, that nobody can finish off our culture, our customs."[42] The inscription of a K'iche' identity is rooted here in the preserving of an atextual cultural space. This is not to say that such a space does not have textuality but that it exists beyond the conscripting powers of dominant foreign forces that would seek to incorporate and thereby colonize it. Menchú's disclosure of a nondisclosure of ancestral ways of knowing the world is comparable to the atextualizing start and finish of the extant *Popol Vuh*. Menchú has said that she is illiterate in K'iche', so she cannot have read the Ximénez transcription and understood it directly. Nevertheless, she connects her atextualizations to those of her forebears: "it is said that the Spaniards raped the best children of the ancients, the most humble people, and in honor of those most humble people we have to keep guarding our secrets. And nobody will be able to discern those secrets more than us indigenes."[43] Atextualization once again appears as an engaged political response to a context of Conquest that dates from the arrival of the first Europeans in indigenous lands and extends through the late twentieth-century experiences of Menchú.

Additional moments of absenting are registered when she depicts K'iche' practices in childrearing: "This implies one more time the pledge that we all have to keep: the customs, the secrets of our ancestors."[44] Here, Menchú declares anew the limits of revelation, of fully present textuality, demarcated by her predecessors. And entering the stage visible to the reader from an unreachable space, she becomes a revenant of challenging absence. Indeed, Menchú virtually rearticulates the opening page of Tedlock's *Popol Vuh* when she states, "We indigenes have hidden our identity."[45] These echoes resound loudly. Their frequency, as Derrida would say, is that of a phantasmal repetition, "of a certain visibility. But the visibility of the invisible."[46] As Menchú argues, "we have guarded our secrets and that is why we are discriminated against . . . you know that you have to hide this until it guarantees that an indigenous culture is going to continue surviving."[47] Cognizant that aboriginal absence can function as disembodied resistance, she insists on it as strategy. Her manifest silences, like those in the *Popol Vuh* and in the diary of the first voyage of Columbus, utilize withdrawal as oppositionality.

Menchú, though ostensibly narrating her life story, knows that her discourse participates in a transatlanticized tradition of atextualization, that of the five centuries and counting of the existence of America. Indeed, that spectral tradition *is* America, an ideation forged by an ongoing transoceanic production of contestatory absence. When Menchú writes, "A priest arrives at our villages and all we indigenes say nothing," she is only superficially talking about the early resistance movement of the K'iche' before the Guatemalan army and dictatorship.[48] At a more profound level, she is re-performing the rhetoric of absence that her ancestors used when they atextualized the predecessor *Popol Vuh*. Both Menchú and the authors of the *Popol Vuh*, faced with reification before the regulatory gaze of church and state, turn the tables and haunt empire from an atextual space of autonomous indigenous subjectivity.

Such intertextuality among atextualizing K'iche' authors separated by centuries differs from that of the chapter epigraphs that pepper Menchú's testimonial. These citations are taken directly from the *Popol Vuh* and Asturias's *Men of Maize*, a novel that deliberately evokes the ancient K'iche' narrative. Menchú is not responsible for the epigraphs in the book that sometimes bears her name. They were chosen by Elizabeth Burgos, the anthropologist who reshaped and repositioned and converted the interviews she conducted with Menchú in Paris into the written text known in English as *I, Rigoberta Menchú*. Burgos, not Menchú, appears as the sole author of the first edition in Spanish of the testimonial. For that reason among others, arguments have circulated for years about whether the text is representative of indigenous life in Guatemala. Irrespective of that debate, the strategic amorphousness of what Menchú does *not* communicate is arguably as compelling as the degree of accuracy of what she or Burgos *does*. This silencing can be safely attributed to Menchú and not her editor. The role of the latter always would be to concretize the atextual, not to leave it as such. The epigraphs that cite the *Popol Vuh* are one example of that and can be dismissed as unrooted in any indigenous production of spectrality.

As Menchú observes, "since they have not given us a space for words, since they have not given us a space in which to speak and opine and take into account our opinions, we also have not opened our mouths willingly."[49] This articulation of non-articulation, this pro-active absenting, shadows and subverts any colonizer or conquistador who might claim scriptural presence. The atextualization is a spectral resistance that complements more familiar forms of political and military contestation by indigenous peoples. Menchú concludes, "we have hidden our identity because we have known how to resist, we have known how to hide that which the regime has wanted to take away from us. Whether through religions or through the redistribution of lands or through the schools or through the medium of books or through the medium of radios, of modern things, they have wanted to insert other things and take away ours."[50] Once again, that which is made absent cannot be co-opted or corralled by a regime that seeks to incorporate it in its own image.

"How then," Doris Sommer asks, "are we to take Rigoberta's protestations of silence as she continues to talk?"[51] Sommer theorizes that the assertion of secrets without revealing them creates an impassable wall between reader and author. Yet Menchú, by enunciating absence, deliberately walks through that wall. She passes back and forth between absence and presence, ever leaving and ever coming back. Whichever way she goes, she is returning: she is a revenant. And like all ghosts, she purposefully clings to anonymity despite her manifest intentions of appearing on a visible stage. The authors of the *Popol Vuh* withhold their aboriginal names, as does Menchú. Absence is the organic principle of such anonymity, absence that hovers and contests and thus is of the haunting kind. But though these names cannot be concretized by colonizing forces, they do not lack presence. Theirs is a perpetually deferred textuality, one whose floating signifiers pass through spatial and temporal borders and continually return indicating crimes committed and unjudged, justice unmet.

The absences of Menchú and the authors of the *Popol Vuh* are indigenous hauntings that constitute America as foundationally ghosted. That is why Whitman cannot conceive of western Atlantic expansion in "Starting from Paumanok" without acknowledging "what the air holds of the red aborigines."[52] But Whitman misjudges this phantasmagoria. He does not realize that the absent presences he notes are not necessarily the product of imperial nostalgia. They can appear also as indigenous contestation. Disembodiment and atextualization can be inverted by "the red aborigines" as a strategic attempt to preserve a counter-narrative beyond the reach of colonizing scripts. Indigenous absences haunt even Whitman in that poem. That is why he is writing about them: his verses are a melancholic reproduction of what is no longer there, his celebratory posturing notwithstanding. The mere existence of "what the air holds" testifies to a foundational crime, to an expulsion of local bodies that still shadows whatever foreign bodies arrive within the places named. However exiled and exterminated the indigenes, their absent presence signifies that, as the *Popol Vuh* implies, the K'iche' will always haunt the place now named Holy Cross. The revenants will be back, time and again. Columbus comes to learn this well. So does Robinson Crusoe.

3 /   Castaway Colonialism: Daniel Defoe's *Robinson Crusoe* and Álvar Núñez Cabeza de Vaca's *Account*

Robinson Crusoe is immersed in the Conquest. Although once he is shipwrecked he has no communication for years with the outside world, he knows well the international struggles for domination that transpire around him. And he acts as if invested in them because, literally, he is. The reason he was aboard a ship in the first place is that he was heading from Brazil to Africa to obtain slaves for his plantation and those of fellow landholders. Though popular construals often suggest otherwise, Crusoe lives not on an abstract island adrift in atemporality but on a Caribbean island in colonial times. As a result, rather than starting his history there with an isolated script, he reenacts the dynamics of power that continue to develop all around him on the mainland: the plottings of empire and its attendant ghosts. Crusoe may be ignorant of his exact coordinates and therefore seem removed from geopolitics, but he plays the role of conquistador as much as Columbus and the Spaniards who sought to colonize the K'iche'. And haunted by transatlantic absence, he, too, performs America.

Daniel Defoe published *Robinson Crusoe* in 1719, not long after Francisco Ximénez saw, copied, and translated the *Popol Vuh* in Guatemala. There is no direct connection between the two narratives, yet both manifest absence as a contestatory transatlantic phenomenon. With respect to Columbus's diary of his first voyage, Defoe's novel is further removed in time from it than from the Ximénez manuscript but closer in orientation due to its accounting of another European sailor who encounters unfamiliar land in the Caribbean. On the island in *Robinson Crusoe* there are no indigenes available immediately to conquer and it is the European who begins in a position of relative weakness, so it takes Crusoe longer than Columbus to incorporate subjects into empire. In the beginning, Columbus plants his flags over indigenous peoples in their presence. They then withdraw themselves into atextualized absence. Crusoe, in the beginning, has to wait slowly for his prospective servants to materialize from such absence. When they do, his colonization of their bodies proves a foregone conclusion. As Maximillian E. Novak notes, "His claim to power is based on the right of conquest; every person who comes to the island is forced to swear complete obedience to his commands."[1] This is because although Crusoe, when shipwrecked, loses contact with Brazil, he never loses sight of the transatlantic and how it is performed.

The reproductions of *Robinson Crusoe* and its derivatives across the globe in fiction, film, song, television, and other media are uncountable. At elite cultural levels, as but one example, the mid-1980s novel *Foe*, an acclaimed reworking of Defoe's narrative, was among the writings of J. M. Coetzee of South Africa that resulted in his receiving the Nobel Prize in Literature of 2003. And in the realm of pop culture, the castaways of the mid-1960s television series *Gilligan's Island*, seen on reruns by decades of viewers in the United States, are imprinted so indelibly in the national imagination that vernacular references to them usually require no contextualization whatsoever. Verses of the theme song alone, which explicitly references Robinson Crusoe, can be sung from memory by huge swaths of the population. Meanwhile, the written genre of Crusoe narratives is so widespread internationally that a French term came into existence just to describe them: *les robinsonnades*. And sundry toponyms dot the planet in homage to Defoe's novel and its inspirations. Curious examples of an unnamed fictional island leading to nomenclature bestowed upon actual islands include Robinson Crusoe Island in Fiji and Isla Róbinson Crusoe in Chile. The latter is adjacent to Isla Alejandro Selkirk, named after the historical castaway upon whom the character of Crusoe was based. In the vast majority of these diverse rewritings of *Robinson Crusoe*, however, the slaving trajectory of Crusoe at the start and end of the novel is eliminated altogether. The figure of Friday and famous moments of Crusoe's experiences on the island are alternately reproduced, parodied, relocated, modernized, and so on, but the worldwide proliferations of the basic plot often gain popularity at the expense of the truly paradigmatic: Crusoe as conquistador before he reaches the island and as colonial emperor when he leaves it.

Throughout Latin America, Crusoe frequently serves as a touchstone reference, perhaps because the Conquest is explicitly regarded as such and because the colonial legacy remains a pulsing dynamic in current events. Although the Argentine writer Domingo F. Sarmiento is best know for authoring *Facundo: Civilization and Barbarism*, whose ghostly title character is a semi-human, semi-alive, semi-mythic force on the pampas, he launched his next major work, *Travels through Europe, Africa and America, 1845–1847*, with an episode in which he comes across four North American castaways on an island onto which "was tossed the mariner Selkirk, which gave origin to the eternally famous story of Robinson Crusoe."[2] Adds Sarmiento, "the memory of Robinson came to us in every moment; we believed we were with him on his island, in his cabin, during the time of his arduous test."[3] At one point Sarmiento literally steps into this role by discarding his own shoes for makeshift sandals of goat hide and thereby going "shoed à la Robinson Crusoe."[4] Yet here, too, there seems to be a sympathetic evocation of Crusoe that, as in most symbolic replays of the island drama, frames the Englishman as a castaway rather than as a conquistador.

A remarkable range of scholarly works that stretches now across three centuries corresponds to the global breadth of Crusoe reenactments and rewritings in print, on stage, and upon earth. The proliferation of academic criticism on Crusoe and his literary kin in all cultural media likewise shows no sign of abating. Given the massive circulation of Defoe's novel and its successors in so many genres, plus the enormous extent of corollary scholarship, no analysis of *Robinson Crusoe* can engage fully with the extensive scope of relevant texts. The following pages seek only to contribute a particular, but in no sense exclusionary, approach to Crusoe studies by focusing on the interplay of absence, presence and the transatlantic in the novel proper. By sandwiching that interplay in between the spectral dynamics of texts with which Defoe's narrative is never juxtaposed, the *Popol Vuh* and *I, Rigoberta Menchú* and *When the Combes Fought* (the first African novel in Spanish), this chapter hopes to suggest unexpected orientations even in a fiction as familiar as *Robinson Crusoe*.

The transatlantic figurations of the text, like those of the absented Moors and Jews in the opening pages of Columbus, appear long before the protagonist actually traverses the ocean. In Crusoe's case, an imbricated history of not expulsions but enslavements precedes his unplanned arrival on an unfamiliar Caribbean island. Years before the infamous shipwreck on the western side of the Atlantic, Crusoe makes two sea voyages from England to northwestern Africa. On the second, he is captured by a Moorish pirate and becomes his slave for two years. A fellow slave is a "young Maresco" boy named Xury.[5] A "Maresco," or *morisco*, was an individual of Islamic, Spanish, and northwest African heritage. The large *morisco* population resulted from the seven plus centuries of Moorish presence in Spain, the same whose formal power, as Columbus notes in the prologue to his diary, ended in 1492 with the fall of Granada. Xury, though a character virtually unknown by the countless publics that have consumed Crusoe narratives over the centuries, plays a pivotal role in the spectral tensions of the novel. Like the Moors and Jews at the beginning of Columbus's journal and like the predecessor text mentioned at the commencement of written versions of the *Popol Vuh*, Xury disappears soon from the main of the narrative to come and yet frames it throughout. His embodiment into servitude is later filled by various successor slaves and potential slaves in Brazil and the Caribbean and West Africa. These include not only Friday but also such unlikely subjects as a parrot named Poll, a score or so of shipwrecked Iberians, and three English mutineers. Xury sets the stage for all these conquered bodies even though he is long since gone from Crusoe's control by the time of their respective appearances, and even though Crusoe and he share the same initial status as slaves to the Moorish pirate.

The transition by Crusoe from slave to slave master is noticeably rapid. When an opportunity arises for escape from the pirate, Crusoe hatches a plan and commandeers a small boat. On it are only Xury and one of the pirate's relatives. Crusoe throws the relative overboard and would have been content to "ha' drowned the boy" but instead decides that Xury should pledge him fealty or else be tossed into the waves as well.[6] The response from the boy pleases Crusoe greatly, for Xury "swore to be faithful to me, and go all over the world with me."[7] This pledge will be realized even after Xury exits the scene when other slaves substitute symbolically for him in Brazil and the Caribbean and western Europe. The escape by the duo from bondage to a buccaneer therefore does not equate to fraternal freedom. It merely shifts who is in charge of whose body. Although Xury, as Crusoe acknowledges, turns out to be a helpful companion throughout their ensuing wanderings southwest along the Moroccan coast, the dynamics of his servitude are never abandoned. As the first of many underlings of the protagonist, he thus appears on the proscenium of the transatlantic set of the novel. Xury establishes the role of coerced body to Crusoe. Others will follow. And when they evidently do not, their absence will connote to Crusoe an intangible and haunting resistance to his own presence.

After many days at sea and within view of the Cape Verde islands, Crusoe and Xury are picked up by a ship that is captained by a friendly Portuguese. Crusoe promptly sells the youth: "he [the captain] offered me also 60 pieces of eight more for my boy Xury, which I was loath to take, not that I was not willing to let the captain have him, but I was very loath to sell the poor boy's liberty, who had assisted me so faithfully in procuring my own."[8] Though the idea of trafficking Xury is initiated by the captain and Crusoe professes to dislike it, his qualms about re-enslaving the boy are not particularly believable. Crusoe had not been troubled by the idea of drowning Xury or forcing him into servitude at the start of their travels. And the phrase "my boy Xury" resounds easily with Crusoe's multiple references decades later to another obeisant subject, "my man Friday."[9] It suggests that Crusoe sees Xury not so much as a fellow prisoner and then escapee but as chattel. The vision is not unique to the Portuguese captain. As Roxann Wheeler notes, "Xury's status is as a slave not a servant precisely because he is understood to belong to Crusoe who has no contractual rights to his labor or person."[10] Unsurprisingly, the captain and Crusoe quickly reach a compromise in which Xury would be sold and, "if he turned Christian," the captain would free him in ten years.[11] In short, Crusoe sells Xury into a decade of servitude despite never having owned him in the first place. And the arrangement apparently will become lifelong if Xury decides to remain Islamic. Acceptance of a spiritual conquest is therefore the prerequisite for personal freedom. Crusoe placates his own conscience by noting that Xury says "he was willing to go" with the captain, but the boy's assertion is clearly under duress and hardly seems convincing.[12] At no point in the novel is Xury autonomously in charge of his own body, which is passed off from one master (the Moorish pirate) to another (Crusoe) to another (the Portuguese captain). No one manumits him. Crusoe enslaves a slave at his first opportunity and sells him at the next. An individual like that never lives in social isolation, whatever the solitude that may surround him. No man is an island when he is so experienced in the business of the main.

After the sale of Xury, the absence of bodies subject to Crusoe's control is but temporary. Indeed, not owning other human beings will prove unstomachable to him. In fact, and though it might come as a surprise to many people, this is the only period in the rest of the novel in which Crusoe is *not* a slaveholder. After the rescue near the Cape Verdes, the Portuguese captain carries Crusoe from eastern to western Atlantic shores. Their voyage of some three weeks ends with the ship arriving in the harbor of Salvador, Bahia, later to become infamous as the epicenter of the slave trade of Brazil and, arguably, the entire New World. Crusoe sets himself up as a plantation owner but a lack of laborers inhibits his economic growth. And a plantation without slaves is only a farm. In his third year in Brazil, Crusoe concludes that he "wanted help, and now I found more than before, I had done wrong in parting with my boy Xury."[13] Here again he assumes a right of possession of Xury ("my boy") despite his never legally owning him in the first place. Crusoe does not regret the enslavement per se of Xury, just the decision to sell him to the Portuguese captain instead of keeping the youth for himself. The phrase "I had done wrong" speaks not to ethical concerns but to practical and economic ones about capitalizing his plantation. Fortunately for Crusoe, the Portuguese captain helps transfer some of his money from England to Brazil, exchanges it en route for useful European goods, and throws in, as a gesture of friendship, "a servant under bond for six years service."[14] As a result, Crusoe finds his fortunes suddenly and vastly improved "in the advancement of my plantation; for the first thing I did, I bought me a negro slave and an European servant also."[15]

With Crusoe now invested in the commerce of slaves and indentured servants on both sides of the Atlantic, the former role of Xury has been filled by new human bodies. Indeed, Crusoe defines social relationships by such trafficking. While laboring on his plantation prior to acquiring the "negro slave" and the two servants, Crusoe observes that "I lived just like a man cast away upon some desolate island, that has no body there but himself."[16] The foreshadowing is remarkable for its implied equation of "no body" with no *servile* body. Crusoe is definitely surrounded by other people in Brazil, including a friendly neighboring plantation owner named Wells.[17] But before the financial intervention of the Portuguese captain, missing are unpaid laborers like Xury whose disloyalty is punishable by death. It is their absence, not those of peers like Wells, that makes Crusoe compare himself to "a man cast away upon some desolate island." He feels stranded in Brazil because he owns no human beings there. The absence of servant bodies in between the enslavements of Xury and the "negro" constitutes a challenge to his sense of social self. That is why from the moment Crusoe escapes from the Moorish pirate, the novel works toward providing him with real and potential slaves. As a corollary, any time such enslavements are contested by absence, for instance by the famous footprint in the sand, Crusoe finds himself haunted.

The endless reproductions of the novel and its offshoots rarely frame their protagonist as an early and frequent enslaver. Phrases approximate to "the first thing I did, I bought me a negro slave" tend not to appear in performances of even the most obviously derivative castaway narratives. Yet the acquisition of Friday on the island is only the most known of Crusoe's procurements of chattel. Indeed, the whole reason why Crusoe leaves Brazil aiming to re-cross the Atlantic is to secure more slaves for himself and his fellow plantation owners. After Crusoe regales them with "how easy it was to purchase upon the [African] coast, for trifles . . . ne-groes, for the service of the Brasils, in great numbers," they propose to outfit a ship for just that purpose.[18] The plan is for Crusoe to lead the expedition across the ocean without having to pay for any part of it. His compensation, as he notes, will be "that I should have my equal share of the negroes."[19] Again, comments like that do not generally spring to mind as staples of subsequent desert island plots. And Crusoe is no ac-cidental slaver. He operates in the vanguard of venture capital. He is a market leader, for according to him, slave trafficking "was a trade at that time not only not far entred into, but as far as it was, had been carried on by the assientoes, or permission of the kings of Spain and Portugal."[20] For the duration of his absence, Crusoe legally entrusts the management of his plantation to his partners. They oversee his property, both human and geographic, with such success that, as he learns at the end of the novel, his quantity of slaves multiplies prodigiously while he is away. This makes him a very prosperous man even when he is alone on the island. Although he does not know it while stranded for over twenty-eight years, Crusoe never ceases to be a slave owner from the moment he purchases the "negro" as "the first thing I did" upon having enough money to do so.

The apparent absences on the Caribbean island where Crusoe finds himself are destined to be temporary because his world only makes sense within a succession of scripted servitudes. In other words, Crusoe ar-rives on the island embroiled in transatlantic dynamics of empire and embodiment. He is acutely aware of the competing national and sub-national interests involved in the ongoing scramble for booty, human and otherwise, on both sides of the ocean. He knows that the riches on western and eastern shores are constantly in play and falling to who-ever proves most successful at controlling local bodies in any given moment and place. The island is consequently an empire available for any conquistador to seize. Such is the ideological presumption that both produces *Robinson Crusoe* and follows from it. As Rebecca Weaver-Hightower observes about the novel and its narrative progeny, "by help-ing generations of readers to make sense of (perhaps feel better about) imperial aggression, the castaway story, in effect, enabled the expansion and maintenance of European empire . . . castaway tales . . . made imperial expansion and control seem unproblematic and natural."[21] Indeed, when surrounded by nothing, Crusoe is still surrounded by everything. He lives on an island seemingly isolated from all human contact, but he perceives it as part of the transatlantic. Slaving led him both west and east across the ocean and so is inextricable from any lands he happens upon in between. His physical alienation on the island is never matched by a psychological remove. Although the would-be slaves in Africa that he intended to obtain before the shipwreck remain virtual, as do, in a different sense, the actual slaves increasing on his Brazilian plantation in his absence, Crusoe comes up with ways to embody new ones even on the allegedly asocial island.

Shortly after the shipwreck that launched a thousand other shipwrecks, Crusoe notes, "It is not easy for any one, who has not been in the like condition, to describe or conceive the consternation of men in such circumstances; we knew nothing where we were, or upon what land it was we were driven, whether an island or the main, whether inhabited or not inhabited."[22] Earlier consultations of "charts of the sea-coast of America" have helped him but little and, though he and the ship's master had decided to try to gain Barbados, one of "the circle of Carribee-Islands," they fail to arrive at a known place on their maps.[23] Instead of reaching "some of our English islands, where I hoped for relief," Crusoe finds himself a lone survivor on an island that is apparently uninhabited by any indigenous society and unclaimed by any imperial power.[24] Here he will start with nothing and create something; here he will craft the island in his own image. Here, in sum, he will colonize a seemingly empty space. But a peculiar sort of colonization it is, for it initially seems to lack indigenous bodies to play the role of the colonized. They will (dis)appear eventually in the form of a footprint in the sand, an apparition that is bound to return. The alienation of the island proves only ostensible and the flesh-and-blood subjects, uncannily elusive. Crusoe's ongoing struggle to embody the absent and inscribe upon them a manifest Conquest amounts to an attempt to incorporate ghosts into servitude.

The New World seems to Crusoe an organic entity. When he spots land across the water during an early attempt to survey his shipwrecked position, he notes, "I could not tell what part of the world this might be, otherwise than that I knew it must be part of America, and, as I concluded by all my observations, must be near the Spanish dominions, and perhaps was all inhabited by savages."[25] The "America" to which he refers is not defined by specific territories but by the overall hemispheric theater in which various players compete for leading roles. To Crusoe, peering from his island, "America" offers an extensive and iterating staging of peoples in sundry but parallel power struggles. His separation from human society, which would in theory allow him to start his life anew on an island unmarked by history, is contrasted by the combat between Europeans and indigenes that he knows to be raging around him on the visible continent. Crusoe, if not his avatars in popular culture and many of their readers and viewers, is aware that he is not so isolated. Consequently, there is a profound hollowness in his claim, "I am divided from mankind, a solitaire, one banished from humane society."[26] He may be divided from mankind by a bit of water, but he is no solitaire and he is not banished. The society from which he is physically separated, rife with conflict, is not all that humane or human either.

The social absences that envelop Crusoe at first are misleading. On his arrival, the island seems devoid of local and continuous human presences, though it will ultimately turn out that cannibals visit the far shore with some frequency to dine and dance. The island genuinely does lack intermittent presences in the form of European ships sailing on nearby commercial routes. Therefore, the constant arrival of potential escape vessels on Gilligan's Island and other castaway loci has little parallel in their literary ancestor. Crusoe washes up onto a relatively barren stretch of litoral land, which leads him to believe that he is "cast upon a horrible desolate island."[27] Ten months later, however, he surveys more of the island and finds that it is good:

> the country appeared so fresh, so green, so flourishing, every thing being in a constant verdure or flourish of spring, that it looked like a planted garden. I descended a little on the side of that delicious vale, surveying it with a secret kind of pleasure (tho' mixt with my other afflicting thoughts) to think that this was all my own, that I was king and lord of all this country indefeasibly, and had a right of possession.[28]

This area appears as prelapsarian and presocial, brimming with pristine nature. And with no one else present to claim this virginal vernal land that lacks all humans, Crusoe assumes automatically that he has "a right of possession" to it. He is "king and lord of all this country indefeasibly." He seems to be the sole inhabitant of a terrestrial paradise, a figure akin to Adam alone in a "garden" at the start of a new world. Enthralled by his edenic discovery, Crusoe writes that "the green limes that I gathered were not only pleasant to eat, but very wholesome; and I mixed their juice afterwards with water, which made it very wholesome, and very cool and refreshing."[29] Yet Adam begins life in his Garden as truly asocial. Crusoe, by contrast, is a transatlantic slave trader.

There is a qualitative difference between a new world and the New World. Crusoe does not write his life upon the island as if upon a clean slate because his sense of authorship and authority carries over wholesale from his prior slaving experiences. Although he is often interpreted as inscribing a fresh narrative for himself and, metaphorically in his pseudo-adamic role, for all humanity, that narrative essentially recapitulates the preceding one in which he left Brazil "to fetch negroes."[30] Though Crusoe wishes he had not been shipwrecked, he never regrets the mission of the ill-fated journey per se. He remonstrates himself instead for not having stayed at home in order to buy Africans "from those whose business it was to fetch them."[31] The Crusoe of lore is a man alone on an island, but the island is never insular and he is never alone. His world is populated with virtual corpora destined to corporealize in one form or another. And when tangible bodies appear, Crusoe intends to inscribe them into empire. Correspondingly, when indigenes and indigenous textualities leave the *Popol Vuh* and the diary of Columbus's first voyage, their withdrawals always betoken resistance to foreign control. A disembodied footprint in the sand in *Robinson Crusoe* will effect the same. Absence will haunt the "king and lord of all this country," too.

With no humans available to fetch or buy or seize, Crusoe fills their role with a talking bird. Obtaining a servant on an uninhabited island is no easy task, but Crusoe is no feckless enslaver. Soon after recognizing that he is proximate to the geopolitics of the mainland, Crusoe "saw an abundance of parrots, and fain I would have caught one, if possible, to have kept it to be tame, and taught it to speak to me. I did, after some pains taking, catching a young parrot, for I knocked it down with a stick, and having recovered it, I brought it home."[32] He teaches the parrot, whom he names Poll, to speak and call to him. Later he will follow a similar sequence with Friday. Poll, not Friday, is the first indigene on the island to be deprived of his freedom and forced into mimicry. Estimating that Spaniards and indigenes are nearby on the visible continent, and no doubt assuming that the two groups are either battling each other or bound to do so, Crusoe is inspired to act aggressively as a conquistador. Thus he seizes and domesticates his first indigenous subject, Poll. Assuming possession of that local body and enclosing it is the opening order of business for him once he finishes his trip around the island:

"most of the time was taken up in the weighty affair of making a cage for my Poll."[33] Evidently, "my Poll" is the best surrogate available for the missing domesticated human bodies of "my boy Xury," of the slaves and servants in Brazil, and of the "negroes" to be fetched in Africa. The parrot is a stand-in for the role ultimately to be played by "my man Friday."

Other animals form part of a growing collection that Crusoe oversees on the island, including cats who survive the shipwreck and a young goat that his dog captures and which Crusoe hopes to breed. Yet none of them bears both virtual personhood and indigenousness like Poll. The dog accompanies Crusoe faithfully for many years and comes closest to servanthood, but he does not talk and is not native to the island. As another survivor of the shipwreck, the dog does not go through the set piece in which Crusoe comes upon an indigene in his local environment, demonstrates physical power over him, and determines his limits. Unlike Poll and Friday, the dog also does not suffer the colonial imposition of Crusoe's naming him. Only in a personified parrot does Crusoe find before Friday an aborigine of the island to play the role of conquered. And he does so immediately upon deducing that he lives within eyesight of the ongoing Conquest. That projection of Spaniards and indigenes on the mainland resolves him anew into conquering mode.

Poll cannot lend manpower proper to the growth of Crusoe's domain, which is why even after teaching him to speak Crusoe says that he still "wished for my boy Xury."[34] The parrot remains, however, if not quite a person (a characterization that Crusoe might well apply to all his slaves in any case) then certainly an indigenous and subjected personhood. For example, when referring to himself in the third person and as royalty, Crusoe triumphantly writes of his meals, "there was my majesty the prince and lord of the whole island; I had the lives of all my subjects at my absolute command; I could hang, draw, give liberty, and take it away, and no rebels among all my subjects. Then to see how like a king I dined too, all alone, attended by my servants. Poll, as if he had been my favourite, was the only person permitted to talk to me."[35] Just as Crusoe had arrogated the right to have drowned Xury, he now lords life and death, freedom and captivity, over his "subjects" and "servants" such as Poll, a veritable "person." This embodiment of a free being into a conquered subject fits easily within Crusoe's sense of still being adjacent to a colonial world while on his supposedly isolated island. His regal dinners are of a piece with his selling of Xury, his installing of slavery on his Brazilian plantation, and his embarking on a transatlantic slaving mission.

Poll is usually mentioned in scholarship, if at all, for a single scene that takes place when the sleeping Crusoe is awakened "by a voice calling me by my name several times, 'Robin, Robin, Robin Crusoe, poor Robin Crusoe, where are you, Robin Crusoe? Where are you? Where have you been?"[36] These are questions, as often recognized, at the thematic core of the novel. And certainly, these are questions that the footprint in the sand, shortly to appear, and Friday—the disembodied and the embodied, the absent specter and the present servant—will prompt Crusoe to respond in full to eventually. Yet in many ways, Crusoe long has established where he is and where he has been: immersed in a transatlantic Conquest from which he has never been separated by geography or psychology or praxis. New World lands quite possibly controlled by Spain lie within sight; the slaves and servants he still owns in Brazil, though unknown to him, are only increasing; and his colonization of the island already includes a virtual slave in the form of a parrot who sits unctuously by his side as a "person" at dinner.

The significance of the only well-known passage involving Poll is not the posing of metatextual questions but the suggestion of haunting in the brief moments in which Crusoe is unsure of the "voice calling" him. Poll enters the scene in a ghostly environment that the sleeping conquistador mistakenly identifies as a dreamworld. At first, Crusoe cannot locate the source or nature of the disembodied voice and so, waking up, "was at first dreadfully frighted, and started up in the utmost consternation."[37] It is this fleeting moment in which absence overturns his comprehension and control of his world. Once that absence is fleshed into the subject body of Poll, Crusoe can regain confidence in his role as colonizer. Still, the mere shock of the spectral sound defers that resumption a bit more: "even though I knew it was the parrot, and that indeed it could be no body else, it was a good while before I could compose my self."[38] Such is the power of ghosts: their disembodiment allows them to threaten the corporeal integrity of those who seek to cage them. The resolution of the parrot's voice into Poll proper is tantamount to colonization. The span of absence in which that reduction does not occur is that in which colonization fails. This passage appears just a half score of pages before the discovery of the ghostly footprint in the sand and foreshadows it, literally. For so long as an indigenous body remains obviously intangible, Crusoe the conqueror is haunted out of his wits.

The many conscious acts of taking possession of the bodies of others both before and after the shipwreck imply that, each time, Crusoe reenacts a shadow play whose lines he knows well. Brazilian plantation owner that he is, Crusoe begins speaking of his two "plantations" on the island, then three.[39] His is a role, not a renaissance. He begins his castaway life bereft of an audience but not of a script. This, moreover, is no one-man performance. At first there appears to be nothing and no one in the empty theater that is the island, but just because some things cannot be seen does not mean they are not there. The atextualized predecessor of the *Popol Vuh* is one example of that. The Moors and Jews absented in the opening pages of Columbus's diary are another. And Crusoe, like Columbus, equates his arrival on unfamiliar shores to ownership of them. He, too, operates on the presumption that, without competing European claimants, all lands he steps on are his. Adam may have been cast out of the Garden but Crusoe and Columbus frame themselves as cast into it. Informed by the transatlantic, they then take possession of all the trees they find there. The fruits are those of empire.

They likewise take possession of the individuals they come across. Conquests require bodies to fill designated roles. A conquest without subjects is not a conquest at all. Defoe's novel rectifies the initial lack of a conquered on the island with the training of Poll to pay Crusoe obeisance, and then of Friday to do the same. In the case of Columbus when he lands on other Caribbean islands, indigenes, too, are immediately categorized as colonized subjects. Only those who disappear before him escape the reach of his conquest by haunting it from their atextual spaces. This is akin to the spectral resistances manifested at the commencement and conclusion of written versions of the *Popol Vuh*. Crusoe, however, does not find on his arrival an available corps of indigenes whom he can subsume into servitude. But over time and whenever possible, he goes about appropriating residents of the island. Though he arrives on its shores a wreck of a seafarer, he is never a wreck of a conquistador.

That is why a trace of absence is as pivotal to the haunting of empire in *Robinson Crusoe* as it is in the *Popol Vuh* and *I, Rigoberta Menchú* and Columbus's diary of his first voyage. The outline of a foot that the castaway sees in the sand, the hint of the human that terrifies him so, marks what is almost the halfway point of the book. Most individuals today who never have read Defoe's novel, but are familiar with its basic tropes, are likely to assume that the title character and Friday pair up throughout as an early version of the Lone Ranger and Tonto. Yet this is not the case. Friday does not enter the plot until the last third of the novel, well after the footprint. In fact, Crusoe spends only the final four of his twenty-eight years on the island with him. When Friday does appear on stage, his role is to provide a human body on which Crusoe can reinscribe the Conquest from which he has been separated only in the most insular sense of geography. After all, Crusoe was shipwrecked on a slaving voyage and believes his island to be near Spanish expansionism on the visible mainland. Unlike Friday, however, the footprint is invisible. The key dialectic of the book is therefore not the relationship between the two famous characters, Crusoe and Friday, but the tension between the colonizer and the specter of the sands. The trace of a disembodied otherness spooks Crusoe because he cannot incorporate it. The footprint, like those in Columbus and in the bookending passages of the *Popol Vuh*, suggests an indigenous presence on the island that precedes Crusoe and that is not subject to his grasp because its very corpus is intangible. His dominion over the island is threatened by that which he cannot seize upon, that which eludes his ken and his capture. He could control the bodies of Xury and Poll and, had it not been for a hurricane, of the men and women he intended to purchase in Africa. But he cannot control what is not there.

Crusoe invokes a spectral discourse the moment he comes across the footprint. His vocabulary is suddenly full of apparitions and shades. "I stood like one thunder-struck, or as if I had seen an apparition; I listened, I looked round me, I could hear nothing, nor see any thing."[40] His senses reveal only terrifying absences. He adds soon that he "was ready to sink into the ground at but the shadow or silent appearance of a man's having set his foot in the island."[41] The imagery is ghostly. A shadow, a silent appearance, a deferred full presence contrast with the corporeal inability of Crusoe himself to melt away. The ectoplasm of opposition envelops him. The absent presences of America unnerve him. "When I came to my castle," he recounts, "for so I think I called it ever after this, I fled into it like one pursued."[42] Chased by the perception of a ghost, he terms his home as a "castle." Like Columbus, he suspects that specters constitute disembodied resistance to his presence. The questioning voice of Poll resolved quickly into a submissive body, but the footprint does not seem likely to do the same. Terrified, Crusoe tries to convince himself that maybe the footprint is really his own. He supposes that he "had played the part of those fools who strive to make stories of spectres and apparitions, and then are frighted at them more than any body."[43] So, feeling braver, he goes back and measures the footprint. It is not his. The "spectres and apparitions" are real after all. And so he reflects, "I had lived here fifteen years now, and had not met with the least shadow or figure of any people yet."[44] This language is suitably uncanny, for what he confronts now is not actual humanity but the "shadow or figure" of such. Therein lies its contestation of his colonization.

After the appearance of the apparition, Crusoe is haunted to the point at which he feels his own self in danger of disarticulation. As Michel de Certeau notes,

> Robinson Crusoe already indicated himself how a crack appeared in his scriptural empire. For a time, his enterprise was in fact inter-rupted, and haunted, by an absent other that returned to the shores of the island, by "the print of a man's naked foot on the shore." The instability of the limits set: the frontier yields to something foreign. On the margins of the page, the mark of an "apparition" disturbs the order that a capitalizing and methodical labor had constructed.[45]

Here, de Certeau recognizes that the trace of "an absent other that re-turned" rewrites Crusoe's script of appropriation. The narrative of col-onization that Crusoe thought he was authoring on the island is now matched, perhaps even overwhelmed, by a ghosted one that manifestly he is not. The absent textuality haunts Crusoe's "scriptural empire" be-cause he cannot incorporate the unincorporated. Poll can be thwacked and taught to speak, but no ghost is a parrot. Specters are simulacra that challenge by virtue of their very difference from those who face them. Only when Friday materializes as an embodied indigene does Crusoe again regain confidence in his drama of Conquest. As de Certeau ob-serves, "Robinson will see someone (Friday) and will recover the power of mastery when he has the opportunity to see, that is, when the absent other shows himself. Then he will be once again within his order."[46] Fri-day, of course, will do more than show himself. He will parrot Crusoe faithfully as well.

Ghosts force their witnesses to question a prevailing and accepted narrative by putting forth an alternative narrative whose parameters challenge existing arrangements of power. The footprint haunts the re-gime that Crusoe thought he had established over Poll and the rest of his menagerie and over the island itself. Only a human body brought to servitude will be able to trump the indigenous apparition indicated by the outline of a foot. But, unfortunately for Crusoe, the first people who do arrive on the island are as uncontrollable as ghosts. In the in-terval between the appearances of the footprint and of Friday, Crusoe realizes that cannibals who live on the mainland occasionally come over to eat their victims. Operating beyond his power and jurisdiction, they naturally appear to him as spectral: "these savage people who sometimes haunted this island."[47] The verb "haunted" carries a phantasmal sense here beyond an otherwise equivalent verb like "frequented" in that the indigenes, in their ungovernability, are ghostly. Crusoe cannot compel their presence on his terms and this further unnerves his "life of anxiety, fear, and care which I had lived ever since I had seen the print of a foot in the sand."[48] As Peter Hulme observes, "The period between the discovery of the footprint and the arrival of the cannibals is the period of greatest anxiety for Crusoe, the period in which, one might say, his notion of self is most under threat . . . the single, isolated footprint in the middle of the beach [is] more like a pure trace of the idea of otherness than the actual track of another human being."[49] The very suggestion of an inassimilable "otherness" constitutes the contestation of Crusoe as colonizer. That is why the ghostliness of the footprint disturbs him so. It unsettles his very settlement.

By drawing lessons from his past in Africa and Brazil and on the island, Crusoe hits upon a solution: he will force the ghosts into embodiment, absence into presence, the unincarnated and free into the incarnated and subject. They will no longer haunt the island once he chains them down. Thus he plots, "I fancied my self able to manage one, nay, two or three savages, if I had them, so as to make them entirely slaves to me, to do whatever I should direct them."[50] The later conscription of Friday into servitude, so often the centerpiece of popular and scholarly attention, seems almost incidental. The patterns into which Friday fits are so engrained already. As with Poll, Crusoe bestows a name on him and teaches him to speak English and to accept his place in a colonial hierarchy: "I made him know his name should be Friday, which was the day I saved his life; I called him so for the memory of the time; I likewise taught him to say Master, and then let him know, that was to be my name."[51] Adds Crusoe, "[I] let him know I would give him some cloaths, at which he seemed very glad, for he was stark naked."[52] Having tagged and draped this absent conquered that finally has appeared in flesh and blood, this surrogate embodiment of the footprint in the sand and of the haunting cannibals, Crusoe now begins "to instruct him in the knowledge of the true God."[53] The evangelical Conquest long commenced on the mainland now reiterates on the island as well. And Crusoe, a method actor with ample training on the world stage, performs his role of conqueror yet again.

The above passages involving Friday are among the most cited and dissected in *Robinson Crusoe* and do not need further exegesis here. It is important to underline, however, that from the moment Crusoe spots him in flight from other cannibals and decides to save him, he sees Friday as an embodied subject in the mold of characters from Xury to Poll. The castaway is actually cast away from very little. On seeing Friday running and swimming for his life, Crusoe immediately thinks, "now was my time to get me a servant."[54] After the successful rescue, this plan comes to fruition when Friday sets Crusoe's foot "upon his head; this it seems was in token of swearing to be my slave for ever."[55] A short time later, recalls Crusoe, Friday "made all the signs to me of subjection, servitude, and submission imaginable, to let me know how he would serve me as long as he lived."[56] These renowned scenes are rarely linked to Poll. Yet one of the first things that Crusoe does with Friday is impress and intimidate him by shooting a wild parrot. The metaphorical import is clear: Friday must follow Poll into the tamed mimicry of servitude or else face the force that felled the wild parrot, a surrogate for Poll's previous freedom. As Crusoe recounts the scene, "I made him understand that I would shoot and kill that bird; according I fired and bad him look, and immediately he saw the parrot fall, he stood like one frighted again."[57] Now it is a colonizer who scares a present indigene into submission and not, as in the case of the footprint, an absent indigenous specter who terrifies a would-be colonizer. Since the wild parrot, "not being quite dead," is still fluttering on the ground, Crusoe orders Friday "to run and fetch the bird I had shot."[58] The wild parrot, like its alter egos Poll and Friday, now is a controllable body and thus despite hovering between life and death offers no ghostly ability to contest Crusoe's will to possess him.

With the potential resistance of indigenous specters—the footprint in the sand, the haunting cannibals, even the wild parrot—now assimilated into the flesh of Friday, the imperial theater that is the novel has a thicker cast of servants and slaves in place. Friday, though a local Caribbean indigene, achieves a triple incorporation as a deferred realization of the African aborigines whom Crusoe intended to procure when he sailed from Brazil, as an embodiment of the footprint in the sand, and as a cannibal who does not haunt the island like the others. That is, Friday functions as an enslaved and material convocation of three different iterations of absence. Writes Peter Hulme, "Friday is certainly a slave inasmuch as he has no will of his own."[59] And Stephen Zelnick remarks, "Neither Xury nor Friday is a negro. . . . And yet the whole problem they refer to *is* African slavery."[60] This is not to say that all servitudes in the novel are the same. Xury the *morisco* and Friday the indigene are not ultimately resolvable to each other, nor is Friday, of course, to that other servile indigene of the island, Poll the parrot, nor is any of the above to the humans owned by Crusoe on his Brazilian plantation. Yet all conjoin in that Crusoe produces their diverse bodies so that they might serve him. To this extent they reiterate each other. With sundry specters now corporealized via Friday into what de Certeau terms Crusoe's "scriptural empire," with undomesticated apparitions now supplemented by a tamed body, the conqueror can proceed apace with his Conquest.[61] This is the performance of transatlantic America: absences convoked servitude and escaping from the same.

A different performance of the Conquest by another shipwrecked European, Álvar Núñez Cabeza de Vaca, provides a counterpoint to Crusoe's own rendition. The two men share the postapocalyptic experience of washing up shipwrecked on unknown shores. Like Crusoe, Cabeza de Vaca loses virtually all that he has and therefore, seemingly, all that he is. His situation is complicated by the multiple aboriginal presences that continually surround him. Indigenes alternately dress him, enslave him, provide him with food, trade with him, treat him as a healer with magical powers, and teach him their language. Whereas Crusoe seeks to inscribe indigenousness within the semiotics of European civilization, Cabeza de Vaca finds himself instead being written within indigenous textualities. His account of his adventures is thus often read today as an inversion of the triumphalist imperial chronicles of the New World. In the most dramatic case of role reversal, Europeans and not indigenes are the ones who eventually fall to eating each other. This possibility is alluded to briefly in *Robinson Crusoe* but never consummated.[62] Cabeza de Vaca and his few fellow survivors, despite being shipwrecked like Crusoe, never appear as new Adams in a new Eden. This is because other people are already there and because they hardly find themselves in Paradise.

Yet just as much as Crusoe and Columbus, Cabeza de Vaca is familiar with his script ahead of time. Its outline never leaves his mind, regardless of the travails he suffers. He knows all along that the role he is supposed to play is an imperial one. As a result, despite the dearth of chances to step onto stage in that capacity, he does so whenever possible. For instance, when styled as a healer by one group of indigenes, Cabeza de Vaca notes that "The manner in which we performed cures was by making the sign of the cross over them and blowing on them, and praying a Pater Noster [The Lord's Prayer] and an Ave Maria [Hail Mary]."[63] Though more fettered by circumstance than Crusoe, Cabeza de Vaca here takes advantage of an opportunity to inscribe his own Fridays into a prefabricated religious textuality. This is reminiscent of all the evangelizations by Columbus and Crusoe, enacted as well as anticipated. It amounts to a momentary success by Cabeza de Vaca at playing the part he assigns himself before his ship even goes down.

As much as Crusoe, Cabeza de Vaca knows that an empire must have subjects. Otherwise, it is not so much an empire as a desert island. Consequently, when Cabeza de Vaca eventually nears outlying Spanish settlements, he is dismayed to learn that all the indigenes in the area have fled to the mountains: "We traveled through much land and we found all of it deserted, because the inhabitants of it went fleeing through the sierras without daring to keep houses or work the land for fear of the Christians."[64] This absenting, familiar from the diary of Columbus's first voyage, is a strategic move by indigenous peoples to remove themselves from the advancing Spanish empire. Recognizing this, Cabeza de Vaca proposes that a peaceful Conquest replace the militaristic, enslaving one that is underway: "it is clearly seen that all these peoples, to be drawn to become Christians and to obedience to the Imperial Majesty, must be given good treatment."[65] His goal is not the mitigation of the Conquest per se nor a toleration of plurality. Instead, he wants to conjure forth as many indigenous bodies as possible so that they might "be drawn to become Christians and to obedience to the Imperial Majesty." Depopulation does not an empire make.

A local Spanish mayor pleads with Cabeza de Vaca to convoke the vanished bodies: "the land was abandoned and not cultivated and all of it greatly destroyed, and the Indians went about hidden and in flight through the highlands without wanting to come and settle themselves in their villages; and [he asked] [sic] that we have them called together and order them on behalf of God and Your Majesty to come and settle the plain and work the land."[66] Such desires for indigenous incorporation are, as in the case of Crusoe, eventually realized:

> after the children [of the most important indigenous lords] had been baptized, we departed for the *villa* of San Miguel, where, when we arrived, Indians came who told us how many people were coming down from the sierras and populating the plain and making churches and crosses and doing everything we had commanded them . . . the Indians were down from the sierras and had populated the plain, and they [the Christians] had found populous villages that earlier were abandoned and deserted, and that the Indians came out to receive them with crosses in their hands and took them to their houses and shared with them what they had.[67]

The land is disembodied no more. The indigenes, fully present, now act in the role of Friday. And Cabeza de Vaca at last oversees his theater like Crusoe. Though once haunted by vanished co-authors, the imperial script can now scroll forward without ghostwriters. After all, the absent corpora implied by footprints presented a presence contestatory to any attempted Conquest. Bodies can be chained but not specters. And colonies beset by elusive subjects are not colonies at all.

The passages in *Robinson Crusoe* that invoke Spaniards are often cues to situating Crusoe within larger imperial contexts. This is notable early in the book via the episodes involving Xury, who as a *morisco* is a living legacy of centuries of struggle between northern Africans and southern Europeans for control of Iberia. And later on the island, Crusoe comments repeatedly on the Spanish involvement in the European scramble for the New World, the same sprawling drama in which the similarly shipwrecked Cabeza de Vaca once transformed himself into a conquistador. Crusoe is so attuned to the territorial struggles ongoing in the lands visible from his island that he articulates political positions on them. For example, he dwells several times on the widespread accounts of hyperbolic Spanish atrocities in the New World. These influential stories are collectively known as the Black Legend. While reflecting that ignorant local cannibals ought not be held accountable for their gastronomic habits, Crusoe argues to himself that

> therefore it could not be just for me to fall upon them. That this would justify the conduct of the Spaniards in all their barbarities practised in America, where they destroyed millions of these people, who, however they were idolaters and barbarians, and had several bloody and barbarious rites in their customs, such as sacrificing human bodies to their idols, were yet, as to the Spaniards, very innocent people; and that the rooting them out of the country is spoken of with the utmost abhorrence and detestation by even the Spaniards themselves at this time, and by all other Christian nations of Europe, as a meer butchery, a bloody and unnatural piece of cruelty, unjustifiable either to God or man; and such, as for which the very name of a Spaniard is reckoned to be frightful and terrible to all people of humanity, or of Christian compassion.[68]

Crusoe later describes Spaniards as people "whose cruelties in America had been spread over the whole countries, and was remembered by all the nations from father to son."[69] His heartfelt belief in the Black Legend suggests that a geopolitical as well as psychological investment is at stake for him. Wheeler rightly cites such passages as proof that "In this depiction of the Spanish in particular, the novel reveals profound anxiety about the control of the Atlantic islands."[70] All horrified invocations by Crusoe of Spanish praxis serve as reminders that his physical separation from the rest of the New World is not paralleled by a mental isolation from what transpires there.

Spain was the first and largest of the transatlantic empires and the Caribbean was the site of its earliest presences. It makes sense that Crusoe, stranded in body but not in mind, positions himself vis-à-vis Spanish expansion in the New World. His denigration of Spanish "barbarities" is in line with longstanding attempts by northwestern European powers to privilege their own imperial behavior as civilized. This comforting story is implicit in the justifications by Crusoe, ever aware of being English, of his own colonizations. Peter Hulme thus concludes that Crusoe, in order to distance himself from Spaniards, utilizes the "ready-made rhetoric of the Black Legend."[71] And Kathryn Rummell, commenting on *A New Voyage Round the World*, a fictional narrative that Defoe published five years after *Robinson Crusoe*, writes, "Defoe's use of the Black Legend, then, allows him to advertise his colonial scheme in South America by asserting that the Spaniards are unfit to colonize. His manipulation of the Spanish stereotype [is] in order to further his own colonial designs."[72]

The surfacing of the Black Legend in *Robinson Crusoe* ties Defoe to the writings of Bartolomé de las Casas, whose *A Very Short Account of the Destruction of the Indies* narrates the early sixteenth-century obliterations of indigenous populations in lands held by Spain throughout the New World.[73] The *Very Short Account* served for centuries as a foundational source of the Black Legend. In the opening pages, for example, Las Casas depicts conquistadors as approaching vulnerable indigenous populations "like extremely cruel wolves and tigers and lions who had been hungry for many days. And they have done nothing else for the last forty years through today, and still today they do it, other than cut them into pieces, kill them, distress them, afflict them, torment them and destroy them by strange and new and varied manners of cruelty, the likes of which have never before been seen nor read nor heard."[74] As Chris Schmidt-Nowara observes of Las Casas, "no single author is so closely identified with the origins of the Black Legend, particularly in regards to Spanish cruelties in the Americas."[75] Rummell believes that Defoe personally owned a 1642 translation of the *Very Short Account* from Lyon.[76] And she describes Defoe as a "consummate imperialist" who "capitalizes on European translations of Las Casas in order to castigate the Spaniards. . . . I would argue that he knew Las Casas' work fairly well."[77]

Las Casas also is important as an implicit referent for the island in *Robinson Crusoe* because he contextualizes the castaway within the macrohistorical transatlantic roots of absent presences in the Caribbean. As editor of the surviving version of Columbus's diary of the first voyage, Las Casas co-authors the inaugural script of the appearances of disappearance in the New World. He is directly responsible for keeping in the diary the myriad descriptions of absenting indigenes. Possibly, by excising other parts of the journal, he even increased the relative prominence of those passages. And the footprint in the sand that unnerves Crusoe so is a descendant of the footprints in the sands that unnerve Columbus. Both men are spooked by visible invisibility. Both arm themselves against specters. Both discover their Caribbean colonizing projects to be haunted. The intertextualities with Las Casas's ghosted corpus, including the diary and the *Very Short Account*, indicate that *Robinson Crusoe* is profoundly enmeshed within an extensive chronological and spatial transatlantic production of absence.

The Black Legend always doubled, none too subtly, as a Protestant critique of Catholic comportment as well as of malevolent imperial behavior per se. Expansionist nations like England with deep investments in the Reformation were eager to gain discursive and territorial advantage over a rival power like Spain by characterizing the colonial procedures of the latter as brutish. Crusoe often has been portrayed as paradigmatically Protestant, from his attitudes toward labor and the material development of his island world to his instruction of Friday into Christianity without reliance on church institutions. Defoe, a Dissenter (a rubric covering non-Anglican English Protestants), was intensely embroiled in various religious disputes of his day. He prolifically issued pamphlets taking controversial stands on them. He lambasted as hypocritical, for example, those Dissenters who occasionally opted to take communion with Anglicans. And the connections between Catholic theology of the Eucharist and the popularity of the Black Legend in Protestant lands are not as distant as might seem. The church interpretation of the consumption of the host and wine as a literal intaking of body and blood could be used by antagonistic polemicists to correlate Catholic nations like Spain with cannibalistic practices. At times, this seems to be a subtext of Crusoe's twinned fears of Spanish savagery and of indigenous anthropophagy.

Nevertheless, Defoe does not uniformly represent Spaniards as barbaric, either in his most famous novel or in subsequent works such as *The Farther Adventures of Robinson Crusoe* and *A New Voyage Round the*

World. His associations of Spanish imperialism with the Black Legend often do not concretize in Crusoe's specific interactions with particular Spaniards. For example, when he discovers a Spanish captive about to be killed and eaten by cannibals, Crusoe unhesitatingly frees him, speaks to him in Spanish, and arms him in order to together fight off his foes. In the melee that follows, Crusoe approvingly describes the Spaniard "as bold and as brave as could be imagined."[78] Later, Crusoe refers to the newcomer's countrymen on the mainland as "our friends, the Spaniards."[79] The importance of the scattered presences of Spain and Spaniards throughout *Robinson Crusoe* is therefore not that they conform consistently to stereotypes of a colonial power competing with Britain (or with Crusoe as the British empire personified) but that they repeatedly puncture any presumption that the island is segregated from the complex flows of the imperial transatlantic.

Spaniards arrive at the island, in fact, the same way that Crusoe does, via a shipwreck. In his twenty-fourth year on the island, a vessel founders on offshore rocks and seventeen Spaniards and some Portuguese manage to make it to the mainland in a smaller boat. Crusoe visits the wreck only after the survivors have left it, so he remains unaware of their fate for some time. He does identify the ship as Spanish and guesses, correctly as it turns out, that it crashed en route from Argentina to Cuba.[80] Several years later, one of the Spanish sailors turns up on the island as the intended and aforementioned repast of the cannibals. He is the first European to arrive alive ashore since Crusoe. As such, he is a potential ally as well as a potential foe. Inchoate at this point are the prospects of a symbolic restaging of the Conquest in which an Englishmen and a Spaniard, representing their respective homeland empires, vie for dominance of the island and its resources. Consequently, Crusoe exults after he saves the Spaniard and asserts control of all the denizens at hand, who now include Friday, the Spaniard, Friday's father (who arrived coincidentally with the Spaniard as another edible captive) and, metaphorically, Poll and the other domesticated animals: "My island was now peopled, and I thought myself very rich in subjects; and it was a merry reflection which I frequently made, how like a king I looked. First of all, the whole country was my own meer property; so that I had an undoubted right of dominion. 2ndly, my people were perfectly subjected: I was absolute lord and lawgiver; they all owed their lives to me and were ready to lay down their lives, if there had been occasion of it, for me."[81]

Flush with unassailable power over land and inhabitants alike, Crusoe has culminated a colonial trajectory that only temporarily was in tatters when he washed up to the island nearly three decades earlier. Eventually, he sends the Spaniard back to the mainland to fetch the other shipwrecked Iberians so that they all might build a boat together and escape the region for good. Wary of betrayal by potential geopolitical rivals, Crusoe makes the Spaniard swear that all the Iberians would "be directed wholly and absolutely by my orders . . . [bound by] a contract from under their hands for that purpose."[82] Crusoe has such a dim view of collective Spanish action that he would prefer to take his chances with hungry cannibals more than with dangerous Catholics: "I had rather be delivered up to the savages, and be devoured alive, than fall into the merciless claws of the priests, and be carry'd into the Inquisition."[83] Crusoe may be away from other theaters but he is never alienated from them. He steps into every scene with an ease achieved only by knowing a very old script by heart.

While the Spaniard is gone—Crusoe now refers to him as "my Spaniard," a locution resonant of "my boy Xury" and "my Poll" and "my man Friday"—an English ship run by mutineers lands on the island. Aided by Friday, Crusoe rescues its captain and the sailors loyal to him, and seizes the malcontents. Throughout this sequence, the stratagems with which Crusoe handles the mutineers are highly theatrical. This underlines the performative nature of his presence on the island from the very beginning. As James H. Maddox observes, "In this episode, Crusoe is not only spectator but also playwright and director, as he confidently shows the captain how to regain control of his errant crew. Nowhere else does Crusoe pass over so completely into play, as he bustles about, manipulating this little drama, which, he abundantly hints, so much resembles his own past history. . . . Crusoe has reached the pinnacle of power: he sits back and watches a replay of his own story."[84] Crusoe is a veteran player in such stagings. The previews of colonization with Xury, the slaves in Brazil, the anticipated slaves in Africa, Poll the parrot, and the disembodied indigene of the footprint, all transmogrified into Friday, are now something akin to a daily matinee. And the castaway sits comfortably in the director's chair.

The English ship secured, Crusoe departs aboard it for Europe. He leaves behind the three most incorrigible mutineers as punishment and advises them that the shipwrecked Iberians will be arriving soon from the mainland. The timing of these events is remarkable. After twenty-eight years of Crusoe as the solitary European on the island, suddenly Spaniards and Portuguese and Englishmen appear at virtually the same time. The coincidence is inexplicable unless read as a projection of the broad outlines of the Conquest onto the island. In other words, first Crusoe the slave trader arrives at a terrestrial paradise. Then he colonizes the bodies of Poll and Friday. Then he sets up a contest among three of the principal imperial powers in the New World. By this point, the Englishmen, too, have sworn complete subjecthood to Crusoe. Their captain tells him that his ship "is all yours, and so are we and all that belong to her."[85] Crusoe, the emperor who had no clothes, now oversees a full empire at last.

The novel could have finished neatly with Crusoe leaving the island. It does not. The itinerant ending tends to be backgrounded by scholars as superfluous to the main story of a man on an island. The general public, in most renditions of the novel in print and on screen, is not even alerted to the existence of the post-island adventures of Crusoe in Europe in which he confronts a needlessly provoked bear and hundreds of hostile wolves. These events probably strike most readers of Defoe as bizarre, for the episodes appear to have no explicable relationship to the rest of the plot. It is suggestive, however, that during the denouement Crusoe travels among England, Portugal, and Spain. These are the imperial homelands whose individual personifications he has just left behind on the island. And the scenes with the wild animals are equally resonant of the Conquest that Crusoe concretized even when allegedly cast away from Western civilization. The adventures on the borderlands of Spain and France involving the bear and the wolves are marked with Crusoe's continued references to "my man Friday" and Friday's cries of "O master."[86] Together now on a mainland, the slave owner and slave continue to slaughter the undomesticated. Europe proves a reproduction of the island that proved a reproduction of Europe.

Poll, the original indigenous servant on the island, might also be accompanying Crusoe during these reenactments of man versus nature. When Crusoe departs for Europe on the English ship, he makes a point of taking with him "my parrot" as well as Friday.[87] Whether this particular bird is Poll is unclear. There are two other parrots that Crusoe also had trained after Poll to say his name.[88] At one point, Crusoe recounts that Poll "lived with me no less than six and twenty years: how long he might live afterwards, I know not . . . perhaps poor Poll may be alive there still, calling after poor Robin Crusoe to this day."[89] This description could be consistent with Poll as the parrot who leaves with him on the English ship. Since Crusoe does return eventually to the island, Poll could have traveled with him eastward to Europe and then crossed the Atlantic with him again before flying away. But whether the parrot that

Crusoe takes with him to Europe is Poll or not, two things are certain. First, that parrot, like Friday, is an indigenous resident of the island who travels across the ocean calling out an avian version of "O master" to Crusoe. Second, afterward and forever in Crusoe's mind, Poll, wherever he is, continues to do so.

By the final pages of the novel, all the specters of the island have been incorporated into servitude. All the threats of the footprint have vanished. The colonization by the castaway complete, Crusoe sells his Brazilian plantation and reaps the financial windfall of the labor of all the slaves he came to own there while his partners were managing his estate.[90] And now at the end of his narrative, Crusoe returns to the Caribbean:

> I visited my new collony in the island, saw my successors the Span-
> iards, had the whole story of their lives, and of the [English] villains
> I left there; how at first they insulted the poor Spaniards, how they
> afterwards agreed, disagreed, united, separated, and how at last the
> Spaniards were obliged to use violence with them, how they were
> subjected to the Spaniards, how honestly the Spaniards used them;
> a history, if it were entred into, as full of variety and wonderful ac-
> cidents as my own part; particularly also as to their battles with the
> Caribbeans, who landed several times upon the island, and as to
> the improvement they made upon the island it self, and how five of
> them made an attempt upon the main land, and brought away elev-
> en men and five women prisoners, by which, at my coming, I found
> about twenty young children on the island.[91]

In short, the novel ends with another reenactment of the Conquest. In the beginning, quite unlike Adam, Crusoe sells Xury into slavery. Then he owns servants and slaves in Brazil. Then he seeks additional slaves in Africa. Then he subjugates Poll. Then the absent body of the footprint in the sand frightens him to his colonial core. He regains his own foot-ing by the incorporation of Friday. This consolidates his sense of posses-sion of the island itself, for even when he departs from it for Europe, he "reserved to my self the property of the whole."[92] Behind him he leaves a miniature imperial replica of the Conquest in which Iberians and Englishmen and indigenes struggle against each other for dominance. This time the Spaniards best the English while the "Caribbeans" seem more persistent warriors than their cannibal predecessors. And despite his Black Legend concerns, Crusoe sympathizes with the Iberians more than the mutineers who are his compatriots. Such changes to the basic script of the Conquest are to be expected. No reproduction of any performance is ever one with its previous versions. The significance of this final drama in the novel is that in *Robinson Crusoe* it is iterative, not that it is identical.

The often overlooked conclusions of Crusoe in Europe and then back to his "new collony" on the island confirm powerfully the imperial production in which he was acting before he first struggled up a Caribbean shore. The novel ends as it does because Robinson Crusoe, despite his reputation, is never stranded on a desert island. On the contrary, he is always invested in a transatlantic that stretches from western Europe and western Africa to the Western hemisphere and every direction in between. His island is a microcosm of the transatlantic, his conquest a microcosm of the Conquest. That is why he remarks, while gazing over the waves one day, that he "fairly descry'd land, whether an island or a continent, I could not tell."[93] The reason he cannot tell is because there is an iteration here of America, a repeating production of colonization. Islands and continents are similar, if successive, sets in the same play, respectively small and large but always simulacra of each other. Crusoe acts out the script of America, the plot of the transatlantic. He is not so much a castaway as a conquistador.

As Roxann Wheeler writes, "*Robinson Crusoe* is best understood as a colonial narrative. The novel establishes Crusoe's method of rising in the world as possible because of a developed colonial labor force and of the demands of trade . . . the Africans he trades in, the Maresco Xury whom he sells as a slave, and the Carib Friday whom he relegates to perpetual servitude."[94] A trace on a shore, however, spectrally resists colonization. Bodies can be enchained and inscribed but ghosts cannot. They elude empire while those of flesh and blood are incorporated into it. The indigenous atextualizations in the *Popol Vuh* and in Columbus's diary of his first voyage reveal such broad powers of haunting. So does the footprint in the sand, the identity of whose body Crusoe never does come to learn.

The specters of the transatlantic are never insular. They roam west and east across the ocean and back again, south and north and back again as well. Seas cannot be conceived without such wanderings. And so the temporal and geographic distance between one foundational text and another on facing shores of the same Atlantic may be far less than immediately apparent. This is not to say that all mutual reflections are the same. Not all mirrors produce exact simulacra. And not all ghosts, even when they gesture of parallel crimes and justice unmet, appear in the same way and form. As long as the western African people whom

Crusoe aimed to purchase before his shipwreck remain free, their ghosts haunt his colonizing project. The knowledge that some of them appear in the first African novel in Spanish, albeit in different figurations, would cause him to fortify feverishly his "castle" anew.[95] He would keep his arms positioned in bulwarks and ready to fire. The thing about specters, though, is that passing through walls is inherent to who they are. And weaponry, however advanced, is of little use against those who are not there.

4 / Apparitions of Africa: Leoncio Evita's *When the Combes Fought* and José Martí's "Our America"

In 1898, Spain and the United States fought a brief series of battles in the Caribbean and Southeast Asia. The clash, known as the Spanish-American War, resulted in the Spanish colonies of Cuba, Puerto Rico, the Philippines, and Guam being transferred to the United States. In subsequent interpretations of the significance of the war, major figures in both imperial nations produced a slew of texts that entered canons of historiography, autobiography, fiction, journalism, and philosophy. Virtually unread, by contrast, is the treatment of the conflict in the first African novel written in Spanish, *When the Combes Fought*, by Leoncio Evita.[1] That the ghosts of such a pivotal planetary year might appear on eastern Atlantic shores should not be surprising. Africa, after all, is the destination of Crusoe when he sails from Brazil in hopes of obtaining slaves. In many senses, he treats the island of his shipwreck as something of a sublimated Dark Continent. And imperial dramas are reinvested with absence and presence every time their originary plots are reenacted, even if on unexpected coasts and in little known literary traditions like that launched by Evita.

The Spanish-American War of 1898, despite the hyphen and implied dialectic, was never simply a matter involving two nations and a particular year. It was a global conflict from the very beginning, disputed by a European and a North American power but fought on islands on opposite sides of the world, in the Caribbean and Southeast Asia. Furthermore, substantive local revolutionary forces in both regions had been battling for independence before the foreign master changed from Spain to the United States. And the Spanish-American War did not take place only in 1898, at least not at symbolically. For Spain, the actual military contest to retain control of its colonies paled in importance before the larger narrative at stake, that of the end of the direct Spanish presence in the New World that had existed since Columbus.

The Spanish empire, once the largest in world history, had been fading for centuries. Its reach shortened precipitously in the first quarter of the nineteenth century when societies from Mexico to Argentina rebelled and formed independent nations. By the last quarter of the century, empires like France and Great Britain dwarfed Spain on land and sea across the planet. And in the 1898 war, Spain lost ground to yet another expansionist rival, this time the relatively young United States. Intellectuals throughout Spain viewed this defeat as the final blow to a national identity that, since 1492, had been moored in empire. These writers and thinkers, conventionally known as the Generation of '98 and considered to include figures such as Azorín, Miguel de Unamuno, Pío Baroja, and Antonio Machado, paid little specific attention to the United States as the victorious enemy power. It was the loss of the last Spanish colonies in the Americas and Asia, not the advent of the latest triumphant adversary, that occasioned a soul-searching into the putatively postimperial nature of Spain. For the Generation of '98, the war produced the final scenes of an overseas drama that had lasted for four centuries. From this standpoint, the import of the Spanish-American War of 1898 extended far beyond 1898 and did not concern the "American" opponent much at all.

The acquisition by the United States of overseas colonies pursuant to 1898 has seemed to some historians as an aberration, even something of an accident, for a nation whose tradition of foreign policy was supposedly isolationist. To the extent, however, that imperialism can be defined broadly as expansion into territories over the wishes of those who live in or control them, the United States already had a long history by 1898, into which the new possessions in the Caribbean and Southeast Asia fit neatly. After all, the thirteen original colonies consistently had expanded westward and southward through war and diplomacy and purchase. The United States gained control of huge swaths of France (the Louisiana Purchase in 1803), Spain (Florida in 1819), Mexico (Texas to California in 1845–53), Great Britain (the Pacific Northwest in 1846), Russia (Alaska in 1867) and, in so doing, innumerable aboriginal lands. Cuba, Puerto Rico, Guam, and the Philippines were not even the only islands acquired in 1898 by the United States, for that was the same year as the annexation of Hawaii. Despite having recognized Hawaii as an independent state since 1826, the United States toppled the indigenous kingdom of Queen Liliʻuokalani in 1893 and, five years later, incorporated the distant archipelago officially into the nation. Also in 1898, leading figures of the United States, realizing that the national ability to fight naval wars was undermined by the time it took for ships to sail between the Pacific and the Atlantic, commenced an enduring push for control of the isthmus that would become the site of the Panama Canal. Yet Colombia, of which Panama was then part, was unwilling to sign a canal agreement on terms that were overly favorable to the United States. Washington consequently encouraged and assisted an independence movement in Panama. Within a month of separation from Colombia in 1903, local Panamanian officials agreed to the canal conditions desired by Theodore Roosevelt, the veteran of the Spanish-American War of 1898 then occupying the Presidency.

In the ongoing aftermath of 1898, the Spanish-American War as a narrative has played out discursively in a variety of performances. These include the introspective novels and poems of the Generation of '98, the equally self-obsessed war memoir *The Rough Riders* by Roosevelt, and sundry professional and amateur histories. In some of these texts, the conflict scarcely involves Spain. In others, it scarcely involves the United States. In almost none of them does it involve Africa. It seems unlikely, of course, that a Pacific and Caribbean war fought by North American and West European powers would do so. Yet the war never has ceased to be staged in a global theater. And the absence of Africa proves to be, once again, a foundational ghost of the transatlantic. A novel from the lone Spanish sub-Saharan colony does speak, mostly unheard, of the war. From that position of absence, it haunts canonical accounts. As with the specters in Columbus's diary and the *Popol Vuh* and *Robinson Crusoe*, the apparitions of *When the Combes Fought* upset expected hierarchies of power between conquistadors and indigenes and subvert seemingly prevailing narratives of colonialism.

The macroscopic geopolitical context of Equatorial Guinea is not generally familiar, not even to scholars who specialize in the Spanish-speaking world. The history of the nation is suffused with successive colonial spaces. The country consists of an island called Bioko, a larger area on the rather distant mainland known as Río Muni, and a few islets such as the faraway Annobón.[2] The capital, Malabo, is situated on Bioko, the most urbanized part of the nation and the primary focus of colonial attention and development over the centuries.[3] Río Muni features one tiny coastal city and the rest is largely tropical jungle. The nation as a whole is isolated as the only hispanophone land in sub-Saharan Africa. It is not contextualized in any substantive way by other geopolitical remnants of Spanish southward expansion, which include the cities of Ceuta and Melilla on the north African coast, the Canary Islands off the north-western shores of the continent, and Western Sahara.[4] Equatorial Guinea is surrounded by francophone Cameroon and Gabon on the mainland, anglophone Nigeria nearby, and the lusophone island nation São Tomé and Príncipe.

Historically, the first European power to arrive on the scene was Portugal, whose navigator Fernando Pó surveyed Bioko and parts of the mainland in 1472. The Portuguese empire nominally controlled the area until swapping some of the land with Spain in 1778 for certain territories in Brazil. During the nineteenth century, Spain continued to be the ostensible colonial power, though Great Britain, France, and Germany also put in occasional claims. Finally, the Berlin Conference of 1884–85 and then an additional treaty in 1900, just two years after the collapse of the rest of the Spanish empire, ratified Spanish dominion over the lands constituting present-day Equatorial Guinea. As the twentieth century wore on, various Spaniards arrived intent on the usual economic, military, and religious colonizations. On October 12, 1968, the anniversary of the day Columbus consummated the first transatlantic journey, Equatorial Guinea became independent.

The nation has been ruled since by two dictators. The first, Francisco Macías Nguema, fell in 1979 in a coup d'état to his nephew, Teodoro Obiang Nguema Mbasogo, who remains in power. The Macías tyranny caused the deaths of tens of thousands of Equatoguineans and the flight of up to perhaps a third of the country, probably more than 100,000 people, to neighboring countries and Spain. The educated elite were among the chief targets of the government. As Ibrahim K. Sundiata writes, "Anti-intellectualism was the cornerstone of Macias Nguema's cultural policy. . . . From 1969 to 1976, 75 educators and educational administrators were killed. This included three ministers, a secretary-general, and a director-general of education. The use of the term *intellectual* was prohibited and in 1973 a member of the cabinet was fined for using it."[5] The Obiang regime, fueled since the 1990s by petrodollars, continues to run the country as a police state. Equatorial Guinea does not have an independent press or a single independent bookstore. Thanks to the oil exploitation, however, the nation is not entirely isolated from the rest of the world. According to Peter Maass in 2005, "It is now possible to fly nonstop from Malabo to Texas on a weekly flight known as the 'Houston Express.'"[6]

The literature of Equatorial Guinea, like the country itself, is not well-known. This is particularly the case with its written manifestations from the colonial era. Longstanding oral traditions that exist among the nation's constituent societies, such as the Fang from Río Muni and the Bubi from Bioko, have received scrutiny by a handful of anthropologists, but Leoncio Evita's *When the Combes Fought* of 1953 is the first of only two novels by Equatoguineans that were published prior to independence. Thereafter, a tradition of creative writing was slow to emerge, owing largely to the dictatorial conditions that led to the suppression, exile, or murder of potential authors. Nonetheless, *When the Combes Fought* is a landmark text as the first African novel in Spanish, no matter that its successors were belated in appearing. Moreover, it is a profoundly transatlantic novel that rewrites the Spanish-American War of 1898 in a counterhistorical way that lets Spain symbolically emerge victorious. The protagonists include a Spanish general and his nephew who flee the Cuban anticolonial movement of the 1890s and head for western Africa. There they replace two United States missionaries as the commanders of a local indigenous society, enter a conflict involving cannibals, and declare triumphantly that all nearby African lands shall come under Spanish rule. Metaphorically, the general and his nephew thereby substitute Spain's loss of its remaining Caribbean and Pacific holdings in 1898 with the genesis of a brand-new African empire. The end of history yields to a new beginning of history, with Spain's New World, now dead, to be resurrected in Africa. But this transatlantic fiction will be haunted. Notwithstanding Evita's apparent paean to imperialism, indigenous ghosts will render uncanny the colonial project in Equatorial Guinea, too.

The final line of *When the Combes Fought*, spoken by the Spanish general with long experience in his own nation's occupation of Cuba, seems anything but complicated: "Let us go, my son, we cannot dream, we cannot rejoice until all of these beautiful lands are under the sovereignty of Spain."[7] Here, Equatorial Guinea is imagined implicitly as a logical extension of the Conquest. The novel, in consequence, seems to offer straightforward support for Spanish expansion. Certainly, there is no hint that the ending is meant to be read ironically or satirically. As a result, the few critics who have turned their attention to *When the Combes Fought* have read it almost uniformly as a collaborationist text. For instance, Mbaré Ngom describes the novel as "a powerful instrument of propaganda for the Spanish colonial administration . . . the novel not only defends the necessity of the colonization but also justifies it. Thus, it fits within what is called the literature of consent."[8] Ngom points out that the publisher of the novel, the High Council of Scientific Investigations, was "a propaganda apparatus of the Franco regime of the era."[9]

Donato Ndongo-Bidyogo, a prominent Equatoguinean author and scholar, adds that Evita's novel "was the loyal reflection of what was expected of black Guineans: that they accepted entirely the postulates of the colonizer so much that they denied the essence of their being."[10] In his prologue to the 1996 re-edition of *When the Combes Fought*, Ndongo-Bidyogo also stresses that the novel "seems to have been written at the pleasure of the colonizers."[11] There is little room left by this analysis for any contestatory reading of the novel. Ndongo-Bidyogo goes so far as to assert that "Undoubtedly, then, the book pleased the colonialists since it, though written by a black man, contributed to laying the foundation for the edifice of the colonization by influencing the elements that sustained the colonial superstructure."[12]

In general, according to Ngom, the literary tradition of hispanophone Africa shares little of the polemics often found in its francophone, anglophone, and lusophone counterparts: "different from what happened in other sub-Saharan African territories under colonial domination, there was not a combative or anticolonial literary production" in Equatorial Guinea.[13] The possibility of a direct linkage with the Négritude movement of Léopold Senghor and Aimé Césaire is explicitly denied by Ndongo-Bidyogo.[14] Ignacio Tofiño-Quesada even suggests that the lack of anticolonialism in Evita's text deprives it of its own ethnic identity: "Although an Equatoguinean wrote the novel, it is essentially Spanish: its language, its attitudes, and its point of view are those of the colonizer. At a time when Senghor and Fanon were publishing and colonialism was being widely criticized, Evita offers an apology of the colonialist action of Spain in the Gulf of Guinea."[15]

Carlos González Echegaray, the Spaniard who edited *When the Combes Fought*, certainly saw the novel as the product of a sufficiently domesticated indigenous subject. He wrote the following in his preface to the first edition:

> when Leoncio Evita gave me his novel to read and asked me to write a prologue for it, I did not give him my word that I would write it until I was convinced that it was something distinct from the unconnected and absurd tales that some pseudointellectual "blacks" write more for their personal satisfaction than with the hope of seeing them published. But my surprise kept growing as I continued reading, upon finding myself with a clearly acceptable

little work that well could have been written by any beginning writer born in our patria.[16]

In other words, Evita's "little work" is "acceptable" to González Echegaray because it does not seem to him overly Equatoguinean but rather so Castilian that a Spaniard could have written it. It is neither too wild ("unconnected") nor too uncontrollable ("absurd"), which is to say that it hews close enough to an imperial episteme to be comprehensible. Indeed, praises González Echegaray, the novel is so Spanish that Evita is not really black anymore: "the novel is conceived and felt 'in white' and only when the plot develops among indigenes, only in part and as a spectator does the writer sense his race."[17]

This astonishing conclusion is undermined by the admission by González Echegaray that he deliberately edited out indigenousness whenever it appeared to undercut colonial norms. "Regarding the style, I have corrected some constructions that are excessively foreign to our syntax and some errors of improper application of Castilian words, but I have left the work in its own style, which at times can appear rough in form and naive in content but which is a stylized example of the half-Castilian spoken by our Negroes."[18] That is, he peremptorily removed violent ruptures with standard Castilian but permitted minor variants to stay in order to show the quaintness of the stunted language used by "our Negroes." Evidently, to the extent that Evita writes normative Spanish, he is an acceptable imperial subject; but to the extent that autonomous indigenous voicings appear in his discourse, he is at best a semi-evolved cultural bastard who needs to be further civilized. The ungraspable aboriginality that Evita produced was forced into an incarnated and therefore controllable form by González Echegaray. There is an absent and anterior *When the Combes Fought*, much like that indicated in the opening and closing passages of the *Popol Vuh*, that challenges the definitiveness of the available document by its very illegibility. The published text is haunted by the missing predecessor, which does not exist in alienation from the version at hand but rather, like Rigoberta Menchú, constantly goes back and forth between spectral and material worlds in a way inaccessible to colonizers from Columbus to González Echegaray. The autonomous space of the previous version of *When the Combes Fought* is a ghostly one, contestatory in its unedited indigenousness of everything acceptable to the claim-staker from abroad who wants to frame an imperial possession—Evita as well as his novel and homeland—to the metropole.

González Echegaray ends his preface with the conviction of all unrepentant colonizers that the colonized truly merit their fate: "an evolved indigene deserves the character and the colonization of the Spaniards with their small defects of temperament—violence, irreflection, pride— and their fundamental virtues—generosity, faith, simplicity, enthusiasm—and, especially, their indefatigable valor, which has always attracted the enthusiastic admiration of the indigenes like to a magnet."[19] By implying that some Africans are evolved but others are not, González Echegaray effectively defines evolution as a process of Europeanization through which individuals like Evita become able to approximate Spanish praxis. Their movement toward supposed civilization does not entail the dissolution of cultural differences altogether—there is no space in the prologue for the possibility that indigenes actually might become Spaniards like González Echegaray—but rather the assimilation of Evita into a context wherein the threats of his foreignness can be controlled. The magnetism of colonialism that González Echegaray lauds does not merge distinct bodies but instead keeps one safely attached to the other. The unedited Evita and the antecedent *When the Combes Fought* exist beyond the pull of that magnet, like so many other indigenes and indigenous textualities on the other side of the Atlantic.

The echoes of Columbus and Crusoe here are many. S. Onomo-Abena, who has written the most extensive analysis of the González Echegaray prologue to date, concludes that it "is an ethnocentric discourse marked by disdain of the *Other* to whom is denied religion, history, writing and culture."[20] Yet the editorial effort seems not so much to pronounce the nonexistence of otherness but to tame its abundances and excesses. González Echegaray recognizes that Evita writes from the beyond and that is precisely why he strives to bring the novel under domination. He wants to force its free indigenousness into colonized presence. Writing decades later in his preface to the 1996 re-edition of *When the Combes Fought*, González Echegaray remains convinced that its textual body never had escaped his control: "Naturally, throughout the novel as in my prologue—'*mea culpa*'—the influence of 'official' thought about the colonization can clearly be seen. We thought officially and tried to install in the natives a monolithic 'imperial' thought based on the theoretical precepts of the Laws of the Caribbean Colonization and of the past glories of Spain."[21] This raises what could be called the Paumanok paradox: the contradiction inherent in any assertion of triumphant colonial textualities, given that the claim implicitly acknowledges that alternative indigenous narratives exist that, though suppressed, remain potent enough in their absent presence to contest the completeness of the claim itself.

Contrary to the presumptions of González Echegaray, the aboriginal actors of *When the Combes Fought* haunt an imperial theater. The plot of the novel revolves around two pairs of foreigners and indigenes who inhabit Equatoguinean space at the turn of the twentieth century: the Spanish general and his nephew, a missionary couple from the United States, a local indigenous society (the Combes) led by King Roku, and a group of clandestine cannibals. The novel opens with the missionary John Stephen and his wife Miss Leona being awakened at night by shrieks from the dormitory in their compound where seven African girls sleep. Stephen grabs his rifle and heads out into the dark, "converted already into a true nocturnal hunter."[22] Furious at the disturbance, "Instinctively he shot at a lost point in the darkness where he seemed to see two flashing eyes" and swears "Africa!" under his breath.[23] Entering the dormitory, he demands of the terrified girls, "'What does this insubordination mean?'—the voice of the white man sounded metallic."[24]

Already in this initial scene, the hierarchies of hegemony are manifest. For Stephen, Africa is not so much a continent as a curse, while cries of fright from African girls are but rebellion against his imposed order. The voice of the missionary is as "metallic" as the gun he fires into a "darkness" that encompasses both the uncontrolled night and the uncontrolled locals. The reaction of the girls to the missionary's penetration into their bedroom is unequivocal: "Their little ebony faces revealed excessive fright, which the presence of the white man greatly accentuated."[25] Of this scene, Joaquín Mbomio Bacheng writes, "In this way and in the first lines of his narrative, Evita already presents us with the image that the white man projects in the African world with its characteristic features: power (represented by the rifle), domination and severity towards the black individual. The white man, even a missionary like brother John, does not permit any type of insubordination from a black individual."[26] The cause of the dormitory commotion turns out to be a hole in a wall that is attributed to an attacking animal.

Within this frame of the novel, an array of darknesses haunt the missionary. A chaos of disembodied voices has broken up his sleep, causing him immediately to don the role of "true nocturnal hunter." The blackness of night unnerves him and so he shoots at it, but this is literally a shot in the dark. He has no idea what is threatening his presence and he cannot control it. Like Crusoe, of course, he will try to kill the apparition should he sight it again, but rifles are impotent against specters. He declares that the frightened girls are insubordinate by virtue of their screaming, then tells Miss Leona, "I fired in order to impose silence. I thought that there was no other way of making those rebellious girls shut up."[27] In effect, indigenous African noises form for the missionary an unsettling semiotic subtext to his attempts at imperial inscription. After silencing the girls and returning to his bed, he hears "an unclassifiable range of murmurs, crackles and noises."[28] The missionary has crossed the Atlantic to enlighten an allegedly dark continent, but Africa is already shadowing him. The diverse bodilessnesses in Columbus and Crusoe and Cabeza de Vaca appear here as a hole in a wall, as lost points in the night, as uncategorizable sounds in the dark. Unknown alterities, whether human or animal or environmental, present themselves atextually like Rigoberta Menchú and the authors of the *Popol Vuh*, asserting their codes and simultaneously withdrawing them from colonial ken.

The two groups of indigenes in *When the Combes Fought*, though depicted on different sides of good and evil, share the same potential resistances to colonization as other animate and inanimate aboriginal forces in the novel. Whenever either local society presents an unreadable textuality to imperial agents of Spain or the United States, a tangibly intangible spectrality appears as oppositional. That common contestatory ghostliness links the indigenous peoples of the novel, even when they are seemingly antagonistic toward each other. Such is the case of Vilangua, son of King Roku of the Combes, in the scenes following John Stephen's shot in and at the dark. In this sequence, Roku worries about his son, who was lost in the woods two days earlier.[29] When the king comes across a bloody and tattered sack that his son had carried, he assumes that Vilangua has been killed by a leopard.[30] In ensuing days, presumptive leopards finish off chickens, goats, and lambs domesticated by the Combes, and then dogs, and then finally more Combe individuals.[31] Yet eventually and unexpectedly Vilangua reappears, "looking like a ghost," and tells his father a strange tale about how he had been assaulted in the woods by a man disguised as a leopard.[32] Vilangua managed to kill this first attacker but then two other leopard men appeared and kidnapped him. He was taken to a sinister village inhabited by "people of rudimentary aspect who in nothing resembled the blacks of the coast. They went around almost naked."[33] These underdeveloped, underclad people imprison Vilangua in a hut and spend the rest of their time wildly dancing, making strange noises on musical instruments, and eating sandwiches made of "iboga (cocaine) mixed perhaps with human entrails."[34] Despite the relegation of these cannibals to infernal caricatures pitted against Vilangua, their fundamental oppositionality is not to him or to the larger Combe society but to the imperial forces that already have begun

seeking to domesticate Africa. Festive cannibals, their carnivalesque ca-
vorting an uncontrolled threat to every colonizing order, are a common
trope in Conquest fiction. Robinson Crusoe, for instance, notes of the
indigenes preparing to eat Friday that "they were all dancing in I know
not how many barbarous gestures and figures, their own way, round the
fire."[35] As Crusoe realizes and Vilangua implies, such dancing is not
aimless and its "gestures and figures" are not meaningless. All the physical movements betoken ritual, not randomness, which is to say an alternative narratological order rather than no order at all. The footprints of
the cannibals mark a corpus of content illegible to those foreigners who
try to overwrite it. The cannibals dance in a visibly invisible code.

Vilangua deduces that his captors are fattening him up for a sacrifice.
Fortunately, he manages to escape the night before he is going to be killed
and eaten. At this point, the outlines of a spectral America re-emergent
in Africa are hazy but perceptible. First, there is an evangelist with a gun
who has been unnerved by multiple apparitions such as the ostensible
eyes in the darkness, the unseen wild animal that made the hole in the
wall, and the disembodied array of voices and local sounds. Next appears
a disappeared indigene, Vilangua, who seemingly returns from the dead.
Third, alleged cannibals are on the loose, as in Crusoe and Columbus.
The subsequent addition to the plot of a shipwreck, a Spanish general,
and a Cuban revolution will develop further the novel as a reenactment
of not only the war of 1898 but also of a palpably ghosted transatlantic.

On hearing Vilangua's tales from the beyond, Roku goes to Stephen
and asks that the missionary lead the imminent Combe counterattack.[36]
Stephen declines on the ground that he is neither a hunter nor a killer,
though this is belied by his opening performance as a "true nocturnal
hunter."[37] He adds that are "some Spanish hunters" in the area who
might prove useful.[38] With Roku's consent, the missionary strikes out
for the Spaniards in a canoe, accompanied by two African guides. When
a hurricane tosses the three overboard, they are fortuitously sighted by
Carlos, a brash young Spaniard who, along with his aging uncle Martín,
are the two adventurers whom Stephen is seeking. Carlos rides out to
rescue Stephen. Riding is a particularly accurate term here, as Africans
row while Carlos whips them and shouts, "Imbeciles! Row hard. Come
on! Or I will step on your guts!"[39] Back in the Spaniards' hut, Stephen
recuperates and the older man introduces himself as "Martín Garrido,
Spaniard, ex-official of the Spanish navy and now lover of Africa."[40] This
remarkable self-characterization is matched by another from Stephen: "I
am the bearer for you of a task assigned by a black princeling."[41]

After a brief conversation, the Spaniards agree to pacify the leopard men on Roku's behalf, using firearms if need be.[42] They do have military experience, for

> Martín Garrido was an old official of the Spanish Navy. He spent the better part of his life in the sea of the Antilles. Thus when he retired he did not return to Spain but instead made his residence in Santiago de Cuba. . . . Toward the end of the year 1894, when the Cuban insurrection was beginning to be in the air, Martín went aboard in San Juan a Dutch ship, which after arriving in various ports in Cuba, headed out for the black Continent. During the crossing, the Garrido men met Adonis, a crewman who, years after the abolition of slavery, was returning to his country, but the enchantment of the Spaniards converted him into an inseparable servant.[43]

In short, Martín acquired his martial chops in the Spanish imperial navy as it clung onto its last Caribbean holdings. He thus almost certainly would have participated in the Spanish struggle against the 1868–78 Cuban rebellion. Regardless, he decided to spend his sunshine days in Santiago, a retirement aborted by the second coming of that "insurrection." This was the version championed by the Cuban essayist and poet José Martí in the early 1890s. Essentially a refugee from the imminent collapse of the Spanish empire in Cuba, Martín headed for Africa. Old generals do not necessarily fade away. For just as Martín and Carlos reprise black servitude with Adonis after the abolition of slavery, they will also reincarnate the spirit of the Spanish empire after its death knell in the western Atlantic. Indeed, Martín and Carlos are holding the Spanish imperial banner upright even "during those nine years in which Spain, beset by wars, had abandoned matters in Africa."[44] Since these two men are ostensibly the ultimate heroes of *When the Combes Fought*, Evita explicitly situates the novel as an intervention from Equatoguinean space into the 1898 imperial conflicts happening elsewhere on the planet. With the entrance of Martín and Carlos, the stage is now set for all the players in an African version of the Spanish-American War.

In this reenactment, the novel demonstrates that the performance of America is not confined to the cartographic contours of the Americas. As a reiterating drama, or what Diana Taylor would term a scenario, America can appear on Atlantic shores far from those on which colonialists from Columbus to Roosevelt stand and claim as theirs. Each representation of America assumes a recurring plot and twists upon it, recurring characters and reshapings of them. The result is a performance that is novel and yet hauntingly familiar. Such envisioning of America as a subversive and theatrical repetition can reconfigure all traditional taxonomies of New World history and literature. And as Taylor notes, "The apparent discreetness [sic] of nation-states, national languages, and official religions barely hides the deep intermingling of peoples, languages, and cultural practices."[45] Performance studies attuned to transnational flows can unveil those connections, whether material or theoretical.

Taylor, however, generally limits herself to imagining American scenarios as hemispheric phenomena. Apart from a chapter on the transatlantic theatricalities surrounding the death of Princess Diana of the United Kingdom, Taylor's *The Archive and the Repertoire* surges past national frames but stops at the geographic borders of the New World. The stages of her scenarios, for the most part, are not transatlantic or global. Yet in a post-Columbian age marked by currents that reach all shores, staying mostly on the longitudinal landmass between the Pacific and the Atlantic may not prove expansive enough. "A hemispheric perspective," writes Taylor, "stretches the spatial and temporal framework to recognize the interconnectedness of seemingly separate geographical and political areas. . . . Now is a time for remapping the Americas. . . . Decentering a U.S. *America* for a hemispheric *Americas* seems urgent and overdue. This remapping would also show histories and trajectories omitted from earlier maps."[46] Recent scholarship that likewise has reenvisioned the Western hemisphere from novel cartographic perspectives includes Laura Lomas's *Translating Empire* of 2008. Her focus on migrant Latina/o subjectivities, such as her interpretation of Martí's reading of Whitman as an imperialist poet, rearranges hemispheric vectors in ways that compellingly complement Taylor's work. And as Ralph Bauer notes in a comprehensive overview from 2009 of interamerican scholarship, "Since 2000, we have witnessed a veritable explosion of scholarly activities in hemispheric studies."[47] All these academic efforts are necessary because reimagined chartings of the New World are imperative. But a West European novel like *Robinson Crusoe* and a West African novel like *When the Combes Fought* ought have their place in the remapping project, too. Both are American novels that would be excluded even from a project that decenters the United States in favor of "a hemispheric *Americas*." The decentering of America that Taylor describes as "urgent and overdue" should be planetary as well as performative in scope, transatlantic as well as hemispheric.

Notwithstanding the engagement of *When the Combes Fought* with broad geopolitical dynamics, little involvement of that sort can be found in the life of its author. Indeed, anyone hoping to arrive at postcolonial interpretations based on the extraliterary context of Leoncio Evita would find the novelist and his work unhelpfully isolated. According to an interview Evita gave sometime in the 1990s, the novel was the only one he wrote.[48] Moreover, he was quite a young man at the time, for he was born in 1929 and the text came out in 1953. Throughout his life, apparently, Evita did not take much part in politics, anticolonial or otherwise. As a youth he was trained in technical drawing and in 1952 he became a teacher at an art school. A year later, the same in which *When the Combes Fought* was published, he moved to Cameroon to work as a technical drawer in a construction company. Evita did not return to Equatorial Guinea until 1960, "due to the political instability in Cameroon."[49] Nothing in this career path seems to speak to the macrohistorical concerns of his novel.

Rafael Evita Enoy, his brother, was evidently more immersed in international currents. After teaching at a Catholic mission in Equatorial Guinea and studying theology in Rome, he obtained a degree in economics at the University of Fribourg in Switzerland and subsequently moved to Washington, D.C., where he taught Spanish at Howard University.[50] In the early 1960s he was active in the leadership of MONALIGE, the National Liberation Movement of Equatorial Guinea, an important resistance group.[51] At the largest conference in history on Equatorial Guinea, an event held at Hofstra University in 2009, the writer J. M. Davies, speaking on behalf of a generation of exiled Equatoguinean intellectuals, read aloud a poem to "Friend and brother Evita/Giant among giants," dedicated to the recently deceased Rafael.[52] By contrast, Leoncio Evita was barely mentioned at any point in the conference. Perhaps this is because, decades after the publication of his lone novel, he was still focusing on manual arts like "artistic drawing and wood shop."[53] And when asked about his literary influences, he cited such canonical European figures as Gustavo Adolfo Bécquer and Honoré de Balzac.[54]

Nevertheless, Evita's stance on his own novel cannot be deemed entirely apolitical. He recalls that "The colonial situation that prevailed when I wrote my novel gave me a great stimulus to keep writing and broaden my knowledge. Personally I felt satisfaction for having opened that small breach in the 'dike' of the monopoly of the intellectual discrimination that reigned."[55] The emphasis here, however, seems to be not on the content of the first Equatoguinean novel but on the triumph represented by producing it despite colonial conditions. Evita adds that "Traditional literature is my source of inspiration" although it is the conversion of that oral culture into a novel, a genre of European roots, that strikes him as his singular achievement.[56] Regardless, Evita does assert, "I do not believe in 'art for art's sake.' The African writer should take a position of commitment or combat through his literary creation."[57] Whether Evita is viewed as a politically engaged writer or not, none of his commentary on *When the Combes Fought* is of the stridently contestatory sort that might counteract the seemingly vigorous collaborationism of the novel's concluding scene and its projection of a glorious Spanish empire about to dawn in Africa.

Whatever the nature of his personal ideologies, Evita wrote within a larger sociohistorical context charged with colonialism. Donato Ndongo-Bidyogo, describing education in a typical Equatoguinean classroom in the late 1940s and early 1950s, notes that

> The geography was only that of Spain (the expulsion of the Arabs, Ferdinand and Isabella, the discovery of America and the Empire and little more): "Are we Spaniards?" asked the teacher of the class. "Wee are Spaaniards by the grace of Gooood!!" "Why are we Spaniards?" asked the teacher. "Wee are Spaaniards because we have had the joy of being born in a country called Spaain!!" Upon entering the school you had to make formations, do five or ten minutes of military calisthenics, sing "Face to the Sun" with the arm raised high, and also sing "Full of Fervent Ardor," "I Am a Fascist, Fascist until I Die or Conquer," and finally "Long Live Spain." . . . That was not cultural assimilation. It was cultural assimilation at gunpoint.[58]

Evita, presumably, experienced a similar education in his formative years just before writing *When the Combes Fought*. This in itself does not lead necessarily to either a collaborationist or anticolonial reading of the novel, but the presence of such pedagogy does testify to the strength of Spanish ideology in Equatorial Guinea in the era leading up to the text's composition. The teaching techniques resembled those in classrooms in Spain itself during those years of autocracy under Francisco Franco. Transferred to an African context, fascism blended readily with colonialism.

In reaction to foreign dominance, stirrings of anticolonialism began consolidating among Equatoguineans in the late 1940s. At a meeting in 1950, "It was decided to found an organization whose goal was to make the people conscious of the abuses of the Europeans and to present an increasingly firm resistance against the colonial power."[59] A few years later, about the time of the publication of Evita's novel, that organization became known as the MONALIGE. This was the same movement in which Rafael Evita would occupy a leading role in the early 1960s. Local forces of opposition were therefore developing prior to the moment in 1955 when Spain joined the United Nations. Admission to that organization left the metropole vulnerable to the growing international disapproval of colonialism in Africa. Nonetheless, as Ndongo-Bidyogo observes, "in the colonial Guinea of 1953, the gag still bound black mouths and heads were still bent to the floor."[60] He adds that Evita "could not rebel against" Spanish rule.[61]

There is nothing inherent in the sociohistorical conditions surrounding the writing of the novel that bears directly on the question of whether to read *When the Combes Fought* against its climax or not. The plot takes place half a century before the era of its publication and makes no explicit reference to contemporary political debates. Reader-reception analyses also are of little use in situating the text within a local context, since the novel was printed only in Madrid and probably few copies were disseminated. It is quite possible that no indigene in Equatorial Guinea saw the novel other than the author and his immediate circle. González Echegaray, the prologuist, notes that the intended audience for *When the Combes Fought* was not Equatoguinean in any case: "I thought that I was doing a good service for a new image of the Guinean, that he was capable of writing a novel in Spanish whose primary readers were going to be Spaniards from the metropolis, more demanding of quality than the countrymen of the author."[62] Clearly, an indigenous public for the novel in Equatorial Guinea was of little concern to its editor, while in Spain, the published version no doubt disappeared quickly from the horizon.

Given the absence of a definitively relevant context for the book's production as well as the firm belief of many commentators that the text is collaborationist, any contestatory interpretation of *When the Combes Fought* must rely perforce on a contrarian exegesis of the novel itself. And irrespective of the imperial project that González Echegaray thought he was advancing as editor, the entrance of the Spaniards into *When the Combes Fought* marks the scriptural reversal and cartographic upheaval of 1898 Caribbean reality. With the missionary Stephen, a fading presence, acting as interpreter, King Roku gives Martín and Carlos jurisdiction over the Combe warriors. He tells them, "You are the absolute heads of the mission," a quiet paradox given that the local sovereign is the one issuing rights to the Spaniards.[63] The war party, including all principal members of the cast except Roku, sets out for the cannibals. One morning two Combe warriors fail to wake up, but Martín glosses over the setback. The expedition then loses additional personnel when Miss Leona mistakenly accuses Vilangua of entering her tent at night with shady intentions and he, along with a Combe sentinel, flees into the forest.[64] Soon thereafter, Miss Leona is found dead in her bed.[65] And in the following days more Combes are found dead in the morning. Unknown to the Spaniards, however, all these characters have been drugged by the leopard men. The cannibals then exhume the various coffins in secrecy and take Miss Leona and the Combes, all still alive, to the sacrifice-fattening hut. Martín, not knowing this, is at a loss for action, especially when Stephen, Carlos, and Penda, the king's counselor, inexplicably disappear one day. The Spanish general assumes that all the warriors and Miss Leona have perished of natural causes. He does not consider foul play and seems frozen by the turn of events. He is utterly impotent to counteract or even comprehend the daily diminution of his war party. His imperial hubris, acted out once on western Atlantic shores and now again on eastern, is suffering what should be a fatal blow. A novel that is going to conclude with a supposedly nascent Spanish empire has as its supposed imperial hero a military man haunted by individuals he cannot see and environments he cannot understand.

One morning, two mysterious Africans appear and point a shotgun at Martín. They tell him that they can lead him to Carlos, Stephen, and Miss Leona if he obeys them. Martín is absolutely terrified: "the threatening look of the black man with the shotgun paralyzed him."[66] Moreover, he cannot recognize the indigenes because they are wearing red and white body paint. After they leave, he remains "still not recovered from his fright."[67] The Spaniard had entered the narrative as a veteran, well-suited for a conquering expedition despite the collapse of empire he had left behind in Cuba. Now, however, Equatorial Guinea, too, has proven uncontrollable. Once again the locals are forcing his hand, not vice versa. Once again the aging Martín, and by symbolic extension the geriatric Spanish empire, is on the wrong end of the gun. The novel had begun with Martín's imperial twin, Stephen, shooting at the darkness. Now, the darkness is threatening to shoot back. And when Martín meets the two Africans that afternoon as they had ordered, he must submit again to their demands:

"Call your men," muttered the subject who had spoken to him before.

"Who are you and how am I going to trust you?" Martín protested.

The savage who had until then remained in silence emitted certain orders in a language rather familiar to the white man, although he understood nothing of what the black man said.

"He says, boss," the other savage interpreted, "that you lose too much time chatting. Call your men, for one must walk a lot in order to arrive."

Martín emitted a prolonged whistle, and as soon as the first of his men appeared, the little black man said:

"Walk!"

"March!" transmitted Mr. Garrido to his people.[68]

This must seem to Martín a drama redux of Cuba. An experienced commander in the Spanish navy, he is supposed to be in control of this Conquest. And yet he is the one taking, not originating, marching orders. He is the one whose requests for information are abruptly rebuffed. Instead of inscribing an empire into being, Martín finds himself inscribed upon at will. He cannot comprehend the semiotics around him, cannot grasp the narrative at hand, cannot read the body paints that render his rulers unidentifiable. All is legibly illegible to him. Friday has corporealized out of nothing, but Crusoe is directed to follow.

The two Africans lead Martín to the site of the leopard men, who yet again are dancing around a bonfire and beating their drums. Martín, either unable or unwilling to act, orders one of the remaining Combe warriors to attack a hut where prisoners seem to be held. This unnamed indigene refuses to does so but transmits the order to another, who enters the hut and fatally stabs a dancing executioner about to plunge an iron bar into Miss Leona's breast. The warrior takes the bar and throws it out the window, whereupon it lands in the chest of another cannibal and kills him. Martín yells for the Combes to attack the leopard men and a vigorous battle ensues. Carlos, Stephen, and Miss Leona are freed from the hut, apparently by the Combes, at which Carlos shouts in utter joy and in complete misunderstanding of the circumstances, "But it is you, Uncle Martín, the angel of our redemption!"[69] Miss Leona adds timidly, "Mr. Garrido, have you come to carry us to glory?"[70] Both automatically assume that Martín deserves credit for the victory. In actuality, his leadership has been inept and humbled from the beginning. The two mysterious Africans who are the real leaders turn out to be Vilangua and the sentinel. With the cannibals now vanquished, Martín and Carlos watch Stephen and Miss Leona depart for the lands from which they started at the beginning of the plot. The retired naval officer then turns to his nephew and utters the ludicrous final line of the narrative: "Let us go, my son, we cannot dream, we cannot rejoice until all of these beautiful lands are under the sovereignty of Spain."[71] The novel, which opens with the United States missionary Stephen firing his gun into Africa at night, ends literally and metaphorically with a new commencement of Spanish imperialism at "the first dawns of day."[72]

When the Combes Fought thus displaces 1898 onto African soil. It envisions through Martín and Carlos the Spanish empire fleeing from its defeat in the western Atlantic only to re-project itself triumphantly in the eastern Atlantic. This time Spain will metaphorically win the war it historically lost, substituting the United States, personified by Stephen and Miss Leona, as the principal imperial power. The novel proposes a new New World, this time in Africa, with contour lines lifted from the old New World across the ocean. Yet old ghosts haunt even new New Worlds. The spectral contestation of this transposed and inverted America is represented by Vilangua, the indigene who so ably shadows both the United States missionary and the Spanish general. This complicates dramatically the close of the novel. The imperial triumph it predicts and embraces is wildly delusional. Evita, writing in 1953, knew full well that a glorious Spanish empire had not come to be in Africa, nor had it ever any chance of existence. Based only on the text itself, this is also a fantasy, for the Spaniards are dramatically subverted by both groups of indigenes, the cannibals and the Combes. After all, the leopard men drug and kidnap Carlos and most of the Spanish-led war party. Martín never understands what is going on. Meanwhile, Vilangua and the sentinel turn the veteran general into their own foot soldier. Allegorically, the "Cuban insurrection" that Martín fled has succeeded in dismantling the Spanish empire yet again, with Vilangua and the sentinel (and arguably the cannibals as well) standing in for the Cubans.[73] Their signifying body paints signify nothing to Martín, hence their atextual ghostliness. And none of the imperial principals ever seems to gain any comprehension whatsoever of their African environment in general. Stephen is as much in the dark at the end of the novel as he is at the start. The manner in which the novel culminates, however, effectively denies all this. The intended heroes are clearly Martín and Carlos and the expanding empire they personify. Yet the sheer preposterousness of the conclusion renders it thoroughly unbelievable.

A literal reading of that finale has dominated academic analyses of the novel as a whole. Mbaré Ngom, the most prolific scholar of Equatoguinean literature, concurs with González Echegaray that *When the Combes*

Fought is "conceived and felt in 'white'" and written "from the European perspective."[74] Ngom adds that it "rejects consciously or unconsciously its own ethnic identity."[75] The essentializing gestures of such comments are problematic. Phrases like "conceived and felt in 'white'" and "the European perspective" do not stand up as critical terms. More viably, and in apparent contradiction to the thrust of the previous critique, Ngom also writes, "In using an alien language—Spanish, the language of the dominant order—early Equato-Guinean writers wanted to break the silence, marginality, and invisibility to which the literature of the Spanish colonizers had confined them."[76] Although Evita seems not to have led a life particularly animated by ideology, the fact that he wrote a novel at all does create an inherently politicized space in which otherwise ignored and overlooked voices can emerge. *When the Combes Fought*, as the first novel in Spanish by an African, is an indigenous incursion into imperial terrain. Narratively, it constitutes a counter-occupation. The energy that González Echegaray invested into squashing aboriginal elements of the text that a Spanish audience might find unpalatable is proof enough that the novel is a radical artifact merely by virtue of existing.

The agreement by Ngom and González Echegaray that Evita eschews his social identity in *When the Combes Fought* also is belied by the common framing of the novel as an Equatoguinean example of *costumbrismo*. This genre, which is more or less canonical in both Spain and Latin America, comprises fictional texts whose plots and characters are primarily mechanisms designed to relate unfamiliar ethnographic information to the reader. The careful depiction of local customs and color in *costumbrista* literature takes precedence over the nuanced development of plots and characters. Authors design scenes principally to reveal particular provincial backdrops such as village and rural homes, native flora and fauna, local diets and clothes, parochial economic and religious and culinary practices, and so on. *Costumbrista* fiction therefore may seem like a fairly neutral type of literature, given its reduced literary pretensions and its foregrounding of quasi-scientific reportage. Yet ideological tensions are inevitable given that *costumbrismo*, by definition, seeks to convey information to metropolitan readers about a place and a population that are peripheral to power. The (pseudo)anthropological motives of the *costumbrista* writer, regardless of whether that person hails from social centers or margins, participates inevitably in projects that produce or interrogate colonizations of unfamiliar cultural spaces. Any author who intends to convey a sense of the beyond to consumers in a capital is engaged automatically in a profoundly political enterprise.

At a minimum, a *costumbrista* text offers an array of counter-examples to social arrangements dominant elsewhere. The implicit politics that result can be complex and contradictory. *Costumbrismo* may work in opposite directions simultaneously, for instance, if local cultural details offered by an author in a spirit of championing difference are read in the metropole in the rather contrary spirit of voyeuristic exoticism. Celebrations of the peculiarities of a place and a people may not ultimately contest but reassure some readers' prevailing sense of situ and self. But the apparent ideological neutrality of *costumbrismo* may work also by deftly drawing readers into a text that gradually proves far more politicized and unsettling than first expected. The most well-known example of this in Latin America may be the testimonial of Rigoberta Menchú, which opens with explanations of various customs of her K'iche' community before presenting more explicitly charged portrayals of indigenous struggles under the Guatemalan military regime. Readers who begin by learning of K'iche' childrearing practices ultimately find themselves implicated in a militarized drama of torture and murder. Although the conjoined media that carry Menchú's story outward—the Spanish language, the genre of the written testimonial, the anthropologist who interviewed her in Paris, the Western publishing houses—are not original to the K'iche', the book proved no less subversive or influential on behalf of indigenous Guatemalans. Indeed, had Menchú mediated the exact same narrative instead through traditional K'iche' oral means, her political critiques would have gone largely unnoticed. The ideological potential of *costumbrismo* thus may be linked strongly to what Mary Louise Pratt terms autoethnography, which "refers to instances in which colonized subjects undertake to represent themselves in ways that *engage with* the colonizer's terms. . . . Autoethnography . . . involves partly collaborating with and appropriating the idioms of the conqueror."[77] The fact that Evita published in Madrid and described indigenous African customs via a Western genre and a Western language does not necessarily vacate his text of counter-hegemonic discourse.

A reading of *When the Combes Fought* as mostly an ethnographic document of neutral ideological import divests the novel of its radicality as much as does categorizing it as a collaborationist text. Both constitute ways in which scholars have sought, consciously or otherwise, to exorcise its hauntings of empire. Many are the voices that have reached the *costumbrista* conclusion. T. Bruce Fryer, for example, refers to Evita's work as "his *costumbrista* novel."[78] Landry-Wilfrid Miampika describes it as "the precursory novel of ethnographic inspiration."[79] And Augusto

Iyanga Pendi depicts it as a "historical-*costumbrista* novel; the author insists with special attention on depicting the typical customs" of the Combes.[80] Ngom suggests that "In *Cuando los Combes luchaban* [*When the Combes Fought*], the plot is just an excuse for the author to describe in a detailed manner the traditions, customs, and rituals of the Combe ethnic group."[81]

Many scholars probably take their cue directly from Evita, who subtitles his narrative a "novel of the customs of Spanish Guinea" and includes in its pages his own illustrations of a local village and various plot scenes.[82] Evita indicates that his text is "an ethnological novel of the customs of the Combe tribe" and as such a legacy "to future generations . . . of what can be learned of my cultural environment."[83] This position places the author squarely in the *costumbrista* interpretive camp. The opinion of any writer about his own writing, however, can never be taken as the definitive word. Evita's reading of *When the Combes Fought* leaves unproblematized all those elements of the novel that range far beyond a simple plot draped over descriptions of a particular West African society. These include, for starters, the charged displacements of the Spanish-American War of 1898.

Another reason why *When the Combes Fought* often is deemed *costumbrista* may be because a long tradition of such fiction exists in hispanophone literature. The alignment within *costumbrismo* provides a ready frame within which to classify a text otherwise uncircumscribed as the inaugural African novel in Spanish. Yet this also amounts to a gesture akin to that of González Echegaray when he shaped the text to make it conform to styles that he and readers in Spain would find comforting and recognizable. And so it would be a mistake to dismiss *When the Combes Fought* as primarily an ethnographic report composed in the mode of fiction, notwithstanding Evita's subtitle and sketches, just as it would be overly simplistic to consign it to collaborationism on the basis of its climactic paean to Spanish imperialism and its adoptions of tired colonialist tropes such as infernal cannibals. The novel suggests far more than an inverse reenactment of the Spanish-American War of 1898 motivated by collaborationist sentiment and *costumbrista* intent in which this time United States imperialism in the form of Stephen and his gun cedes counterhistorically to Spanish imperialism in the form of Martín and his gun.

After all, neither collaborationism nor *costumbrismo* can account for a scene in which a United States missionary identifies himself to a Spanish military man by saying, as Stephen does after being rescued from the shipwreck, "I am the bearer for you of a task assigned by a black princeling."[84] Carlos cannot comprehend this power reversal and so asks in confusion, "The help that you request, is it for the indigene or for you?"[85] When Stephen responds, "remember that I represent the black man," promptly a "friendly guffaw sealed the deal between the Spaniards and the American."[86] Yet even as they chortle, the two imperial forces agree to work for an African. King Roku, though presented as feckless, is actually the stage manager who cues the imperial players into resolving his problem. And the ultimate commander of the war party is his son Vilangua, not the supposed United States or Spanish principals. Vilangua is the unreadable specter whom Martín follows meekly to the cannibals, not the indigenous and passive colonial subject that the Spaniard believes he is directing.

Vilangua, moreover, is the centerpiece of an oration apparently given by Penda, King Roku's chief counselor, that defends indigenous education and culture.[87] This speech is reminiscent of the ideas of the characters' real-life contemporary José Martí, the key figure of the Cuban revolution from which Martín and Carlos have fled. When Dyewé, the father-in-law of Roku, criticizes the Combe king for not having sent Vilangua to foreign missionaries like Stephen for education, the man who seems to be Penda responds with the following:

> Before Vilangua passed into the hands of those men, he needed, like the black man that he was, to know profoundly the things of his native country, such as hunting, fishing, etc., in a word, to live like a genuine black man. The civilization that we desire so much is like a torch; it lights up a lot, but it burns everything that it encounters in its path . . . as has occurred in other parts of this same world. . . . Is this the life that you want to leave to your children? No! Let future men grow like the species that the forest keeps, without tobacco or clothes, and let them learn to use wild salt, to leap with the monkeys and fight with the buffalo; thus have our ancestors grown and lived. Brothers: consider this final warning: our education, which the whites call savagery, obeys our nature. We cannot transform our customs, nor can we renounce them either, for the simple reason that all intent at erasing our origin will result in damage to the race.[88]

This declamation, set but a few years after Martí's essay "Our America," recalls the Cuban revolutionary's proclamation that "The European University has to cede to the American University. The history of America, of the Incas from here, has to be taught thoroughly."[89] Indeed, in promoting the need for a local education rooted in a local context, the two men issue remarkably similar rhetoric. Penda asserts that "our education, which the whites call savagery, obeys our nature."[90] Similarly, Martí avers that "There is no battle between civilization and barbarism but between false erudition and Nature."[91] Penda also seems to echo Martí when the Cuban writer lauds indigenous heritage by embracing "These children of our America that has to save itself with its Indians."[92]

In other ways, the language of Penda is quite different from that of Martí. The former's urge to "live like a genuine black man" appears in monocultural contrast to the panoramic vision of the latter's "our mixed-blood America."[93] And yet both declarations employ tropes that are comparable on a broad level: a fraternal plea for a return to ancestral roots, an anticolonial (but not exclusive) privileging of autochthonous culture, a vaguely utopian and prophetic tone based on an acceptance of an essentialized past, and a lexicon of warning and salvation. Moreover, all of this is expressed in both cases by an eloquent activist voice that invokes a frequent and seemingly transhistorical first person plural, notwithstanding the shared and particular fin-de-siècle imperial context of Spain and the United States as rival powers. In a surprise twist, however, Penda turns out to be the principal antihero of *When the Combes Fought*. On the penultimate page, he is revealed to be the dancing executioner of the cannibals who nearly dispatches Miss Leona. This suggests that the arguments of his "Our Africa" speech are meant to be rejected. But his passionate plea for an autonomous African subjectivity is given ample, unmediated space for expression. At no point in the novel is it explicitly countered or even addressed. Despite Penda's secret affiliation with the anthropophagi, the sheer rhetorical power of his oration is such that Martí would surely agree with Joaquín Mbomio Bacheng that "the initiative of L. Evita can be interpreted as well as an act of resistance by African culture before the aggression of the colonial system: his work carries in this way a pre-independence message and, all things considered, amounts to a shout for liberty."[94]

To the extent that Penda promotes a revalorization of ancient, local knowledges that Evita never directly rejects, a substantive ideological strain within *When the Combes Fought* would seem to be deliberately parochial in nature. Both in Penda's speech and in the ultimate triumph of Vilangua resides the implication that new modalities arriving on African shores, whether across the waves from Europe or from the Americas, are to be eschewed or at least overcome insofar as possible. But this stance paradoxically reveals the very impossibility of a return to a precolonial identity and a pre-transatlantic past. As Paul Gilroy notes, the "history of the black Atlantic yields a course of lessons as to the instability and mutability of identities which are always unfinished, always being remade."[95] A complete immersion by Vilangua or any other Combe individual into an indigenous education, as desired by Penda, would not allow him "to live like a genuine black man" owing to the fundamental elusiveness of that concept. Whether an essentialized identity was achievable in precolonial times is dubious in any case, but transatlantic dynamics certainly have made unfeasible even a presumptive return to such a sense of self. The traditions promoted by Penda, if taken up again, would now be framed as disavowals of other, foreign traditions. This changes their nature fundamentally. Even if leaping with the monkeys and fighting with the buffalo are conceded to have been once an unproblematized marker of ethnic or racial or social identity, doing so now would accrue to them the imports of an entirely new politics of resistance within a dialectics of colonialism and anticolonialism.

Furthermore, although Penda delivers his speech orally and at a traditional gathering, his words are relayed only through the environment of a language he does not speak, Spanish, and in a written form he does not know, the novel. Vilangua also is transformed, in his case as an allegorical Cuban who speaks Spanish in a reenactment of multiple indigenous responses in the Americas that have played out on disparate stages from 1492 through 1898 to today. Gilroy, sighting the ships real and metaphorical that have circulated among Atlantic shores along previously unrecognized vectors, emphasizes the importance of acknowledging "the inescapability and legitimate value of mutation, hybridity, and intermixture" that characterizes modern ethnic identities.[96] He shows, particularly in his tracings of black musics that metamorphosed through different singers and social contexts on both sides of the ocean, that transatlantic travels render both essentialized and radically de-essentialized notions of cultural purity as inadequate to depicting the protean transculturations that typify reality. Gilroy adduces many substantive proofs of these hybridizations as emergent from documented sea voyages of one kind or another, but the actual experience of ocean-crossing by a person or text is not prerequisite to creating transatlantic subjects and subjectivities. Penda and Vilangua live in the transatlantic as much as the Mayan authors of the *Popol Vuh*, even though none of them ever steps foot in a vessel headed for the other side of the ocean and even though their words, too, rarely travel so far. Indeed, the indigenous protagonists of *When the Combes Fought*, like those of the *Popol Vuh*, are inconceivable now outside a transatlantic framework, notwithstanding their never leaving their continent of origin. Gilroy would not be able to trace any physical movements across the ocean within the time span of Evita's novel because its plot unfolds entirely in a reduced area of West Africa. All the characters live on eastern Atlantic shores when the story begins. Nor does Evita himself stand out as a transatlantic figure, for the farthest he traveled from Equatorial Guinea seems to be neighboring Cameroon. Moreover, his novel appears sui generis as the first of hispanophone Africa, lacking any direct genealogical relationships to fictions from across the ocean. Nonetheless, the characters of *When the Combes Fought*, including those who know no geography but their own, recreate centuries of transatlantic drama as the absences and presences and hauntings of America appear and disappear once again.

Superficially, Evita allegorizes an illusionary inversion of the 1898 war in which, this time, the United States yields to Spain and not vice versa. The result appears to be a counterhistorical reproduction of the western Atlantic set in the eastern Atlantic. Crusoe, too, stages a dramatic struggle, albeit less conclusively, among indigenous and anglophone and hispanophone colonists as a final microcosmic proxy for the Conquest. Whereas Crusoe produces his reenactment on a southern Caribbean island, Evita moves the play onto the West African mainland. Yet his conclusion of a Spanish imperial triumph is upset in that Roku and Vilangua are the de facto directors of both the United States missionary and the Spanish general. The heroes of *When the Combes Fought* are not the imperial protagonists but instead the quasi-colonial subjects, who actually are nothing of the sort. The novel, as a result, turns out not to be a collaborationist text from a marginal and colonized space but instead, despite its final line, a transatlantic critique of a planetary struggle between rising and falling world powers.

The negotiation of this critique through the echoes of Cuban resistance movements may be viewed as a model of what Françoise Lionnet and Shu-mei Shih term "minor transnationalism," that is, as "a space of exchange and participation wherever processes of hybridization occur and where it is still possible for cultures to be produced and performed without necessary mediation by the center."[97] This definition of minor transnationalism (Lionnet and Shih offer several) suggests that cultures peripheral to metropolitan centers can interrelate in their oppositionalities without necessarily defining themselves vis-à-vis the loci of hegemonic power. Evita does not have to work through the canonized Generation of '98 in Spain in order to establish the literary contours of turn-of-the-century Spanish Guinea. He can play off Cuban environments instead. Indeed, he does not insert Iberia directly into his story at all, for he circumvents the peninsula by engaging the Equatoguinean 1898 in east-west flows of the Atlantic rather than north-south. Ignoring the imperial hub altogether, he produces a plotting that is subtly radical in its displacements of the expected lines of oceanic contact.

The minor and major transnationalisms of *When the Combes Fought* imply that traditional academic and national framings of 1898 need to be resituated, perhaps decentered entirely, to account for renderings of an ocean that already at the time had been trespassed for four centuries. In recent years, scholarly movements to include Cuban and Puerto Rican interventions in 1898 have impacted the older, more static perceptions of a binational imperial clash with binational results, such as the literary productions of the Generation of '98 writers in Spain and the national political campaigns of Theodore Roosevelt in the United States. *When the Combes Fought* demonstrates that the geographic and temporal parameters of 1898 must be reenvisioned from Africa as well. The binary transatlantic tensions implied by the phrase "the Spanish-American War" are incommensurate with the historical and literary record.

To situate Vilangua as an emblematic New World indigene who haunts that conflict is not to appropriate away his identity as an African, but rather to complement it. Specters of the transatlantic appear in many locations and in many forms. A performance of America may take place on any seaboard and aboard all the ships in between. Iterated dramas of absence can be staged in a multitude of spaces and times. Columbus and Las Casas and Cabeza de Vaca know this, as do Rigoberta Menchú and the authors of the *Popol Vuh*. Crusoe, who directs his own transatlantic show of Conquest, knows it, too. And the least that can be done when absences appear is to not run immediately, as do colonizers in most instances, to grab the nearest gun. This almost always leads to shots being fired and a dominant incorporation attempted once more. Instead, revenants should be welcomed, greeted, shown that seats await them at the table if they choose, that equally they may wander yet if they want, that their liberty is no longer sought to be enchained. There are many specters of the transatlantic, some more visible than others, some less so, but all should feel free to speak if they wish, and to listen or be listened to as is their desire.

Ghosts, like questions, gesture that we follow. They may lead their witnesses then to the most unexpected of places. The colonial United States, along with cannibal communities in West Africa, could be one.

5 / Subjunctive America: Thomas Pynchon's *Mason & Dixon* and Gabriel García Márquez's *Love in the Time of Cholera*

If Columbus co-authored the opening pages of a ghosted America, Charles Mason and Jeremiah Dixon added to the narrative with a line they wrote upon the New World. In the reimagination of their enterprise by Thomas Pynchon in an eponymous 1997 novel, Mason and Dixon are bit players in a transatlantic drama of Conquest whose plottings they barely grasp, if at all. Like Columbus, they are charged by great royal powers to cross the ocean in an unparalleled quest to delineate western spaces uncharted by Europeans. Like Crusoe, they leave from Britain and make their way first to Africa before turning west. And like all the characters in this book, they find an America born of indigenous markings that disappear only partially before a foreign and conquering project of inscription. In the case of Mason and Dixon, this writing takes the form of a line of latitude that they are commissioned to draw between the British colonies of Maryland and Pennsylvania. This line is one more imposed narrative, one more colonization that will prove haunted by that which it presumes to erase.

Mason is an astronomer, Dixon a surveyor, and their paired scientific skills allow them to score with mathematical precision an eerily straight border that begins south of Philadelphia and scrolls forth westward. Like all parallels, the Mason-Dixon Line is written in invisible ink, but that hardly undercuts its powers and presence. Thousands of trees disappear in its path, thousands of indigenous people, too. The mapping project, a triumph of the Age of Reason, is therefore imbued with an ongoing production of the spectral. Pynchon's *Mason & Dixon*, though written five centuries after Columbus's diary, shares with that text a profound preoccupation with an America created by absent presences. The novel recognizes that the successive originary moments of the Conquest are marked as much by what is suppressed as by what is impressed.

The historical Mason and Dixon played their role at a pivotal moment, the 1760s. This was just before the first successful national liberation movement of the hemisphere, that of the United States. The cartographic enterprise rooted itself in a New World metropolis, Philadelphia, the future home of the Declaration of Independence and the hub of the independence struggle. By virtue of this temporal and geographic centrality, Pynchon returns to a foundational moment of transatlantic inscription and finds that the performance of conquistadors has been haunted from the beginning. In terms of literary genealogy, *Mason & Dixon* does not launch a particular tradition in the fashion of *When the Combes Fought* (as the first African novel in Spanish) or Columbus's diary of his first voyage (as the landmark transatlantic text), but it does, like the *Popol Vuh* and *Robinson Crusoe*, reimagine a signal scene of New World commencement and the ghostliness that suffuses it. In this sense, Pynchon's novel inaugurates the tradition of an America whose every inauguration, necessarily, is a reinauguration. Figuratively and perhaps factually, *Mason & Dixon* is no less accurate or seminal than Columbus's diary, whose avowals of veracity are often suspect and whose claims to originality are often questionable given the evident influence of predecessor texts by Marco Polo and others.

As with Columbus, many conflicts have been waged over the implications of Mason and Dixon long after the deaths of the historical individuals in question. Although the Mason-Dixon Line in its particulars was intended only to resolve a boundary dispute between proprietors in two colonies within the same empire, the division it created came to represent the borderline between the northern and southern United States. This gave it great symbolic importance, for the line in the earth led to a dialectical binarism—North and South transmuting into North *versus* South—and all the apparent oppositionalities that customarily if dubiously follow: free/slave, capitalist/feudal, urban/rural, and so on. As John H. B. Latrobe declared in 1854, just a few years before the United States Civil War:

> There is, perhaps, no line, real or imaginary, on the surface of the earth—not excepting even the equator and the equinoctial—whose name has been oftener in men's mouths during the last fifty years.

In the halls of legislation, in the courts of justice, in the assemblages of the people, it has been as familiar as a household word. Not that any particular interest was taken in the line itself; but the mention of it was always expressive of the fact, that the States of the Union were divided into slaveholding and non-slaveholding—into Northern and Southern. . . . Its geographical thus became lost in its political significance; and men cared little, when they referred to it, where it ran, or what was its history—or whether it was limited to Pennsylvania, or extended, as has, perhaps, most generally been supposed, from the Atlantic to the Pacific.[1]

The Mason-Dixon Line became an invisible wall between neighbors, looked to as a preserver of cultural difference and, as a result, an artificer thereof. For example, when Southern regionalists fought and lost a war in the name of "Dixie," it was Jeremiah Dixon whose surname probably was being invoked. Though the origin of the word is hazy, Dixie as a synonym for the southern United States was "first recorded in American English in 1859 in the folk song *Dixie's Land* by Daniel Decatur Emmett . . . three sources of the name have been advanced: 1). that *Dixie* is a modification of Dixon abstracted from *Mason and Dixon's line* (1779, the boundary between Pennsylvania and Maryland, surveyed 1763–67 by Charles Mason and Jeremiah Dixon; the line was regarded as separating the slave states from the free states.)"[2] The first usage of "Dixie" therefore came long after the lives of the surveyors but, significantly, on the eve of the 1861–65 conflict in which the divisive North/South imagery of the Line materialized in pitched war.

The interpretive possibilities of the Mason-Dixon Line extend beyond even the nation it would come to separate. The southern United States, though a full participant in the hemispheric hegemony of the country as a whole, shares with Latin America a history of plantations, slavery, belated industrialization and, most importantly, traumatic defeat at the hands of the same northerners. Due to such similarities, Gabriel García Márquez has said that William Faulkner influenced him for reasons "more geographic than literary. I discovered them long after having written my first novels, traveling through the south of the United States. The scorching towns filled with dust, the people without hope that I encountered in that trip, resembled a lot those whom I evoked in my short stories."[3] The global South, at some metaphorical and arguably literal level, is divided from the global North by the Mason-Dixon Line. Although this case can only be advanced so far, one import of the surveyors' work is clear: the Line, like all those written, bears multiple meanings more profound and nuanced than anything its authors might originally have intended or recognized.

As Latrobe notes, the true significance of the Mason-Dixon Line arose from its metonymic suggestiveness rather than its documented reason for existing. Officially, the Line stretched only far enough to settle a border quarrel in the 1760s between parties in colonial Pennsylvania and Maryland, but that fact paled before the symbolic powers with which it was increasingly invested. The Line accrued additional resonance as a postcolonial era began upon the birth of the United States. The narrative of the new nation developed with every settlement further west, including in lands beyond Pennsylvania and Maryland. In this way, the Line acquired an ability to run beyond itself, as Latrobe suggests, "from the Atlantic to the Pacific." In Pynchon's novel, correspondingly, at one point Mason and Dixon find themselves in a surreal sequence in which they are even inscribing the Line unto infinity.

At the time of the historical surveying, the geographic contours of the future United States were unknown and unknowable. In the 1760s of Mason and Dixon, the thirteen British colonies from Massachusetts to Georgia were but a sliver of the unforeseeable extent of the twenty-first century nation of which they would be part. For example, whole swaths of what would become the states of California, Arizona, New Mexico, and Texas were part of the Spanish empire. Extending the Line to California thus would have equated to extending it to Mexico. And each westward marking by Mason and Dixon amounted to the addition of new pages to a protonational narrative. The surveyors' line was therefore literary as well as technical, symbolic as well as scientific. Such projecting of expansionist lines would prove common in nineteenth-century authors who, participatory in the rhetoric of Manifest Destiny, envisioned a growing country ordained to be writ larger. Kirsten Silva Gruesz notes in Walt Whitman, for instance, "the prematurely continental shape of his vision of an America stretching 'over the Texas and Mexican and Floridian and Cuban seas.'"[4] Pynchon, unlike his protagonists, works posterior to the heyday of Manifest Destiny, but his Mason and Dixon do sense that their authorship of the Line is palimpsestic and, in the etymological sense, topographic. They know they are inscribing places that already existed as other places in alternative local narratives. As with the end of the written *Popol Vuh* when "Santa Cruz" ("Holy Cross") is indicated as the Spanish name of a local town, the inscription is not merely onomastic but synecdochical to a broader story of colonization. In Pynchon's novel, the efforts of Mason and Dixon do not constitute omnicide per se, but they do prepare a narrative of elision by other means. Since genocide and ecocide are a sine qua non of America, Pynchon implies that what appears to be a neutral and scientific determination of a line of latitude is actually an iteration of the tragic foundational drama of the transatlantic.

Mark Knopfler, who turned *Mason & Dixon* into a song in which Mason and Dixon never quite arrive in the New World, appears to be on the same page as Pynchon. Knopfler is the former lead singer and guitarist of the rock band Dire Straits. His literary and cinematic sensibilities have been long evident in songs like "Romeo and Juliet" of 1980 and the groundbreaking, metatextual video of "Money for Nothing" in 1984. The title track of his solo album *Sailing to Philadelphia* is a duet sung by Knopfler and James Taylor playing the protagonists of Pynchon's novel. The album reached the top of sales lists in several countries and was named a Top Ten Album of 2000 in *Rolling Stone* as well.[5] Jann Wenner reviewed it as "a work of masterful songwriting and guitar playing . . . so rich a listen, so valid a masterpiece."[6] The most intriguing feature of the title track is that the lyrics stop before the surveyors reach Philadelphia. Instead of voicing their thoughts while working on the Line, Mason and Dixon sing of their visions of the New World as they travel across the Atlantic toward it. In other words, America emerges as the destination and repository of all of Mason and Dixon's thoughts but it remains for them an inchoate imaginary. They will be the ones to render it determinate, to write a defining line upon it. They will be the ones to reinvest America with absence and presence in a foundational moment to come that already has taken place many times before.

As in the novel, the lyrical tension between Taylor's Mason and Knopfler's Dixon issues from the resignation of the one and the optimism of the other regarding any resolution of the New World dynamics they are soon to confront. Thus Taylor sings, "You talk of liberty./ How can America be free?/A Geordie and a baker's boy/in the forests of the Iroquois."[7] The recognition here is of a presumptive narrative of liberty based on the denial of the same to those already there, namely, indigenes such as the Iroquois. Taylor's Mason indicates that the presence of the surveyors is inextricable from a potential freedom that only can be achieved at its own expense. Knopfler's Dixon responds, "Now hold your head up, Mason, see America lies there./The morning tide has raised the capes of Delaware./Come up and feel the sun./A new morning is begun."[8] Knopfler's Dixon does not deny the paradox signaled by Taylor's Mason. Indeed, thanks to his Quaker background, the Dixon in

Pynchon's novel is even more cognizant of colonial dynamics than his partner. But his "new morning" sensibilities are read best as an openness to searching for a way, however unlikely, in which to settle the contradiction between the presence of the Iroquois and his own presence as a demarcator hired by imperial powers. The chorus, sung in unison by Taylor and Knopfler, acknowledges the originary moment ahead: "We are sailing to Philadelphia,/a world away from the coaly Tyne./Sailing to Philadelphia/to draw the Line,/the Mason-Dixon Line."[9]

The title characters never do gain Philadelphia in the song. And as in the case of many pop culture derivatives of *Robinson Crusoe*, the elements that are missing are interpretive keys to the source text. Seemingly, the Line remains for Mason and Dixon an endeavor that awaits them for its commencement. Yet their work really is a recommencement, for although the surveyors have never been to the New World they will be iterating the loggings of all its previous foreign mappers from Columbus onward. Foundational acts of writing are not singular but recurring, each new draft a unique but recognizable simulacrum of its predecessors. "Sailing to Philadelphia" is not about the technics of measuring a particular position. It is about the violent implications of measuring positions in the first place. That is why it is not necessary for the song's Mason and Dixon to grasp the narrative significance of the Line only upon the physical chaining of it. The Line is a figuration whose resonances of imposed presence and corresponding absence can be contemplated before they arrive on western Atlantic shores. America, after all, is a repeating drama of foreigners arriving in indigenous land and scripting it theirs. The singing surveyors do not have to reach the New World to sense the outlines of their roles as players in that drama.

All references forthcoming to Mason and Dixon denote Pynchon's fictional characters and not the historical individuals, unless otherwise specified. In the novel, the surveyors are charged with measuring with utmost accuracy a line that, as it unscrolls westward from Philadelphia, gradually leaves behind the urbanized coast and penetrates into territories where the recent presences of aboriginal peoples remain more perceptible. The Line therefore is an imperial intrusion, an insertion of artificial writing that implies a narrative of Conquest to be etched upon the hinterland and over the unmeasured indigenous narratives that abound in its path. Mason and Dixon are cartographers who take over where, on the other side of the ocean and in an apparently distinct but actually parallel context, Martín and Carlos in *When the Combes Fought* leave off. In Pynchon's novel, the seemingly objective and quantitative nature of Mason and Dixon's measurements reveals a project whose implications extend far beyond the scientific. For example, when the surveyors chart the end of the Line, they "set a Post at 165 Miles, 54 Chains, 88 Links from the Post Mark'd West and, turning, begin to widen the Visto, moving East again, Ax-blows the day long. From the Ridges they can now see their Visto, dividing the green Vapors of Foliage that wrap the Land, undulating Stump-top yellow, lofty American Clouds a-sailing above."[10] Despite the foregrounded numerical precision of this passage, its real importance lies not in the particular coordinates of the Line but in the narrative that emerges from it: Mason and Dixon are not apolitical actors because their very mapping is a line of destruction. The trees felled along the Visto divide the land in half. Literally, Mason and Dixon log their position. Indigenous peoples in the way of the Line therefore are sure to read it as a scripting of territorial displacement. As one observant character tells Mason, "clearing and marking a Right Line of an Hundred Leagues, into the Lands of Others, cannot be a kindly Act."[11] Correspondingly, David Seed notes that "The novel demonstrates a postcolonial alertness to mapping as a culturally inflected exercise, an exercise in territorial appropriation where the first casualties to be displaced are the native Americans."[12] Mason and Dixon are not conquistadors in a traditional sense. They have no interest in colonization proper and Dixon, a thoughtful Quaker, is particularly aware of the moral implications of their work as demarcators. Yet they are caught up in advancing the imperial process all the same by facilitating the violent superimposition of a rectilinear foreign narrative over many possible indigenous others. Their work is concomitant with the Conquest.

That Columbus's diary and *Mason & Dixon* should both open with apparitions is therefore not surprising. The two texts, from the beginning, are countered by phantasmal narratives that (dis)appear before foreign and ocean-crossing protagonists. Such production of absent presences is tantamount to the foundational hauntings of the transatlantic. Rather than the exiled Moors and Jews of Spain, however, the death of Mason launches Pynchon's ghost story and, more specifically, the narrative of the Reverend Wicks Cherrycoke, former chaplain of the Mason-Dixon party. The Reverend has come to Philadelphia in 1786 to pay his last respects to the astronomer. There, in the newly conceived United States, "with the War settl'd and the Nation bickering itself into Fragments, wounds bodily and ghostly, great and small, go aching on, not ev'ry one commemorated,—nor, too often, even recounted."[13] Cherrycoke visits Mason's grave daily, as if haunted by those national "wounds bodily and ghostly." These specters are multiple and imprecise. There are those of the nation, so recently born; there are those of Mason, the measurer who writes over the unmeasured; and there are those of Cherrycoke, the recollector of the Mason and Dixon party and the teller of Pynchon's tale. The Mason-Dixon Line was the most deliberately drawn border in the history of the British colonies and yet all that surrounds it is ectoplasm.

The explicit hauntings in *Mason & Dixon* number in the hundreds, the implicit ones in the thousands. As Brian McHale points out, "the American wilderness of *Mason & Dixon* is a haunted landscape."[14] As in *When the Combes Fought*, as in *Robinson Crusoe* and the *Popol Vuh* and Columbus's diary, America is ideated as absence arisen in a context of Conquest that links all sides of a haunted Atlantic world. Cherrycoke re-initiates this world with an oral narrative of Mason and Dixon that lasts the length of the novel. He describes the surveyors in their initial pairings in London, Cape Town, and St. Helena, all of which are rehearsals for the performance they will undertake in the New World. In fact, they do not sail across the Atlantic until a third of the novel is past and do not begin writing the Mason-Dixon Line until more than half the text is through. Yet by that point, as with Crusoe prior to encountering Friday, the intertwinings of absence and presence long have been established within a transatlantic narrative of colonialism and its pursuant ghosts.

The material details of Mason and Dixon's experiences of delineating the border between Pennsylvania and Maryland fill in a spectral structure that already has been invoked many times in the novel. For instance, Cape Town, like Philadelphia, is a colonial port clinging to a vast continent as yet uncharted by Europeans. And Jamestown on St. Helena is a town barely hanging onto a haunted island in a manner comparable to the compounds of Crusoe in the Caribbean and of John Stephen in Equatorial Guinea. Cape Town and St. Helena also share cultures of slavery, a proliferation of irrational apparitions, and multiple twinnings of absence and presence of the sort that will trouble Mason and Dixon on the western Atlantic seaboard as well. Nonetheless, the surveyors keep repeating to themselves throughout all their expeditions that they are men of Science, of the Age of Reason, that they are composers of numerical data and not of imperial text. Both men, however, and especially Dixon, come to recognize that they are co-authoring a ghosted Atlantic into existence. They increasingly understand that by inscribing the direction of European colonization, they are writing over aboriginal worlds that in turn shadow them from positions of absence.

In the most critical of the novel's many metatextualities, Pynchon identifies a foundational tension between declarative and subjunctive Americas, that is, between Mason and Dixon's marking of a rationalizing European narrative on one hand and the corresponding suppression of multiple hypothetical indigenous worlds on the other:

> Does Britannia, when she sleeps, dream? Is America her dream?—in which all that cannot pass in the metropolitan Wakefulness is allow'd Expression away in the restless Slumber of these Provinces, and on West-ward, wherever 'tis not yet mapp'd, nor written down, nor ever, by the majority of Mankind, seen,—serving as a very Rubbish-Tip for subjunctive Hopes, for all that *may yet be true*,—Earthly Paradise, Fountain of Youth, Realms of Prester John, Christ's Kingdom, ever behind the sunset, safe till the next Territory to the West be seen and recorded, measur'd and tied in, back into the Net-Work of Points already known, that slowly triangulates its Way into the Continent, changing all from subjunctive to declarative, reducing Possibilities to Simplicities that serve the ends of Governments,—winning away from the realm of the Sacred, its Borderlands one by one, and assuming them unto the bare mortal World that is our home, and our Despair.[15]

In this passage, the mapping of unknown coordinates, or "changing all from subjunctive to declarative," is revealed to be an imperial project. Every measurement that Mason and Dixon take inserts the colonies further into the empire, the unscripted periphery into the text of the metropole. This process suppresses all local narratives beneath the indicative indications of the surveyors' measuring instruments and the foreign hegemon that funds them. To write is to embody; to chart a foreign position is to incorporate a previously absent aboriginal space. Subjunctive America, the antithesis of the declarative empire, is that unmapped atemporal locus where plural realities and possibilities exist side by side. It is therefore resistant to foreign cartography, which seeks to determine the indeterminate and incarnate the atextual. The colonialism inherent in border drawings and in the Mason-Dixon Line in particular is designed to repress all contestatory narratives, both those that already exist and those that could come into being. An imperial project is effectively an exorcism meant to conjure away this ghostly realm and the alternative local narrators and narratives that populate it.

Pynchon implies that the dialectic of the declarative versus the subjunctive represents no parochial tension within the British empire but rather the history of the whole New World, including what became its

Spanish-speaking parts. After all, it was Columbus, not Mason, who thought he might locate the "Earthly Paradise" in the New World. And it was Juan Ponce de León, not Dixon, who sought the "Fountain of Youth." Another Pynchon character speaks of "a great current of Westering. You will hear of gold cities, marble cities, men that fly, women that fight, fantastickal creatures never dream'd in Europe,—something always to take and draw you that way."[16] Such images recall the thoughts and writings of innumerable early conquistadors who crossed the Atlantic. These are not dreamscapes pertinent only to the lands that would be yoked into the United States but also to subjunctive America in the broadest transatlantic sense. Despite the legal identity of the Mason-Dixon Line as an intracolonial marker, the dynamics of imposed inscription and incomplete erasure is not restricted to Britannia's thirteen colonies on the southeastern mainland. In fact, non-British imperial presences pervade *Mason & Dixon* from French armies near the Great Lakes to irredentist Swedes in the mid-Atlantic region, Spanish privateers in Delaware, and Spanish Jesuits in Quebec. Indeed, the reach of Spanish power repeatedly surfaces, especially via the frequent and sinister Jesuit presence but also in such passages as when the Mason-Dixon party chooses Castilian as the language for "The Anthem of the Expedition, as it moves into the Unknown . . . in among all the ghosts already thick in those parts."[17]

That a Spanish song should be sung by British imperialists in Pennsylvania is not surprising. Dixon knows as well as Crusoe and Martín that the Atlantic is effectively a single theater, its particular national players but usurpers determined to dominate the same subjunctive world. That their anthems borrow from each other makes sense: so do their respective wills to hegemony. It is not a coincidence that immediately after the singing of the Castilian anthem, Dixon suggests to Mason,

> "We shouldn't be runnin' this Line . . . ?"
> Mason regards his Cup of Claret. "Bit late for that, isn't it?"
> "Why aye. I'll carry it through, Friend, fear not. But something invisible's going on, tha must feel it, smell it . . . ?"
> Mason shrugs. "American Politics."
> "Just so. We're being us'd again. It doesn't alarm thee . . . ?"[18]

Mason and Dixon perceive that they are pawns in a far larger contest, complicit in some small way with imperial struggles taking place on an oceanic scale. The "something invisible" is not confined to Pennsylvania and Maryland. The whole of the Atlantic is in play.

Elsewhere in the novel, Pynchon repeatedly makes it clear that the suppression of the subjunctive by the declarative is common to the breadth of the Conquest. For instance, Zhang, a geomancer, rails against "the inscription upon the Earth of these enormously long straight Lines" such as that of Mason and Dixon.[19] Based on his knowledge of "Spanish California," he suggests of the surveyors' work that "To mark a right Line upon the Earth is to inflict upon the Dragon's very Flesh, a sword-slash, a long, perfect scar, impossible for any who live out here the year 'round to see as other than hateful Assault."[20] Zhang links here the "hateful" Line to mappings of Spanish imperialism in North America even though the vast spaces separating "Spanish California" from Pennsylvania were unknown and perhaps inconceivable in the 1760s. Like the Mason-Dixon party singing in Castilian as they move westward, Zhang recognizes that the distinctions between the far-flung periphery of one European empire and another pale before the common attempt to narrate the New World with colonizing script. As a feng shui expert, he wants humans to coexist harmoniously and naturally with geography, but this is exactly what the Line and its parallels in Spanish California are meant not to do. The metatextual role of Zhang leads David Cowart to refer to him as "chief spokesman against the Line."[21] The geomancer sees the surveying by Mason and Dixon as representative of not a border squabble between two British colonies but of the far greater affront that is imperial delineation itself. He concludes that the impositions of foreign markings are "Tellurick Injuries" akin to "the distinction between Blade and Body,—the aggressive exactitude of one, the helpless indeterminacy of the other. In that difference lies the Potency of the Sin."[22] In this metaphoric discourse invoked by Pynchon throughout the novel, inscriptions are wounds, lands are bodies, and imperialism is "the aggressive exactitude" of the blade, be it of the pen or the sword. Mason and Dixon, by wielding their instruments upon earth and paper, by incising the unscored, render a subjunctive land declarative.

This subjunctive America comprises not one narrative or narratological element but many, an aggregate that is extraordinarily varied and irreducible. Whatever the distinctions of these elements, they share a particular feature: opposition to an overpowering reality imposed from without by a Columbus, a Crusoe, a Cabeza de Vaca, a Stephen, a Martín, which is to say, the Conquest. Subjunctive America, like the predecessor *Popol Vuh* now unreachable within the context of the transatlantic, is filled with plural realities and unrealities. Indeed, it is the very unresolvability of this plurality that makes it subjunctive in the first place. Among the novel's cast of surreal characters are talking dogs, talking clocks, and an invisible time-traveling talking mechanical duck. There are also vegetables of hyperbolic size, an enormous runaway cheese, a legendary golem, and a remarkable array of real and imagined ghosts. Not all of these figures surface in the New World section of Mason and Dixon's journeys. Those who do, however, are as believable and as valorized as those who appear in Britain or Africa or the seas in between. Dixon tries his very best to be at peace with these ghosts, to listen to them and the alternative narratives they tell and represent. He does not attempt to incorporate them so as to control them, unlike Columbus and Crusoe, unlike William Carlos Williams in "The Discovery of the Indies," unlike González Echegaray in the prologue to *When the Combes Fought*, unlike various critics of Rigoberta Menchú. Instead, Dixon accepts the atextualizations that he faces and, though participatory in the dynamics that lead to their spectrality, allows that they haunt him. Were he to encounter in some form Xury or Menchú or Friday or Vilangua or the authors of the *Popol Vuh*, it seems likely he would do the same.

The surreal and the absurd are only subcategories of the subjunctive. Unenclosed possibility per se is what Mason and Dixon declaratively overwrite with their Line. Indigenous peoples, therefore, form part of subjunctive America as much as any fantastic phenomena of the New World, not because they are equally implausible but because they, too, constitute an alterity at risk from encroaching linearities. In their case, of course, Mason and Dixon's engagement in "changing all from subjunctive to declarative" is particularly egregious because the alterity in danger of annihilation is not a dreamscape or mythical being but human beings of flesh and blood.[23] Mason and Dixon first encounter this tragedy directly when news reaches them in a Philadelphia coffeehouse of a massacre of unarmed indigenes by the Paxton Boys, a motley group of frontiersmen. When a mechanic notes, "Now the entire Tribe is gone," and Dixon asks "Were there no Soldiers to prevent it?" the mechanic responds, "Colonel Robertson and his Regiment of Highlanders refus'd to stir, toasting their Noses whilst that brave Paxton Vermin murder'd old people, small children, and defenseless Drunkards."[24] Notwithstanding their experiences on the other side of the Atlantic with slavery in Cape Town and hauntings in St. Helena, the surveyors did not expect to find in the New World what another character describes as a "Wicked Policy of extermination."[25] As news of the eradication of "the entire Tribe" in Lancaster sinks in, "Mason and Dixon look at each other bleakly. 'Well. If I'd known 'twould be like *this* in America . . .'"[26] They are allegedly in western Atlantic lands as apolitical men of science, hired measurers and little more, but it begins to dawn on them that they partake in the same westward expansion that has produced the genocidal Paxton Boys. Mason and Dixon have not begun yet to write their Line but erasures already have taken place near its projected script. Alternative narrators and narratives of the New World have been rubbed out in more than one figurative sense.

The moral implications of their role in this drama come to haunt them. As if to face the ghosts of the exterminated indigenes, Mason and Dixon travel to Lancaster to visit the site of the massacre. Suspected by locals after asking too many questions, they disguise their moral concerns in the language of the Enlightenment. "'We're men of Science,' Dixon explains, '– this being a neoclassickal Instance of the Catastrophick Resolution of Inter-Populational Cross-Purposes, of course we're curious to see where it all happen'd.'"[27] This is a purposeful feint by Dixon, for he knows that he cannot pose his questions in terms of ethics. Doing so would risk delegitimizing not only the presence of the frontiersmen he meets but also, by extension, his own presence in the New World. He invokes European scientific discourse to cloak his moral concerns, an ironic manipulation given that he gradually realizes that it his very science that is being used in the service of genocide. He knows that something is out of joint here, that a foundational crime has been committed in Lancaster that can be extrapolated to the whole of the Atlantic. And so, upon seeing the exact site of the butchery, he wonders aghast, "What in the Holy Names are these people about?"[29] The world he is charged with delineating seems now an incomprehensible holocaust. He prays silently for the disappeared, but this brings him no relief. There is a wrong to be set right here and Dixon suspects that he himself is not "credible" enough to play that role.[28] Somehow, he gathers, he is part of the same imperial theatrics as the Paxton Boys. Somehow he, too, is guilty of this massacre that horrifies him.

Mason is wrenched by the events at Lancaster as well. And likewise, he sees the massacre as a parable of America: "Acts have consequences, Dixon, they must. These Louts believe all's right now,—that they are free to get on with Lives that to them are no doubt important,—with no Glimmer at all of the Debt they have taken on. That is what I smell'd,— Lethe-Water."[30] Mason grasps that the Paxton killings are the crime of Conquest in a microcosm and not an isolated event in an insular frontier town. He knows, too, that the forgetting of that crime does not equate to justice. A "Debt" is left pending, "taken on," that same debt that, as Derrida notes, is common to all specters, for haunting always signifies unbalanced accounts.[31] As Mason and Dixon leave Lancaster in a haste, forced to flee because their inquiries have antagonized the locals, "Behind,—below,—diminishing, they hear, and presently lose, a Voicing disconsolate, of Regret at their Flight."[32] This disembodied Voice mourns their departure because, rare on this edge of empire, Mason and Dixon perceive the ghosting of America taking place. Though directly culpable in the extension of that edge, they glimpse what is being elided before it and beneath the scriptings of their instruments. They are haunted by their cognizance of the Voice but do not turn back to try to enchain it on their own terms. Crusoe, by contrast, when haunted momentarily in his sleep by the voice of Poll the parrot, rushes to resolve it into a recognizable body. Mason and Dixon mourn the Conquest in their own ways despite advancing it, which is why the key passage of the novel's nearly 800 pages of text—the paragraph that speaks of "changing all from subjunctive to declarative"—lies at the heart of the Lancaster chapter.[33] Immediately prior to that passage, Mason and Dixon arrive in Lancaster to inquire about the massacre; immediately after it, they visit the site of the killing and wonder what it means.

At that point, Mason and Dixon still have not begun to inscribe the Line. But when they do, they know that their narrative will be splotched with bloodstains with every turn of the page. Wherever the surveyors go, they discover aboriginal populations absenting or absented before them. In Williamsburg, for instance, Mason "is introduc'd, at the State House, to a Party of Tuscarora Chiefs, upon a Mission to bring out the last of their people from the Carolinas. . . . The Escort have some apprehension about crossing Pennsylvania, with an hundred, perhaps two hundred, Tuscaroras, for they have heard of the Paxton Massacres."[34] For the most part, however, as the surveyors write their Line ever westward, they do not see more sites of killings so much as ghosted lands where indigenous peoples used to live. Like Columbus, they become conscious of constantly arriving at places from which aboriginal bodies recently have vanished. The Line, like Columbus's charting of navigational coordinates, is not an isolated and objective measurement but a literary plotting of a collective narrative of Conquest.

When Mason notes of the Line that "'it's a living creature, 'tis all of us, temporarily collected into an Entity, whose Labors none could do alone,'" Dixon responds,

A tree-slaughtering Animal, with no purpose but to continue creating forever a perfect Corridor over the Land. Its teeth of Steel,—its

Jaws, Axmen,—it's Life's Blood, Disbursement. And what of its intentions, beyond killing ev'rything due west of it? do you know? I
don't either. . . . . What else are these [indigenous] people suppos'd to
believe? Haven't we been saying, with an hundred Blades all the day
long,—This is how far into your land we may strike, this is what we
claim to westward. As you see what we may do to Trees, and how
little we care,—imagine how little we care for Indians, and what we
are prepar'd to do to you.[35]

Dixon recognizes that the Line repeatedly forces into absence the indigenous ecologies and peoples that flourished before its narrative came to
prevail. And as in Whitman's "Starting from Paumanok," there appears
to be little if any autonomous space in which the affected can oppose or
manipulate such disappearances. Yet the mourning by Dixon of his own
participation in the production of absence forms a type of contestatory
script within the dominant colonial narrative he is charged with measuring out. The absent presences he signals are challenging in that they
still represent extant alternative narratives, however now overwritten by
the powers that be. In his sympathy with those lives already suppressed
by the Line and those facing a similar prospect, Dixon goes much further than Whitman in "Starting from Paumanok." The Line that bears
his name is a "tree-slaughtering Animal" bent on "killing ev'rything due
west of it."

Charles Clerc, author of the first full-length critical text on Pynchon's
novel, nonetheless lauds the drawing of the Line and depicts it as ethi-
cally neutral: "Progress cannot be forestalled; the line brought civilization, which in itself hardly qualifies as bad or evil."[36] Any such reading
that does not problematize concepts like "civilization" and "progress" is
ideologically naive and differs substantively from that accepted by Mason and Dixon themselves. Clerc adds that "perhaps life is better off with
divisioning, property demarcation, walls, a Mason and Dixon Line. So
maybe what Zhang argues isn't necessarily the correct view. He decries
the line, but, remember, the line brings order."[37] This begs the question
of what sort of "order" the Line imposes. After all, people and flora are
banished or exterminated before it. Life in that case is not "better off."
The eradication of indigenous worlds is not morally neutral. On the contrary, the arrival of "civilization" with its "divisioning" and "walls," all
established by the Line, is omnicidal.

The imposition of "progress" and "order" in *Mason & Dixon* is relatively monolithic compared to the multiplicity of aboriginal societies

and landscapes whose erasure it portends. This is the case, too, in another foundational novel of America, one which Pynchon has praised profusely, Gabriel García Márquez's *Love in the Time of Cholera*.[38] Foundational texts are not only those that appear at some historical moment canonically denoted a beginning (e.g., a flag-planting in the Caribbean or West Africa, a bell-ringing in Philadelphia or Dolores) but also all those written in any era that gesture at the production of absent presences. If any García Márquez novel were to fit this category, it would seem to be *One Hundred Years of Solitude* with its enormous scope and overarching meditations on time and space and phantasmagoria in the New World.[39] Yet two short passages in *Love in the Time of Cholera* are even more compelling precisely because they are traces rather than epics. These sections describe the natural environments that contextualize river journeys taken by the protagonist, Florentino Ariza, half a century apart.

On the first trip, Ariza observes a lush abundance of flora and fauna on the banks: "a forest tangled with colossal trees. . . . The din of the parrots and the racket of the invisible monkeys."[40] This plenitude of aboriginal life causes him to spend his days on the boat "watching the immobile alligators sunning themselves in the large beaches with their jaws open to trap butterflies, watching the flocks of frightened herons that rose suddenly in the swamps, the manatees that suckled their litter with their big maternal teats and surprised the passengers with their womanly cries."[41] But a lifelong romantic obsession later, Ariza takes another trip up the river. This time he discovers that the indigenous landscape he remembered was now little more than a ghost:

> the irrational deforestation had finished off the river in fifty years: the ship boilers had devoured the forest tangled with colossal trees . . . the hunters of pelts from New Orleans tanneries had exterminated the alligators that played dead with open jaws for hours and hours in the gullies of the shore in order to surprise the butterflies. The parrots with their din and the monkeys with their crazy shouts had died off as the fronds came to an end. The manatees with big maternal teats who suckled their litter and cried in the voices of a desolate woman on the beaches were a species extinguished by the reinforced bullets of the pleasure hunters.[42]

In decades of desk work for a riverboat company, Ariza had labored like Columbus and Mason and Dixon in the name of extending commerce and transportation to an uncharted region. Like them, his efforts helped map over an aboriginal landscape to the point of erasing it. All that remains is absence. Ariza's beloved Fermina Daza, on the river for the first time, "had the impression that it was a delta populated by islands of sand."[43] Nevertheless, despite the apocalyptic annihilations of alligators and manatees and colossal trees, some trace of a presence remains: the very absences perceived by Ariza. In other words, the disembodied landscape is a spectral one.

The initial description of a verdant and fecund fluvial ecosystem is devoid of human aboriginal life. This may be read as an elision in favor of foregrounding an exoticized jungle landscape. García Márquez is not particularly known for portrayals of indigenous peoples, who have only bit parts even in a novel as comprehensive as *One Hundred Years of Solitude*. The riverboat passages suggest, however, as does Pynchon, that New World aboriginality can be conceived more amply to include not only humans but also myriad other beings, with "indigenous" as an inclusive and polyvalent term. As Alfred Crosby implies in *The Columbian Exchange*, a pivotal account of the devastations produced by the arrival of Europeans in the New World, the post-1492 annihilations of indigenous ecosystems and human societies should not be isolated into discrete foci and atomized into disparate fields of study. The ghosts of all exterminated life deserve space on the same stage.

The boats of the river company in *Love in the Time of Cholera* that cut a swath through the indigenous landscape mark violently and monolithically an otherwise diverse narrative space. This is what the journals of Columbus and Crusoe and the axes of the Mason-Dixon party do as well. All declaratively write new lines over alternative and plural others. All thereby forge America in absence. It does not matter whether one line is written in Spanish and another in English, whether one appears in a diary or a novel, or in the twentieth century or the fifteenth. America cannot be restricted within parochial boundaries of either space or time, for specters slip old chains and float past borders and through walls. It makes sense that on the river in *Love in the Time of Cholera*, "The oldest ships had been built in Cincinnati in the middle of the century using the legendary model of those who trafficked on the Ohio and the Mississippi"; and that hunters from New Orleans had exterminated the alligators; and that a "hunter from North Carolina" had killed the last manatee.[44] After all, the disembodiment of aboriginal life is unique to neither the Latin American riverboat company nor to North American industrialists and hunters nor to British surveyors or Genovese navigators. All are mutually complicit, each in a particular but not exclusive way, in the spectralization of America. Subjunctive America has been overwritten by declarative forces but it has not been erased altogether. So long as a footprint in the sand remains, so long does America haunt.

Clerc, the early critic of Pynchon who approves of the order imposed by the Line, positions himself on the side of the imperial indicative. But wherever the Line does not extend, there remains the possibility of ontological plurality that is subjunctive America. As observed by Reverend Cherrycoke during his stint as the Mason-Dixon party chaplain, "We have Mileage Estimates from Rangers and Runners, yet for as long as its [the Line's] Distance from the Post Mark'd West remains unmeasur'd, nor is yet recorded as Fact, may it remain, a-shimmer, among the few final Pages of its Life as Fiction."[45] Although some indigenes accompany the party in order to keep an eye on it, the end of the imperial measuring—the western terminus of the violent conversion of the subjunctive to the declarative—is accompanied by their absenting into the unmapped: "On November 5th, two things happen at once,—the Visto is completed, and the Indians depart,—as if, as long as a Tree remain'd, so might they."[46] These indigenes vanish, but just as with those who disappear before Columbus and Martín and Carlos, theirs is not a chaotic and cowardly flight. Instead, it is a strategic move into atextuality, into a spatiality and temporality not determined by foreign measurements and narratives. Faced with the Mason-Dixon Line, the indigenes reconstitute themselves in an enduringly subjunctive America where they retain the full breadth of possibility and wherefrom they haunt those who seek to delineate them.

Latrobe in 1854 writes of indigenous absence. He concludes, "mount the highest tree adjacent to the cairn [that marks the end of the Mason-Dixon Line], that you may note the highest mountain with the range of vision, and then, ascending its summit, take in the whole horizon at a glance, and seek for a single home of a single descendant of the sylvan monarchs, whose war-path limited the surveys, and you will seek in vain."[47] Latrobe senses no revenants here among the vanished "sylvan monarchs." He is unaware that their absence, by virtue of their very presence in his text, forms a contestatory subscript that has not been erased. He does not "seek in vain" for aboriginal presence, despite his claim otherwise, for that presence is visible in its absence. The spectrality of indigenous peoples, however, is not lost on Mason: "'I respect them, and their unhappy history. But they put me in a State of Anxiety unnatural,' he complains to the Rev^d, 'out of all Measure. Unto the Apparition of Phantoms.'"[48] Shortly thereafter, as the surveyors near the end of the

Line, they consider anew their haunted context: "With Indians all 'round them, the Warpath a-tremble with murd'rous Hopes, its emptiness feeling more and more unnatural as the hours tick on, into the End of Day, as the latent Blades of Warriors press more closely upon the Membrane that divides their Subjunctive World from our number'd and dreamless Indicative."[49] Will the ghosts of the westering imperial script seek revenge? Will they demand satisfaction from Mason and Dixon? Will they reenact the skirmish of January 13, 1493, when indigenes materialized on their own terms to strike against empire in flesh and blood?

To respond in the affirmative would be to give up the ghost. The spectrality at play is no more particular to Mason and Dixon than it is to the Paxton Boys or Columbus. The ghosting of the Conquest imbues indicative temporalities and spatialities without need of incorporation. And focusing on discrete acts of armed response in specific situations tends to leave subjunctive resistances unnoticed. The most influential indigenes in the diary of the first transatlantic voyage are the absent ones who cause Columbus to build a fort and tower and moat when he claims there are no antagonists around. Similarly, the most powerful revenants in Pynchon's novel are those who respond not with physical action but ectoplasmic. As one indigene says to Mason, "Long before any of you came here, we dream'd of you. All the people, even Nations far to the South and the West, dreamt you before ever we saw you. . . . Now you begin to believe that we have come from elsewhere, possessing Powers you do not. . . . Those of us who knew how, have fled into Refuge in your Dreams, at last."[50] Of course, indigenous peoples have resisted the genocidal impositions of the transatlantic in every manner conceivable. But among these efforts, often overlooked, are aboriginal hauntings from subjunctive worlds that pervade the declarative mindsets of the conquistadors and their heirs. These hauntings are ultimately unresolvable, for they are invisible and atextual and unable to be written into, and therefore out of, imperial existence. The indigenous flight into western dreams is not only a "Refuge" but a strategic counter-occupation as well. Conquistadors, their wills to incorporation haunted by all that escapes delineation, are shadowed by such revenants.

The specters of America will never be put to rest until the Conquest can be undone, which is to say that they shall wander forever. As Zhang predicts, shivering in the night, "Our Sorrows shall persist and obsess for as long as we continue upon the ill-omen'd Line."[51] The Line, of course, is more than that of Mason and Dixon, for humanity continues upon it today. The Line is all those lines spoken, written, and acted out by the

agents of empire on all sides of the Atlantic. The surveyors come to realize this too: "Having acknowledg'd at the Warpath the Justice of the Indians' Desires . . . Mason and Dixon understand as well that the Line is
exactly what Capt. Zhang and a number of others have been styling it all
along—a conduit for Evil."[52] And so with the Line drawn and its foundational crime committed, Mason and Dixon comprehend most fully the
enterprise they have prosecuted and its synecdochical relationship to the
collective injustice that is the Conquest. As they return in an imaginary
trip to the starting post of the Line, a single thought lingers in the air:
"Will somebody repent, ere they arrive?"[53] Such repentance has been a
concern of the surveyors since before they began the Line, when Dixon
subvocalized a prayer for the massacred indigenes in Lancaster. Yet now
that they have mapped positions into empire, there is no chance of un-
writing what they have inscribed. They can only ask forgiveness for it. It
is a stage of consciousness that Columbus never reaches, nor Crusoe, nor
Cabeza de Vaca, nor Stephen, nor Martín, nor, perhaps, Francisco Ximénez. Back in England, both Mason and Dixon find themselves "dream-
ing of America, whose Name is something else, and Maps of which do
not exist."[54] Subjunctive America, over which they demarcated, now
atextually enters their thoughts and reveries. And the surveyors' senses
of sorrow at the part they played in the immense sprawling performance
of the transatlantic are what has allowed subjunctive America to persist
invisibly within them. Their openness to being haunted reflects their underlying will to redemption.

To accept the existence of America as haunted is to strive, as Mason
and Dixon do in their own ways, for repentance. Pynchon's project may
be seen as participating in this work of mourning, this search for justice,
by returning to the scene of a foundational crime and writing it anew,
this time cognizant of the moral implications of the imperial theatrics
underway. At the same time, the novel is caught up in the absenting it
mourns by primarily envisioning the Atlantic through Mason and Dixon,
cartographers of the Conquest, rather than through the indigenes who
become absent before them. Yet if Pynchon is complicit to that extent in
the narratives of the mappers rather than of the mapped, perhaps this is
inevitable in the production of any text, including the present book, that
seeks to reimagine the Conquest through its hauntings. Although Pynchon offers the perspective of British surveyors working in the service of
empire, he does so in large part for his protagonists to doubt and question the very script of colonization that they are performing. He does
allot agency and voice to indigenes, and even if such is filtered through

his own pen via the perceptions of a fictionalized Mason and Dixon, he remains explicitly aware of that. Given that all those who conceptualize or reconceptualize the transatlantic are unavoidably directing, narrating, and acting out a scriptural colonization, the best that can be hoped for in such circumstances is that the author and the text are as conscious as possible of the problematics of their own positioning in doing so. Only this may be what redeems, insofar as possible, Pynchon's Mason and Dixon as individual moral agents. This is, at best, what perhaps redeems, insofar as possible, any performance of America.

Epilogue: The Elision Fields: Mary Shelley's *Frankenstein*

Frankenstein is the great American novel. There may be no such thing, of course, yet Mary Shelley's early nineteenth-century creation haunts the transatlantic all the same. The timing of its apparition in the throes of the Age of Revolution is impeccable. The era of upheaval was not that of Napoleonic Europe but of the New World, where an epoch of national conjurations, beginning with the United States in 1776 and extending through fin-de-siècle Haiti, was emanating throughout Spain's mainland colonies in the 1810s. Certainly, *Frankenstein* owes its existence to a thoroughly European environment, from its conceptualization in Switzerland to its sundry anglophone and francophone settings. And Shelley had no intention of writing an American novel. But the text does mention the New World twice, both times in a fashion that would seem offhand and inconsequential were it not for the remarkable suggestion of transoceanic dynamics contained therein. These two traces, footprints in an otherwise unarticulated American narrative, appear at the most pivotal moments of the novel: when the "monster" acquires language and when he asks for a companion. These scenes situate him within a transatlantic theater of absent presences and a cast of phantoms that wander all around.

Frankenstein is hardly ever read as an American text, as much because of its legendary occasion of origination as its overall European setting. Throughout the rainy summer of 1816 in Geneva, Shelley and several key European literary figures read German tales of the supernatural. The group included the poets Percy Bysshe Shelley (also her husband) and Lord Byron as well as John Polidori, who would become an important early author of the vampire genre. At one point, Byron came up with the idea that every member of the group should write a ghost story.[1] Mary Shelley, who at the time was not twenty years old, eventually would produce *Frankenstein* as a result of this proposition. The novel was completed in May 1817 and published on the first day of 1818.

In acceding to Byron's injunction that she conjure forth a ghost, Shelley could have borrowed from a plethora of New World characters. In Europe, an era of relative stability had begun with all Napoleonic uprisings concluded definitively. Waterloo and the Congress of Vienna had ended a year prior to the night that, in the description of Thomas Pynchon, Byron and the Shelleys spent "watching the rain come down, while they all told each other ghost stories."[2] The ongoing Age of Revolution in the Americas, on the contrary, featured any number of potentially frightening protagonists. These included contemporary insurrectionists in Mexico, Simón Bolívar in South America, the successors of Toussaint L'Ouverture in Haiti, and many others. Later writers certainly availed themselves of these options. Even by Shelley's time, the southern United States had developed a multilayered discourse for dealing with the ghost of L'Ouverture, whom plantation owners saw as a nightmare in every mainland slave revolt of the early 1800s.

The first reference in *Frankenstein* to the New World occurs when the monster learns to speak by eavesdropping on a tutoring session occurring on the other side of a wall: "The book from which Felix instructed Safie was Volney's *Ruins of Empires*. . . . Through this work I obtained a cursory knowledge of history and a view of the several empires at present existing in the world; . . . I heard of the discovery of the American hemisphere and wept with Safie over the hapless fate of its original inhabitants."[3] Gaining language and consciousness of imperialism at the same time, the monster empathizes with absent indigenous predecessors who likewise were dismissed as semi-human illiterate barbarians. "These wonderful narrations," he adds, "inspired me with strange feelings. . . . For a long time I could not conceive how one man could go forth to murder his fellow, or even why there were laws and governments; but when I heard details of vice and bloodshed, my wonder ceased, and I turned away with disgust and loathing."[4] His amazement at how humankind could be "a mere scion of the evil principle" is thereby juxtaposed with his learning of the existence of the conquistadors who produced "the hapless fate of [the] original inhabitants" of "the American hemisphere."[5] The monster sides instinctively with the aboriginal peoples devastated by the Conquest. He weeps for them out of visceral sadness. The manner in which he learns to speak is a critical trace element in a novel that seemingly has nothing to do with America and yet without which it could not exist.

As a youth, Frankenstein (the creator of the monster) was explicitly interested in producing specters. Of his self-education as a teenager, Frankenstein notes, "The raising of ghosts or devils was a promise liberally accorded by my favourite authors, the fulfilment of which I most eagerly sought; and if my incantations were always unsuccessful, I attributed the failure rather to my own inexperience and mistake, than to a want of skill or fidelity in my instructors."[6] The monster is the adult Frankenstein's realization of his childhood dreams of becoming a conjurer of phantoms. Various ghostly qualities characterize the monster. He is made of dead body parts and yet is alive. He constantly disappears and reappears, both into and out of view and into and out of the text of the novel; he returns time and again like all revenants. His absence is always palpably present. He issues injunctions of redress to those who espy him. And he always sees his witnesses before they see him. Lastly, he, like the atextualized indigenes in all texts seemingly circumscribed by the Conquest, is at his most unsettling when he is not present, when his body is unavailable to the Frankensteins of the world and beyond their hopes of incorporation.

Colonizers often have taken the invisibility of the indigenous as proof of the completeness of their Conquests. For example, the supposed disappearance of aboriginal peoples and their cultures before the march of modernity is a common trope in much literature of the United States that appeared in the decades following *Frankenstein*. Jill Lepore has written extensively of how New Englanders of European descent in that era came to accept such putative absence in various forms, including the counterfactual. "Algonquians in southeastern New England did not vanish," she observes, "but at least to whites, they did become invisible."[7] In *The Name of War*, Lepore cites as exemplary two events of December 1829. One is the announcement by President Andrew Jackson of the official governmental policy of Indian Removal, the forced westward relocation of southeastern indigenous societies. The other is the debut of *Metamora*, "one of the most widely produced plays in the history of nineteenth-century theater."[8] *Metamora* climaxes with the death of its indigenous protagonist, who was known to nonindigenous New Englanders as King Philip. The drama, which proved particularly popular in the 1830s and 1840s and especially so its ending, draws its inspiration from King Philip's War of 1675. That conflict was the first major clash in New England between European colonists and aboriginal societies. Lepore interrogates the near simultaneity of the enactment of Indian Removal and the acclaimed restagings in *Metamora* of King Philip's demise and asks, "A century and a half after Philip's death, why did Americans crane their necks in crowded theaters everywhere to see him die yet again—this time defiantly—even as Cherokees fell by the roadside, collapsing with exhaustion?"[9] Her general conclusion is that "An American identity founded on a romanticized Indian required that Indians themselves be 'long vanished hence.'"[10] In other words, the federally sanctioned ethnic cleansing of the southeastern United States and the repeated theatrical performance of previous ethnic cleansing in the northeastern United States participated in the same assumption by citizens of European descent that indigenous absenting in space and time was foundational to their nation. This absenting could be celebrated or mourned, depending on the commentator, but regardless, it was taken as permanent.

Revenants, as Derrida suggest throughout *Specters of Marx*, always come back.[11] And even the most comforting indigenous absence to a colonist continues to be an unsettling spectral presence in its persistent refusal to go away, in its reminder of foundational crimes. The Cherokee and other aboriginal societies decimated by Indian Removal did not die westward on their own terms, but the disembodied of the Trail of Tears continue to haunt any positivist narrative of the United States every time the national history is taught. And although King Philip did not choose to lose the war named after him nor to die in *Metamora* day after day, the proof that his absence challenges the justice of colonization lies in the diverse ways, as Lepore shows, in which he and the events associated with him have been brought back to life in one form or another over the centuries. Only by (re)embodying Philip and killing him off again could nineteenth-century United States citizens of European descent control his (re)presentation by (re)incorporating him into a victorious narrative of colonization. Such control is fleeting, however, because from the instant Philip dies anew he becomes a ghost again. The key moments in *Metamora* are arguably all those *not* in *Metamora*, that is, all those moments of the day when the character of Philip has yet to appear on the stage in flesh and blood, when his absence haunts. The uncanniness of that absence causes the audience to go to the theater, for only there in performance can it be resolved, albeit temporarily, into flesh and blood. Lepore observes that the play is actually rather ambiguous in its treatment of Philip and indigenous issues in general, with Philip on his death-bed assailing those who have usurped his lands. Nonetheless, one thing is quite clear: the popularity of the play was rooted in its resurrection of indigenous absence into presence. Yet this presence dissolves quickly again into absence, which is contestatory because it cannot be scripted from outside and so must be incarnated anew if to be contained at all.

The deaths of ghosts, like that of King Philip, are always but temporary. Frankenstein's monster knows this well. A second reference in Shelley's novel to western Atlantic lands appears when the monster turns from recounting the past (that of his own education and of the "hapless fate of its original inhabitants") to imagining a future in which he personally repopulates a disembodied New World with a female monster whom he asks Frankenstein to make: "If you consent, neither you nor any other human being shall ever see us again; I will go to the vast wilds of South America. My food is not that of man; I do not destroy the lamb and the kid to glut my appetite; acorns and berries afford me sufficient nourishment. My companion will be of the same nature as myself, and will be content with the same fare. We shall make our bed of dried leaves; the sun will shine on us as on man, and will ripen our food."[12] This projected South America is a postlapsarian version of a prelapsarian New World. The monster and his partner are to be doubles of Adam and Eve, likewise created by a deity (in this case, that role is played by Frankenstein) and to be placed in a veritable Garden. There they shall live off the land, sustaining themselves on "acorns and berries" ripened by the sun. There, too, they will be isolated from human company: the mainland is an island.

Yet this edenic New World is haunted. The land where the monster hopes to live is not virginal but emptied, marked by "vast wilds" devoid of "any other human being." Since the monster has learned earlier of "the hapless fate of its original inhabitants," he considers those "vast wilds" to be not unpopulated but depopulated. After all, he acquired abilities to speak upon the narrative muting of aboriginal peoples. Frankenstein's response to him confirms this epic absenting: "'You propose,' replied I, 'to fly from the habitations of man, to dwell in those wilds where the beasts of the field will be your only companions.'"[13] The positivist and the alleged monster, condemned to coexist, coincide in their conceptualization of the New World as an island wilderness devoid of "habitations of man." But the monster is manifestly aware from his own education in imperial history that the island is not so much a potential Eden as a vacated one. No "other human being shall ever see" him again. By proposing to move to the Western hemisphere, he implicitly conceives of himself as the heir of its aboriginal absences. The monster and his mate will become the foundational apparitions of a novel New World, an America reiterated and restaged.

In terms of fact, South America was not absent of indigenes when Shelley was writing *Frankenstein*. Its aboriginal peoples and cultures, of course, continue existing to this day. The scientist and the monster, however, participate in a spectropoetic discourse and not an anthropological analysis. Far more relevant than the lack of accuracy in their transatlantic projections is the existence of those projections in the first place. Shelley was composing the novel at a time of extraordinary tumult in Latin America. And revolutions testify, at the very least, to the presence of human beings. Shelley ignores New World political unrest in *Frankenstein* by setting the novel in an indeterminate time indicated only as "17–" and thus prior to the events in the Spanish colonies that portended the birth of new national bodies.[14] In other words, although she wrote *Frankenstein* amid the creative convulsions of a new postcolonial era in the Western hemisphere—the same one that Pynchon's Mason and Dixon could sense inchoate in the 1760s—she deliberately places the plot in the preceding colonial epoch. This chronological sleight of hand is what allows her to imagine the monster roaming not in modern Latin American cities and revolutionary war camps but amid a ghosted mythoscape of a New World where a vast wilderness haunted by disembodied indigenes supposedly existed. Ultimately, however, Frankenstein does not create an Eve for the monster and so does not allow him to live freely in depopulated indigenous lands across the ocean. No more than Columbus can Frankenstein stand the idea of his subject haunting him from an absent and absented world.

Tzvetan Todorov, whose *The Conquest of America* of 1982 remains one of the most influential analyses of Columbus, wonders what can be gleaned in the diary of the first voyage about how the indigenes thought of the foreigners on their shores.[15] He supposes that the answer is very little, owing to the a priori surety of Columbus that he knew and understood what was happening during his encounters with local peoples. Thus Todorov asks:

> Can we guess, reading Columbus's notes, how the Indians, for their part, perceive the Spaniards? Hardly. Here again, all information is vitiated by the fact that Columbus has decided everything in advance. . . . It is possible, as Columbus says, that the Indians wonder if the Spaniards are not beings of divine origin, which would

certainly explain their initial fear and its disappearance before the Spaniards' altogether human behavior.[16]

This conclusion, whatever its degree of accuracy, misses all that is haunting about the reiterated indigenous absentings of the diary. Columbus may have decided in advance everything that he was prepared to believe and inscribe, but he had no powers to define those who repeatedly left the reach of his arms. He writes with confidence about the indigenous bodies present before him, those he can control with his sword and his pen, but finds himself helpless before those who render themselves absent and therefore beyond the colonizations of his ken. It is indeed possible to discern something about how the indigenes perceived the Europeans, for that message is communicated in footprints, in ghost towns, in silences, in smoke signals, in escapes, in flights not before men seen as gods but, tragically, as men. That Todorov and all foreign readers of those traces cannot specify with precision what their communications mean is entirely the point. Therein reside the diverse spectral resistances to the Conquest. Therein reside the absent presences, the subjunctivity, the atextualized ghosts who counter the conclusions of all who seek to resolve them one way or another. This is why the monster in *Frankenstein* identifies with the indigenes and indigenous ecologies of America. They are where he could be himself.

As a paradigmatically Romantic and Gothic fiction, as a product of Switzerland and Byron and Polidori and the Shelleys, as a gripping critique of the positivist regime of the Enlightenment, *Frankenstein* seems to be an entirely European novel. Yet an American text it is. Ever since Columbus, dividing worlds across the ocean from each other has been untenable. The monster in *Frankenstein* observes that he came into linguistic existence by learning "of the discovery of the American hemisphere."[17] And from Europe he dreams of starting afresh across the ocean. There he would be a successor of the disembodied indigenes whose place he would take in their faraway postlapsarian prelapsarian subjunctive. There he might at last come to rest in elysian fields. There, perhaps, he would spend his days reading the *Popol Vuh*.

Postscripts

The time is out of joint. O cursèd spite,
That ever I was born to set it right!
Nay, come, let's go together.[18]

* * *

To be haunted and to write from that location, to take on the condition of
what you study, is not a methodology or a consciousness you can simply
adopt or adapt as a set of rules or an identity; it produces its own insights
and blindnesses. Following the ghosts is about making a contact that
changes you and refashions the social relations in which you are located.
It is about putting life back in where only a vague memory or a bare trace
was visible to those who bothered to look. It is sometimes about writing ghost stories, stories that not only repair representational mistakes,
but also strive to understand the conditions under which a memory was
produced in the first place, toward a countermemory, for the future.[19]

* * *

Men of Reason will define a Ghost as nothing more otherworldly than a
wrong unrighted, which like an uneasy spirit cannot move on,—need-
ing help we cannot usually give,—nor always find the people it needs
to see,—or who need to see it. But here is a Collective Ghost of more

than household Scale,—the Wrongs committed Daily against the Slaves, petty and grave ones alike, going unrecorded, charm'd invisible to history, invisible yet possessing Mass, and Velocity, able not only to rattle Chains but to break them as well. The precariousness of Life here, the need to keep the Ghost propitiated, Day to Day, via the Company's merciliess Priesthoods and many-Volum'd Codes, brings all but the hardiest souls sooner or later to consider the Primary Questions more or less undiluted.[20]

* * *

There was a big high wall there
that tried to stop me
and the sign was painted,
said "Private Property"
but on the back side
it didn't say nuthin
this land was made for you and me.[21]

NOTES

Introduction

1. Taylor, *The Archive and the Repertoire*, 19.
2. Ibid., 26.
3. Ibid., 32.
4. Ibid., 31.
5. Ibid., passim.
6. Ibid., 57.
7. Ibid., 55.
8. The title of Evita's novel in Spanish is *Cuando los Combes luchaban*.
9. Taylor, *The Archive and the Repertoire*, 50.
10. Derrida, *Spectres de Marx*, passim.
11. Gordon, *Ghostly Matters*, 64.
12. Crosby, *The Columbian Exchange*, 219.
13. The titles in Spanish of the latter two novels are *Cien años de soledad* and *La casa de los espíritus*.
14. Conrad, *Refiguring America*, 147.
15. Gilroy, *The Black Atlantic*, 15.
16. Ibid., xi.
17. Ortega, *Transatlantic Translations*, 185.
18. Gilroy, *The Black Atlantic*, 4.
19. The title of the Menchú text in Spanish is *Me llamo Rigoberta Menchú y así me nació la conciencia*, whose literal translation is *My Name Is Rigoberta Menchú and This Is How My Conscience Was Born*.
20. Gruesz, *Ambassadors of Culture*, 134–35.
21. Whitman, "Starting from Paumanok," 27.

1 / Columbus the Haunted: The Diary of the First Voyage and William Carlos Williams's "The Discovery of the Indies"

1. Columbus, *The* Diario, 4–5.
2. Hulme, *Colonial Encounters*, 17.
3. Zamora, *Reading Columbus*, 6–7.
4. Columbus, *The* Diario, 16–19. "este presente año de .1492. despues de vr̄as altezas aver dado fin a la guerra dlos moros ~~en la mūy grāde çiudad de granada : adōde~~ q̃ reynavā en Europa y aver acabado la guerra en la mȳ grāde çiudad de granada . . . vide salir al rey moro a las puertas dla çiudad y besar las reales manos de vr̄as altezas . . . p̃ensarō de embiarme a mi xp̄oūal Colon a las d̄has p[ar]tidas de yndia p[ar]a ver los d̄hos prinçipes y los pueblos y las tr̄ras y la disposiçion dllas y de todo."
5. Ibid., 18–19. "despues de aver echado fuera todos los judios de todos vr̄os Reynos y señorios : en el mismo mes de enero : mādarō vr̄as altezas a mi q̃ con armada suffiçiente me fuese a las d̄has partidas de yndia."
6. Zamora, *Reading Columbus*, 61.
7. Columbus, *The* Diario, 184–85. "y digo q̃ .v. altezas no deven consentir q̃ aqui trate ni faga pie ningund estrāgero / saluo catholicos xp̄ianos : pues esto fue el fin y el comienço dl proposito que fuese por acreçentami° y gloria dla religion xpiana."
8. Ibid., 68–69.
9. Ibid., 74–75.
10. Ibid., 78–81. "vna almadia grande estava abordo dla caravela niña /. y vno dlos hōbres dla Isla de Sant salvador que en ella era : se echo a la mar y se fue en ella /. y la noche de antes a medio echado el otro y fue atras la almadia : la qual fugio q̃ jamas fue barca que le pudiese alcançar puesto q̃ le teniamos grāde avante /. Con todo dio en tr̄ra y dexarō la almadia y algunos dlos de mi compañia salierō en tr̄ra tras ellos : y todos fugerō coм̃o gallinas."
11. Ibid., 80–81. "ya de otro cabo venia otra almadia pequeña con vn hōbre q̃ venia a rescatar vn ovillo de algodon : y se echaro algunos marineros a la mar porq̃ el no queria entrar en la Caravela y le tomarō."
12. Ibid., "le māde bolver su almadia que tambien tenia en la barca y le enbie a tr̄ra /. y di luego la vela p[ar]a yr a la otra Isla grāde———[?] q̃ yo via al gueste."
13. Ibid., 82–83.
14. Ibid., 80–83. "que eramos buena gente /. y q̃ el otro [q̃?] se avia fugido nos avia hecho algun daño."
15. Ibid., 104–5. "despues de aver comigo fui en tr̄ra : adōde aqui no avia otra poblacion q̃ vna casa /. En la qual nō falle a nadie q̃ creo q̃ con temor se aviā fugido / porq̃ en ella estavā todos sus adereços de casa."
16. Ibid.
17. Ibid., 106–7. "fuimos a vna poblaçion aqui çerca adonde estoy surto media legua : y la gente della coм̃o nos sintierō dierō todos a fugir y dexarō las casas y escondierō su ropa y lo q̃ tenian por el mōte."
18. Ibid., 116–17. "fue a tierra y llego a dos casas q̃ creyo ser de pescadores y q̃ cō temor se huyerō."
19. Ibid., 120–21. "todos los hōbres y mugeres y criaturas huyerō desmāparādo las casas cō todo lo q̃ tenian."
20. Ibid., 124–27. "hallarō q̃ erā toda la gente huida."

21. Ibid., 154–55. "gente avia alguna y huyerō."

22. Ibid., 158–59. "de seys mācebos q̃ tomo en el rio de mares q̃ mādo q̃ fuesen en la caravela niña : se huyero los dos mas viejos."

_23. Ibid., 180–81. "dierō todos a huyr [q?] ni grāde ni chico quedo /. fuerō los tres xpianos a las casas . . . y no hallarō a nadie ni cosa en alguᵃ dllas."

24. Ibid., 186–87. "hallarō grādes poblaciones y las casas vazias porq̃ se avian huydo todos."

25. Ibid., "llegarō algunos dlos xpianos a otra poblaçion çerca dla p[ar]te de norueste y no hallarō en las casas a nadie ni nada."

26. Ibid., 188–89. "llegarō a mūchas casas y no hallarō a nadie ni nada q̃ todos se aviā huydo /. vierō quatro māçebos q̃stavā cavādo en su heredades   asi como vierō los xpianos dierō a huyr / no los pudierō alcançar."

27. Taylor, The Archive and the Repertoire, 57.

28. Ibid., 60–61.

29. Ibid., 143.

30. Columbus, The Diario, 192–95. "diez hōbres hagā huyr a diez mill . acordo bolverse tan cobardes y medrosos son q̃ ni traen armas salvo vna varas."

31. Ibid., 80–81. "como gallinas."

32. Ibid., 178–79.

33. Ibid., 180–81. "los yndios hizierō ademanes de no los dexar salitar en trra y resi [?] resistillos . . . salierō tres xpianos diziēdo q̃ no oviesen miedo en su lengua . . . en fin dierō todos a huyr [q?] ni grāde ni chico quedo /. fuerō los tres xpianos a las casas q̃ son de paja y dla hechura de las otras q̃ avian visto : y no hallarō a nadie ni cosa en alguᵃ dllas."

34. Ibid., 206–7. "todos los yndios huyerō y huian como vian los navios."

35. Ibid., 212–13. "vierō çinco hōbres : mas ⁿᵒ les quisierō aguardar sino huyr."

36. Ibid., 218–19. "oyerō vn grā golpe de gente todos dsnudos como los de atras a los quales llamarō e fuerō tras ellos / p[er]o—[?] dierō los yndios a huyr /. y finalmēte tomarō vna muger q̃ no pudierō mas."

37. Ibid., 220–21. "fuerō a la poblaçion q̃stava quatro leguas y media al sueste : la qual hallarō en vn grādissimo valle : y vazia porq̃ + todos avian huydo con dexando quāto tenian la trra dentro." The right margin adds the following in a column:
"a. como sintierō yr [a]
b. los xpianos
c. todos huyerō."

38. Ibid., 228–29. "vido tābien gente a la entrada dl rio . mas todos dierō a huyr."

39. Ibid., 326–27. "enbio la barca en trra por agua y por ver si avian lengua : p[er]o la gente toda huyo."

40. The title of the book in Spanish is Brevísima relación de la destruición de las Indias.

41. Las Casas, Brevísima relación, 77. "había más de quinientas mil ánimas, no hay hoy una sola criatura. Todas las mataron trayéndolas y por traellas a la isla Española, después que veían que se les acababan los naturales della."

42. Ibid., 90. "hasta consumir y acabar todos aquellos infelices inocentes: que había en las dichas dos islas más de seiscientas mil ánimas . . . y no hay hoy en cada una doscientas personas, todas perecidas sin fe y sin sacramentos."

43. Ibid., 108, 116. "corderos muy mansos" and "mansas ovejas."

44. Columbus, *The Diario*, 288–89. "agora tengo ordenado de hazer vna torre y fortaleza todo mȳ bien y vna grāde Cava : no porꝗ crea ꝗ aya esto menester por esta gente : porꝗ tengo por dicho / que con esta gente ꝗ yo traygo sojugaria toda esta Isla : la qual creo ꝗs mayor ꝗ portugal y mas gente al doblo o mas son dsnudos y sin armas y mūy cobardes fuera de remedio."

45. Ibid., "mas es razon ꝗ se haga esta torre y se este coῆo se a destar /. estando tan lexos ᵈᵉ vr̄as altezas: /. y porꝗ cognozcan el ingenio dla gente de vr̄a altezas: y lo ꝗ pueden hazar porꝗ con amor y temor le obedezcan."

46. Ibid., 66–69. "ellos dever ser buenos s[er]uidores y de buē ingenio ꝗ veo ꝗ mūy presto dizē todo lo ꝗ les dezia : y creo ꝗ ligeramēte se harian xp̄ianos."

47. Ibid., 81. "coῆo gallinas."

48. Williams, *In the American Grain*, 7.

49. Ibid., 25.

50. Olson and Bourne, *The Northmen Columbus and Cabot 985–1503*, 110.

51. Ibid.

52. Ibid., 110–11.

53. Ibid., 111.

54. Ibid., 112.

55. Conrad, *Refiguring America*, 100.

56. Metherd, "The Americanization of Christopher Columbus in the Works of William Carlos Williams and Alejo Carpentier," 236.

57. Ibid.

58. Ibid., 237.

59. Kutzinski, *Against the American Grain*, 31.

60. Marzán, *The Spanish American Roots of William Carlos Williams*, 20.

61. Conrad, *Refiguring America*, 68.

62. Williams, *The Autobiography of William Carlos Williams*, 187.

63. Columbus, *The Diario*, 234–37. "yo con esta gente ꝗ traygo ꝗ no son mūchos : correria todas estas yslas sin afrenta . ꝗ ya e visto solos tres destos marineros desçendir en tr̄ra y aver multitud destos yndios y todos huyr sin ꝗ les quisiesen hazeʳ mal /. ellos no tienē armas y son todos desnudos y de nigū ingenio en las armas y mūy cobardes ꝗ mill no aguardariā tres . y asi son buenos p[ar]a les mādar y les hazer trabajar sembrar y hazer todo lo otro ꝗ fuere menester : y ꝗ hagā villas y se enseñen a andar vestidos y a nras costūbres."

64. Ibid., 288–89.

65. Ibid., 332–33. "se aparejaron de arremeter a los xp̄ianos y prend[e]llos /. fuerō corriēdo a tomar sus arcos y flechas : y vinie donde los tenian apartados : y tornarō con cuerdas en las manos p[ar]a diz ꝗ atar los xp̄ianos."

66. Ibid. "siempʳ los avisava dsto."

67. Ibid. "visto que podian ganar poco . . . dierō a huyr ꝗ no quedo ninguno."

68. Ibid., 334–35. "ꝗ ᑫᵘᵉʳʳⁱᵃ quisiera tomar algunos dllos /. diz ꝗ haziā mūchas ahumadas."

2 / Indigenous Atextualizations: The *Popol Vuh* and *I, Rigoberta Menchú: An Indian Woman in Guatemala*

1. The title of Menchú's text in English is dissimilar from the original Spanish of

Me llamo Rigoberta Menchú y así me nació la conciencia, whose literal translation is *My Name Is Rigoberta Menchú and This Is How My Conscience Was Born*.

2. Tedlock, *Popol Vuh*, original edition, 71–72. The forward slashes indicate that Tedlock sets apart the preceding phrases as poetic verse.

3. Sommer, "No Secrets," 142.

4. Tedlock, *Popol Vuh*, original edition, 72; revised edition, 63.

5. Recinos, "Preface," xiii.

6. The name of the organization in Spanish is the *Academia de las Lenguas Mayas de Guatemala*.

7. *Popol Wuj*, 1–2.

8. Herbert, "Prólogo de la última edición a mimeógrafo," 2. "Fundador y alma de la Academia de la Lengua Maya Quiché . . . da base a una ciencia: La KICHELOGIA, que rompe el silencio impuesto por la Colonia y vuelve a dar una voz a la sociedad autóctona de América."

9. The title of the book in Spanish is *Pop Wuj (Libro del Tiempo o de Acontecimientos)*.

10. The title of the book in Spanish is *Pop Wuj: Poema Mito-histórico Ki-ché*.

11. Chávez, *Pop Wuj: Poema Mito-histórico Ki-ché*, 1. "Y aquí escribimos (ya con letra castellana), aquí fijamos la antigua palabra; principio, es decir, base de todo lo sucedido en el pueblo Los Magueyes, pero de las grandes gentes kí-ches. De manera que aquí tomaremos a enseñarlo, a revelarlo, es decir, a relatarlo. . . . Y si aquí escribimos ya con letra castellana, ya en cristianismo, en esta forma lo divulgaremos porque ya no se verá nada del Pop Wuj, ciencia que vino del otro lado del mar y que es relato de nuestro origen, ciencia de la existencia se decía. Existe el primer libro (el Pop Wuj), es decir, la antigua escritura. Esto es únicamente para lamentarlo, revisarlo, meditarlo. Es muy extenso, porque relata desde que se terminó de cubrir el cielo y la tierra."

12. Rodríguez Beteta, "Adrián Recinos (Una pequeña biografía)," 114.

13. Herrera C., "Adrián Recinos," 41. "El Popol Vuh le ha inmortalizado: / el mundo nos conoce a travēs de ēl."

14. Chinchilla Aguilar, "Principales datos biográficos del licenciado Adrián Recinos," 45.

15. Recinos, "Preface," xii.

16. Recinos, *El Popol Vuh*, 16.

17. Dosal, *Power in Transition*, 87.

18. Chinchilla Aguilar, "Principales datos biográficos del licenciado Adrián Recinos," 46.

19. Recinos, *El Popol Vuh*, 23–24. "Aquí escribiremos y comenzaremos las antiguas historias, el principio y el origen de todo lo que se hizo en la ciudad de Quiché, por las tribus de la nación quiché. Y aquí traeremos la manifestación, la publicación y la narración de lo que estaba oculto. . . . Esto lo escribiremos ya dentro de la ley de Dios, en el Cristianismo; lo sacaremos a luz porque ya no se ve el *Popo Vuh*, [sic] así llamado, donde se veía claramente la venida del otro lado del mar, la narración de nuestra oscuridad, y se veía claramente la vida. Existía el libro original, escrito antiguamente, pero su vista está oculta al investigador y al pensador. Grande era la descripción y el relato de cómo se acabó de formar todo el cielo y la tierra."

20. Tedlock, *Popol Vuh*, revised edition, 27.

21. The titles of the novels in Spanish are *Hombres de maíz* and *Mulata de tal*.

22. Brasseur de Bourbourg, *Popol Vuh*, 3–5. "Ici nous écrirons et nous commencerons l'histoire d'autrefois, le principe et l'origine de tout ce qui s'est fait dans la cité du Quiché, dans les tribus de la nation quichée: Voici donc que nous amènerons la manifestation, la découverte et l'éclatement de ce qui était dans l'obscurité. . . . Voilà ce que nous écrirons depuis (qu'on a promulgué) la parole de *Dieu*, et en dedans du Christianisme; nous le reproduirons, parce qu'on ne voit plus ce Livre national, où l'on voyait clairement qu'on était venu de l'autre côté de la mer. . . . C'est le premier livre, écrit anciennement; mais sa vue est cachée à celui qui voit et qui pense."

23. Raynaud, *Les dieux, les héros et les hommes de l'ancien Guatémala d'après le Livre du Conseil*, 1–2. "Ici nous écrirons, nous commencerons l'ancien récit du début, de l'origine e tout ce que firent dans la cité Quiche les hommes des tribus Quiche. Ici nous recueillerons la déclaration, la manifestation, l'éclaircissement de ce qui était caché. . . . Nous peindrons (ce qui fut) avant la Parole de Dieu, avant le Christianisme; nous le reproduirons parce qu'on n'a (plus) la vue du Livre du Conseil, la vue de l'aube, de l'arrivée d'outre-mer. . . . C'est le premier Livre, peint jadis, mais sa face est cachée (aujourd'hui) au voyeur, au penseur." The word "recueillerons," translated above as "gather," can also signify "inherit."

24. Tedlock, *Popol Vuh*, original edition, 227.

25. Recinos, *El Popol Vuh*, 153. "Y ésta fue la existencia de los quichés, porque ya no puede verse el [*libro Popol Vuh*] que tenían antiguamente los reyes, pues ha desaparecido. Así, pues, se han acabado todos los del Quiché que se llama *Santa Cruz*."

26. Chávez, *Pop Wuj: Poema Mito-histórico Ki-ché*, 112. "Esta fue la existencia de los Ki'chès. Ya no hay en donde verlo, había un antiguo documento de los señores pero ha desaparecido. Aquí termina lo que hoy se llama Santa Cruz del Quiché."

27. Brasseur de Bourbourg, *Popol Vuh*, 347. "Et voilà tout (ce qui reste) de l'existence du Quiché; car il n'y a plus moyen de voir ce (livre), où autrefois les rois (lisaient tout), puisqu'il a disparu. Ainsi donc c'en est fait de tous ceux du Quiché, qui s'appelle *Santa-Cruz*."

28. Raynaud, *Les dieux, les héros et les hommes de l'ancien Guatémala d'après le Livre du Conseil*, 138. "Telle fut l'existence du Quiche, car il n'y a plus, est perdu, ce qui faisait voir ce que furent jadis les premiers chefs. Ainsi donc c'est la fin de tout le Quiché appelé Santa Cruz."

29. Christenson, *Popol Vuh*, 36.

30. Tedlock, *Popol Vuh*, revised edition, 192.

31. Recinos, *El Popol Vuh*, 146. "Sabían bien que había donde podían verlo, que existía un libro por ellos llamado *Popol Vuh*."

32. Chávez, *Pop Wuj: Poema Mito-histórico Ki-ché*, 107. "había libro para saberlo se llamaba 'Libro del Tiempo.'"

33. Tedlock, *Popol Vuh*, revised edition, 161. His original edition relays the passage rather differently: "As they put it in their own words: 'The sun that shows itself is not the real sun.'" Tedlock, *Popol Vuh*, original edition, 182.

34. Recinos, *El Popol Vuh*, 117. "No era ciertamente el mismo sol que nosotros vemos, se dice en sus historias."

35. Chávez, *Pop Wuj: Poema Mito-histórico Ki-ché*, 80. "sólo se mostró [el sol] cuando fue creado; ya sólo el reflejo quedó, ya no era el mismo Sol el que alumbraba, así dice la tradición."

36. Burgos, *Me llamo Rigoberta Menchú*, 271. "todavía sigo ocultando mi identidad

como indígena. Sigo ocultando lo que yo considero que nadie sabe, ni siquiera un antropólogo, ni un intelectual, por más que tenga muchos libros, no saben distinguir todos nuestros secretos."

37. Sommer, "No Secrets," 130.

38. Ibid., 131.

39. Moreiras, "The Aura of Testimonio," 204.

40. Ibid., 205–6.

41. Beverley, "The Margin at the Center: On Testimonio," 33.

42. Burgos, *Me llamo Rigoberta Menchú*, 33. "los padres tienen que enseñarle al niño . . . [*sic*]—más que todo se refiere mucho a los antepasados—que aprenda a guardar todos los secretos, que nadie pueda acabar con nuestra cultura, con nuestras costumbres."

43. Ibid., 34. "se dice que los españoles que violaron a los mejor hijos de los antepasados, a las gentes más humildes y en honor a esas gentes más humildes nosotros tenemos que seguir guardando nuestros secretos. Y esos secretos nadie podrá descubrir más que nosotros los indígenas."

44. Ibid., 38. "Esto implica una vez más el compromiso que todos tenemos que guardar: las costumbres, los secretos de nuestros antepasados."

45. Ibid., 41. "Nosotros los indígenas hemos ocultado nuestra identidad."

46. Derrida, *Spectres de Marx*, 165. "d'une certain visibilité. Mais la visibilité de l'invisible."

47. Burgos, *Me llamo Rigoberta Menchú*, 41. "hemos guardado muchos secretos, por eso somos discriminados . . . uno sabe que tiene que ocultar esto hasta que garantice que va a seguir como una cultura indígena."

48. Ibid., 196. "Llega un cura a nuestras aldeas, todos los indígenas nos tapamos la boca."

49. Ibid., "como no nos han dado el espacio de palabra, no nos han dado el espacio de hablar, de opinar y de tomar en cuenta nuestras opiniones, nosotros tampoco hemos abierto la boca por gusto."

50. Ibid., "nosotros hemos ocultado nuesta [*sic*] identidad porque hemos sabido resistir, hemos sabido ocultar lo que el régimen ha querido quitarnos. Ya sea por las religiones, ya sea por las reparticiones de tierra, ya sea por las escuelas, ya sea por medio de libros, ya sea por medio de radios, de cosas modernas, nos han querido meter otras cosas y quitar lo nuestro."

51. Sommer, "No Secrets," 136–37.

52. Whitman, "Starting from Paumanok," 27.

3 / Castaway Colonialism: Daniel Defoe's *Robinson Crusoe* and Álvar Núñez Cabeza de Vaca's *Account*

1. Novak, *Defoe and the Nature of Man*, 52.

2. Sarmiento, *Viajes por Europa, Africa i América, 1845–1847*, 13. "fué arrojado el marinero Selkirk, que dió oríjen a la por siempre célebre historia de Robinson Crusoe." The title of the first book in Spanish is *Facundo: civilización y barbarie*.

3. Ibid., 14–15. "nos venia a cada momento la memoria de Robinson; creíamos estar con él en su isla, en su cabaña, durante el tiempo de su dura prueba."

4. Ibid., 16. "calzado a la Robinson Crusoe."

5. Defoe, *Robinson Crusoe*, 42.

6. Ibid., 45.

7. Ibid.

8. Ibid., 54.

9. Ibid., passim.

10. Wheeler, "'My Savage,' 'My Man': Racial Multiplicity in *Robinson Crusoe*," 832.

11. Defoe, *Robinson Crusoe*, 54.

12. Ibid.

13. Ibid., 55.

14. Ibid., 57.

15. Ibid., 58.

16. Ibid., 56.

17. Ibid., 55.

18. Ibid., 59.

19. Ibid.

20. Ibid.

21. Weaver-Hightower, *Empire Islands*, ix.

22. Defoe, *Robinson Crusoe*, 62.

23. Ibid.

24. Ibid.

25. Ibid., 121.

26. Ibid., 83.

27. Ibid.

28. Ibid., 113–14.

29. Ibid., 114.

30. Ibid., 199.

31. Ibid.

32. Ibid., 122.

33. Ibid., 124.

34. Ibid., 136.

35. Ibid., 157.

36. Ibid., 152.

37. Ibid., 152.

38. Ibid.

39. Ibid., 160, 173.

40. Ibid., 162.

41. Ibid., 164.

42. Ibid., 162.

43. Ibid., 166.

44. Ibid., 168.

45. Rendall, *The Practice of Everyday Life*, 154. The original French is in de Certeau, *L'invention du quotidien*, 263. "Robinson Crusoé indiquait déjà lui-même comment une faille s'introduit dans son empire scripturaire. Pendant un temps, son entreprise est en effet interrompue, et hantée, par un absent qui revient sur les bords de l'île. C'est 'l'impression (*the print*) d'un pied nu d'homme sur la plage.' Instabilité du bornage: la frontière cède à de l'étranger. Sur les marges de la page, la trace d'un invisible fantôme (*an apparition*) trouble l'ordre qu'a construit un travail capitaliseur et méthodique."

46. Rendall, *The Practice of Everyday Life*, 154. The original French is in de Certeau, *L'invention du quotidien*, 264. "Robinson verra un être (Vendredi), retrouvera le pouvoir de maîtriser quand il aura la possibilité de voir, c'est-à-dire lorsque l'absent se montrera. Alors il sera de nouveau dans son ordre."

47. Defoe, *Robinson Crusoe*, 180.

48. Ibid., 200.

49. Hulme, *Colonial Encounters*, 201.

50. Defoe, *Robinson Crusoe*, 204.

51. Ibid., 209.

52. Ibid.

53. Ibid., 218.

54. Ibid., 206.

55. Ibid., 207.

56. Ibid., 209.

57. Ibid., 214.

58. Ibid.

59. Hulme, *Colonial Encounters*, 205.

60. Zelnick, "Ideology as Narrative: Critical Approaches to *Robinson Crusoe*," 94.

61. Rendall, *The Practice of Everyday Life*, 154.

62. Defoe, *Robinson Crusoe*, 192.

63. Cabeza de Vaca, *His Account, His Life, and the Expedition of Pánfilo de Narváez*, 114–15. "La manera con que nosotros curamos era santiaguándolos y soplarlos, y rezar un Pater Noster y un Ave María."

64. Ibid., 238–39. "Anduvimos mucha tierra y toda la hallamos despoblada, porque los moradores della andavan huyendo por las sierras sin osar tener casas ni labrar por miedo de los christianos."

65. Ibid., 240–41. "se vee que estas gentes todas, para ser atraídos a ser christianos y a obediençia de la Imperial Magestad, an de ser llevados con buen tratamiento."

66. Ibid., 254–55. "la tierra estava despoblada y sin labrarse y toda muy destruída, y los indios andavan escondidos y huídos por los montes sin querer venir a hazer assiento en sus pueblos; y [rogó] [*sic*] que los embiássemos a llamar, y que les mandássemos de parte de Dios y de Vuestra Magestad que viniessen y poblassen en lo llano y labrassen la tierra."

67. Ibid., 260–63. "despés de bautizados los niños [de los prinçipales señores indígenas], nos partimos para la villa de San Miguel, donde como fuimos llegados vinieron indios que nos dixeron como mucha gente baxava de las sierras y poblavan en lo llano y hazían iglesias y cruzes y todo lo que les avíamos mandado . . . eran baxados de las sierras los indios, y avían poblado en lo llano y [los christianos] avían hallado pueblos con mucha gente que de primero estavan despoblados y desiertos, y que los indios les salieron a reçebir con cruzes en las manos y los llevaron a sus casas y les dieron de lo que tenían."

68. Defoe, *Robinson Crusoe*, 178.

69. Ibid., 217.

70. Wheeler, "'My Savage,' 'My Man': Racial Multiplicity in *Robinson Crusoe*," 841.

71. Hulme, *Colonial Encounters*, 199.

72. Rummell, "Defoe and the Black Legend: The Spanish Stereotype in *A New Voyage Round the World*," 24.

73. The title in Spanish of Las Casas's text is *Brevísima relación de la destruición de las Indias.*

74. Las Casas, *Brevísima relación*, 77. "como lobos y tigres y leones crudelísimos de muchos días hambrientos. Y otra cosa no han hecho de cuarenta años a esta parte, hasta hoy, y hoy en este día lo hacen, sino despedazallas, matallas, angustiallas, afligillas, atormentallas y destruillas por las estrañas y nuevas y varias y nunca otras tales vistas ni leídas ni oídas maneras de crueldad."

75. Schmidt-Nowara, "'This Rotting Corpse': Spain between the Black Atlantic and the Black Legend," 158.

76. Rummell, "Defoe and the Black Legend: The Spanish Stereotype in *A New Voyage Round the World*," 17.

77. Ibid., 15, 17.

78. Defoe, *Robinson Crusoe*, 236.

79. Ibid., 257.

80. Ibid., 196, 243.

81. Ibid., 240–41.

82. Ibid., 244.

83. Ibid., 243.

84. Maddox, "Interpreter Crusoe," 41–42.

85. Defoe, *Robinson Crusoe*, 269.

86. Ibid., 286, 288.

87. Ibid., 273.

88. Ibid., 186.

89. Ibid.

90. Ibid., 297.

91. Ibid., 298.

92. Ibid.

93. Ibid., 121.

94. Wheeler, "'My Savage,' 'My Man': Racial Multiplicity in *Robinson Crusoe*," 827–28.

95. Defoe, *Robinson Crusoe*, 162.

4 / Apparitions of Africa: Leoncio Evita's *When the Combes Fought* and José Martí's "Our America"

1. The title of the novel in Spanish is *Cuando los Combes luchaban.* The Combe people are known more commonly as the Ndowe.

2. Bioko was formerly known as "Fernando Poo" or "Fernando Po."

3. Malabo was formerly known as "Port Clarence" and "Santa Isabel."

4. Western Sahara was formerly known as "Spanish Sahara." Spain decolonized in 1976 but governance remains disputed between indigenous people and Morocco. Ceuta, Melilla, and the Canary Islands continue to be considered part of Spain and not colonies.

5. Sundiata, *Equatorial Guinea*, 133.

6. Maass, "A Touch of Crude," 50.

7. Evita, *Cuando los Combes luchaban*, 101. "Vamos, hijo mío, no podemos soñar, no podemos regocijarnos hasta que todas estas hermosas tierras estén bajo la soberanía de España."

8. Ngom, "La literatura africana de expresión castellana," 412. "un poderoso instrumento de propaganda para la administración colonial española . . . la novela no sólo defiende la necesidad del hecho colonial sino que lo justifica. Asimismo, se encuadra dentro de la llamada literatura de consentimiento."

9. Ibid., 418. "un aparato de propaganda del franquismo en su época." The name in Spanish of the publisher is "Consejo Superior de Investigaciones Científicas."

10. Ndongo-Bidyogo, "La literatura moderna hispanófona en Guinea Ecuatorial," 40. "era el fiel reflejo de lo que se esperaba de los negros guineanos: que asumiera íntegramente los postulados del colonizador hasta negar la esencia de su ser."

11. Ndongo-Bidyogo, "Leoncio Evita, o el nacimiento de la literatura guineana," 28. "parece estar escrita al gusto de los colonizadores."

12. Ibid., 29. "Indudablemente, pues, el libro complace a los colonialistas, puesto que, aún escrito por un negro, contribuye a cimentar el edificio de la colonización al incidir en los elementos que sostienen la superestructura colonial."

13. Ngom, "La literatura africana de expresión castellana," 413. "a diferencia de lo que sucedió en los otros territorios del Africa subsahariana bajo dominio colonial, no hubo una producción literaria de combate o anticolonialista."

14. Ndongo-Bidyogo, "Leoncio Evita, o el nacimiento de la literatura guineana," 30.

15. Tofiño-Quesada, "Spanish Orientalism: Uses of the Past in Spain's Colonization in Africa," 145.

16. González Echegaray, "[untitled prologue]," 5. "cuando Leoncio Evita me dió a leer su novela y me pidió que le hiciera un prólogo, no le di palabra de escribírselo hasta que no me convenciera de que se trataba de algo distinto de los relatos inconexos y absurdos que algunos 'morenos' seudointelectuales escriben, más para su satisfacción personal que con esperanza de verlos publicados. Pero mi sorpresa fué en aumento a medida que iba leyendo, al encontrarme con una obrita francamente aceptable, y que bien pudiera haber sido escrita por cualquier escritor novel nacido en nuestra Patria."

17. Ibid., 6. "la novela está pensada y sentida 'en blanco', y sólo cuando la acción se desarrolla entre indígenas, solamente en parte, y como un espectador, el escritor se siente de su raza."

18. Ibid., 5. "En cuanto al estilo he corregido algunas construcciones excesivamente extrañas a nuestra sintaxis y algunos errores de propiedad en la aplicación de los vocablos castellanos, pero he dejado a la obra en su estilo propio, que a las veces puede parecer en la forma, duro, y en el fondo, ingenuo, pero que es una muestra estilizada del castellano medio, hablado por nuestros negros."

19. Ibid., 6. "a un indígena evolucionado, le merecen el carácter y la colonización de los españoles con sus pequeños defectos temperamentales—violencia, irreflexión, orgullo—y sus virtudes fundamentales—generosidad, fe, sencillez, entusiasmo—y, especialmente, su denodado valor, que ha sido siempre el imán de la admiración entusiasta de los indígenas."

20. Onomo-Abena, 226. "Sujeto cultural colonial y producción literaria en Guinea Ecuatorial. Lectura sociocrítica del prólogo de *Cuando los Combes luchaban* (1953) de Leoncio Evita." "es un discurso etnocentrista marcado por el menosprecio del *Otro* al que se niega la religión, la historia, la escritura y la cultura."

21. González Echegaray, "Prólogo a la 2ª edición," 14. "Naturalmente, tanto a lo largo de la novela, como en mi prólogo—'mea culpa'—se advierte claramente la influencia del pensamiento 'oficial' sobre la colonización. . . . Se pensaba oficialmente y

se trataba de imbuir al indígena un pensamiento monolítico 'imperial' a base de evo-
caciones teóricas de las Leyes de Indias y de las grandezas pasadas de los españoles."

22. Evita, *Cuando los Combes luchaban*, 7. "convertido ya en verdadero cazador
nocturno."

23. Ibid., 8. "Instintivamente disparó contra un perdido punto de la tiniebla donde
le pareció ver dos chispeantes ojos."

24. Ibid. "'Qué significa esta insubordinación?'—la voz del blanco sonaba metálica."

25. Ibid. "Sus caritas de ébano delataban excesivo susto, que la presencia del blanco
vino a acentuar muchísimo."

26. Mbomio Bacheng, "Leoncio Evita o *Cuando los Combes luchaban*: Una obra
trascendental," 77. "De este modo, y en las primeras líneas de su relato, Evita ya nos
presenta la imagen que proyecta el hombre blanco en el mundo africano, con sus ras-
gos caracterizantes: el poder (representado por el fusil), la dominación y la severidad
ante el negro. El blanco, aún misionero como brother John, no permite ningún tipo de
insubordinación por parte del negro."

27. Evita, *Cuando los Combes luchaban*, 10. "Hice el disparo para imponer silencio.
Pensé que no había otra forma de hacer callar a esas revoltosas."

28. Ibid., 11. "una inclasificable gama de rumores, chasquidos y sonoridades."

29. Ibid., 11.

30. Ibid., 14–15. The death is not attributed explicitly to a leopard until pages 22–23.

31. Ibid., 29–30, 34.

32. Ibid., 49. "Parecía un fantasma."

33. Ibid., 54. "gentes de aspecto rudimentario, que en nada se parecían a los negros
de la costa. Iban casi desnudos."

34. Ibid., 55. "iboga (cocaína) mezclada quizá con vísceras humanas."

35. Defoe, *Robinson Crusoe*, 204–5.

36. Evita, *Cuando los Combes luchaban*, 60.

37. Ibid., 61, 7. "verdadero cazador nocturno."

38. Ibid., 62. "unos cazadores españoles."

39. Ibid., 71. "¡Imbéciles! Remar fuerte. ¡Venga!, u os pisoteo las tripas."

40. Ibid., 74. "Martín Garrido, español, ex oficial de la armada española y ahora
amante del Africa."

41. Ibid., 75. "Soy portador para vos de un encargo hecho por un reyezuelo negro."

42. Ibid., 76.

43. Ibid., 77. "Martín Garrido era viejo oficial de la Armada Española. Pasó la
mayor parte de su vida en el mar de las Antillas. Así que cuando se jubiló ya no re-
gresó a España, sino fijó su residencia en Santiago de Cuba. . . . A los finales del año
1894, cuando empezaba el aire de insurrección cubana, Martín tomó en San Juan un
buque holandés, que después de arribar en varios puertos de Cuba, tomó rumbo al
Continente negro. Durante la travesía, los señores Garrido conocieron a Adonis, un
cruman que años después de la abolición de la esclavitud, se retornaba a su país, pero
que el hechizo de los españoles convirtió en un servidor inseparable."

44. Ibid. "durante aquellos nueve años en que España, atosigada por las guerras,
tenía abandonadas las cuestiones de Africa."

45. Taylor, *The Archive and the Repertoire*, 271.

46. Ibid., 277.

47. Bauer, "Hemispheric Studies," 235.

48. Ngom, "Leoncio Evita Enoy," 33.
49. Ibid., 32. "debido a la inestabilidad política en Camerún."
50. Nkogo Ondó, personal communication.
51. Nkogo Ondó, "La Guinea Ecuatorial," 7. The acronym in Spanish stands for "Movimiento Nacional de Liberación de Guinea Ecuatorial."
52. Davies, "A Rafael Evita," [no pagination]. "Amigo y hermano Evita/Gigante de entre gigantes."
53. Ngom, "Leoncio Evita Enoy," 32. "dibujo artístico y talla de madera."
54. Ibid., 33.
55. Ibid., 32. "La situación colonial que prevalecía cuando escribí mi novela me dió un gran estímulo para seguir escribiendo y ampliar mis conocimientos. Personalmente sentí satisfacción por abrir aquella pequeña brecha en el 'dique' del monopolio de discriminación intelectual reinante."
56. Ibid., 33. "La literatura tradicional es mi fuente de inspiración."
57. Ibid., 35. "No creo en el 'arte por el arte.' El escritor africano debe tomar una postura de compromiso o de combate por medio de su creación literaria."
58. Ndongo-Bidyogo, *Historia y tragedia de Guinea Ecuatorial*, 66. "La geografía era únicamente la de España (la expulsión de los árabes, los Reyes Católicos, el descubrimiento de América y el Imperio, y poco más): '¿Somos españoles?'—preguntaba el maestro a la clase—'¡¡Soomos españoolees por la Gracia de Dioos!!'. '¿Por qué somos españoles?'—volvía a preguntar—'¡¡Soomos españoolees por haber tenido la dicha de nacer en un país llamado Españaaa!!'. Al entrar en la escuela había que formar, hacer cinco o diez minutos de gimnasia militar, cantar el 'Cara al sol', brazo en alto, el 'Lleno de ferviente ardor', el 'Falangista soy, falangista hasta morir o vencer', al fin, el 'Viva España'. . . . No era eso asimilación cultural. Era asimilación cultural a punta de pistola."
59. Ibid., 72. "Se decidió fundar una organización cuyo fin era concienciar al pueblo sobre los abusos de los europeos y presentar una resistencia cada vez más firme contra el poder colonial."
60. Ibid., 31. "en la Guinea colonial de 1953, la mordaza aún tapaba las bocas negras y las cabezas aún estaban dobladas hasta el suelo."
61. Ibid. "no podía rebelarse contra."
62. González Echegaray, "Prólogo a la 2ª edición," 14. "yo pensaba que hacía un buen servicio a una nueva imagen del guineano, que era capaz de escribir una novela en castellano, cuyos principales lectores iban a ser los españoles de la metrópoli, más exigentes en calidad que los propios paisanos del autor."
63. Evita, *Cuando los Combes luchaban*, 79. "Sois los absolutos jefes de la misión."
64. Ibid., 84–85.
65. Ibid., 86.
66. Ibid., 91. "le paralizó la amenazadora mirada del negro de la escopeta."
67. Ibid., "aun no salido de su pasmo."
68. Ibid., 93. "– Llama tus hombres—masculló el sujeto que le habló anteriormente. – ¿Quiénes sois y cómo voy a fiarme de vosotros?—Martín protestó. El salvaje que hasta entonces permaneció en silencio, emitió ciertas órdenes en un idioma bastante familiar para el blanco, aunque éste no entendió nada de lo que dijo el negro.

– Dice, jefe—el otro salvaje interpretó—, que pierdés demasiado tiempo charlando. Llama a tus hombres, que hay que caminar bastante para llegar.

Martín emitió un prolongado silbido, y apenas apereció [*sic*] el primero de sus hombres, dijo el negrito:

– ¡Caminar!

– ¡En marcha!—transmitió a su gente el señor Garrido."

69. Ibid., 98. "¡Pero si eres tú, tío Martín, el ángel de nuestra redención!"

70. Ibid., 99. "Señor Garrido, ¿no habrá venido usted para llevarnos a la gloria?"

71. Ibid., 101. "Vamos, hijo mío, no podemos soñar, no podemos regocijarnos hasta que todas estas hermosas tierras estén bajo la soberanía de España."

72. Ibid., 100. "los primeros albores del día."

73. Ibid., 77. "insurrección cubana."

74. Ngom, "La literatura africana de expresión castellana: la creación literaria en Guinea Ecuatorial," 412. "'pensada y sentida en 'blanco,'"; "desde la perspectiva europea."

75. Ibid., "rechaza consciente o inconscientemente su propia identidad étnica."

76. Ngom, "Postcolonial Hispanic African Children's Literature," 58.

77. Pratt, *Imperial Eyes*, 9.

78. Fryer, "Aspectos políticos de Guinea Ecuatorial: Raíces hispánicas en África," 4. "su novela costumbrista."

79. Miampika, "Plaidoirie équato-guinéenne: chronique d'une littérature émergente," 14. "le roman précurseur d'inspiration ethnographique."

80. Pendi, "Breve presentación," 21. "novela histórico-costumbrista; el autor insiste con atención especial en la pintura de las costumbres típicas."

81. Ngom, "Postcolonial Hispanic African Children's Literature," 58.

82. Evita, *Cuando los Combes luchaban*, title page. "novela de costumbres de la Guinea Española."

83. Ngom, "Leoncio Evita Enoy," 33. "una novela etnológica de las costumbres de la tribu combé"; "a las futuras generaciones . . . de lo que puede aprender en mi entorno cultural."

84. Evita, *Cuando los Combes luchaban*, 75. "Soy portador para vos de un encargo hecho por un reyezuelo negro,"

85. Ibid., 76. "La ayuda que pide, ¿es para el indígena o para usted?"

86. Ibid. "recuerden que yo represento al negro"; "carcajada amistosa selló el pacto entre los españoles y el americano."

87. The identity of the speaker is unclear. He is identified only as "a small man," but Penda is named immediately after the speech and very well may have delivered it. Given the later plot developments in which Penda turns out to be a leader of a cannibal group that vigorously practices a local belief system, the sentiments expressed in the oration logically make sense as his. Ibid., 26. "un hombre pequeño."

88. Ibid., 26–27. "Antes de que Vilangua pasara en manos de esos hombres, necesitaba, como negro que era, conocer a fondo las cosas de su país natalicio, tales como cazar, pescar, etc., en una palabra, vivir como un genuino negro. La civilización de que tanto apetecemos es como una antorcha; alumbra mucho, pero quema todo lo que encuentra a su paso . . . como ha ocurrido en otras partes de este mismo mundo. . . . ¿Es esta la vida que queréis dejar a vuestros hijos? ¡No! Dejad que los futuros hombres crezcan como las especies que la selva guarda, sin tabaco ni vestidos y aprendan a

emplear la sal silvestre, saltar con los monos y luchar con los búfalos; así han crecido y vivido nuestros antepasados. Hermanos: consideren esta última advertencia: nuestra educación, que los blancos llaman salvajismo, obedece a nuestra naturaleza. No podemos trocar nuestras costumbres, ni podemos renunciarlas tampoco, por la sencilla razón de que todo intento de borrar nuestro origen, redundará en perjuicio de la raza."

89. Martí, "Nuestra América," 161. "La Universidad europea ha de ceder a la Universidad americana. La historia de América, de los incas a acá, ha de enseñarse al dedillo."

90. Evita, *Cuando los Combes luchaban*, 27. "nuestra educación, que los blancos llaman salvajismo, obedece a nuestra naturaleza."

91. Martí, "Nuestra América," 160. "No hay batalla entre la civilización y la barbarie, sino entre la falsa erudición y la Naturaleza."

92. Ibid., 159. "Estos hijos de nuestra América, que ha de salvarse con sus indios."

93. Ibid., 162. "nuestra América mestiza."

94. Mbomio Bacheng, "Leoncio Evita o *Cuando los Combes luchaban*: Una obra trascendental," 73. "se puede interpretar también la iniciativa de L. Evita como un acto de resistencia de la cultura africana ante la agresión que representa el sistema colonial: su obra vehicula de este modo un mensaje preindependentista y se trata, en definitiva, de un grito de libertad."

95. Gilroy, *The Black Atlantic*, xi.

96. Ibid., 223.

97. Lionnet and Shih, *Minor Transnationalism*, 5.

5 / Subjunctive America: Thomas Pynchon's *Mason & Dixon* and Gabriel García Márquez's *Love in the Time of Cholera*

1. Latrobe, "The History of Mason and Dixon's Line; Contained in an Address," 5-7.

2. "Dixie," 292.

3. García Márquez, *Conversaciones con Plinio Apuleyo Mendoza: el olor de la guayaba*, 50. "más geográficas que literarias. Las descubrí mucho después de haber escrito mis primeras novelas, viajando por el sur de los Estados Unidos. Los pueblos ardientes y llenos de polvo, las gentes sin esperanza que encontré en aquel viaje se parecían mucho a los que yo evocaba en mis cuentos."

4. Gruesz, *Ambassadors of Culture*, 48.

5. Fricke, "Top Ten 2000," 106.

6. Wenner, "Mark Knopfler: Sailing to Philadelphia," 110.

7. Knopfler, "Sailing to Philadelphia."

8. Ibid.

9. Ibid.

10. Pynchon, *Mason & Dixon*, 614-15.

11. Ibid., 573.

12. Seed, "Mapping the Course of Empire in the New World," 98.

13. Pynchon, *Mason & Dixon*, 6.

14. McHale, "Mason & Dixon in the Zone, or, A Brief Poetics of Pynchon-Space," 55.

15. Pynchon, *Mason & Dixon*, 345.

16. Ibid., 671.

17. Ibid., 477–78.

18. Ibid., 478.

19. Ibid., 546.

20. Ibid., 542.

21. Cowart, "The Luddite Vision: *Mason & Dixon*," 348.

22. Pynchon, *Mason & Dixon*, 544, 545.

23. Ibid., 345.

24. Ibid., 304.

25. Ibid., 308.

26. Ibid., 306.

27. Ibid., 343.

28. Ibid., 347.

29. Ibid.

30. Ibid., 346.

31. Derrida, *Spectres de Marx*, passim.

32. Pynchon, *Mason & Dixon*, 348.

33. Ibid., 345.

34. Ibid., 571–72.

35. Ibid., 678, 678–79.

36. Clerc, *Mason & Dixon & Pynchon*, 138.

37. Ibid.

38. Pynchon, "The Heart's Eternal Vow," passim. The title in Spanish of García Márquez's novel is *El amor en los tiempos del cólera*.

39. The title in Spanish of García Márquez's novel is *Cien años de soledad*.

40. García Márquez, *El amor en los tiempos del cólera*, 191. "una selva enmarañada de árboles colosales. . . . La algarabía de los loros y el escándalo de los micos invisibles."

41. Ibid., 192–93. "viendo a los caimanes inmóviles asoleándose en los playones con las fauces abiertas para atrapar mariposas, viendo las bandadas de garzas asustadas que se alzaban de pronto en los pantanos, los manatíes que amamantaban sus crías con sus grandes tetas maternales y sorprendían a los pasajeros con sus llantos de mujer."

42. Ibid., 439. "la desforestación irracional había acabado con el río en cincuenta años: las calderas de los buques habían devorado la selva enmarañada de árboles colosales . . . los cazadores de pieles de las tenerías de Nueva Orleans habían exterminado los caimanes que se hacían los muertos con las fauces abiertas durante horas y horas en los barrancos de la orilla para sorprender a las mariposas, los loros con sus algarabías y los micos con sus gritos de locos se habían ido muriendo a medida que se les acababan las frondas, los manatíes de grandes tetas de madres que amamantaban a sus crías y lloraban con voces de mujer desolada en las playas eran una especie extinguida por las balas blindadas de los cazadores de placer."

43. Ibid., 438. "tuvo la impresión de que era un delta poblado de islas de arena."

44. Ibid., 188. "Los buques más antiguos habían sido fabricados en Cincinnati a mediados del siglo, con el modelo legendario de los que hacían el tráfico del Ohio y el Mississippi"; ibid., 439–40. "cazador de Carolina del Norte."

45. Pynchon, *Mason & Dixon*, 650.

46. Ibid., 681.

47. Latrobe, "The History of Mason and Dixon's Line; Contained in an Address," 37.

48. Pynchon, *Mason & Dixon*, 647.
49. Ibid., 677.
50. Ibid., 663.
51. Ibid., 692.
52. Ibid., 701.
53. Ibid., 712.
54. Ibid., 757.

Epilogue and Postscripts

1. Shelley, *Frankenstein*, vi–vii.
2. Pynchon, "Is It O.K. to Be a Luddite?" 45.
3. Shelley, *Frankenstein*, 84.
4. Ibid.
5. Ibid.
6. Ibid., 22.
7. Lepore, *The Name of War*, 185.
8. Ibid., 191.
9. Ibid., 193.
10. Ibid., 224.
11. Derrida, *Spectres de Marx*, passim.
12. Shelley, *Frankenstein*, 105.
13. Ibid.
14. The incomplete date is given in epistles that appear at the beginning and end of the novel on pages 1, 4, 7, 8, 11, 13, and 155.
15. The title of Todorov's text in French is *La conquête de l'Amérique*.
16. Howard, *The Conquest of America*, 41. The original French is in Todorov, *La conquête de l'Amérique*, 57. "Peut-on deviner à travers les notes de Colon, comment les Indiens, de leur côté, perçoivent les Espagnols? A peine. Ici encore, toute l'information est viciée par le fait que Colon a décidé de tout d'avance. . . . Il est possible, comme le dit Colon, qu'ils se soient demandé si ce n'étaient pas là des êtres d'origine divine ; ce qui expliquerait assez bien leur crainte initiale, et sa disparition devant le comportement bien humain des Espagnols."
17. Shelley, *Frankenstein*, 84.
18. Shakespeare, *Hamlet*, 64.
19. Gordon, *Ghostly Matters*, 22.
20. Pynchon, *Mason & Dixon*, 68.
21. Guthrie, "This Land Is Your Land," [originally unpublished stanza].

Bibliography

Bauer, Ralph. "Hemispheric Studies." *PMLA* 124, no. 1 (January 2009): 234–50.

Beverley, John. "The Margin at the Center: On Testimonio." In *The Real Thing: Testimonial Discourse and Latin America*, edited by Georg M. Gugelberger, 23–41. Durham, N.C.: Duke University Press, 1996.

L'abbé Brasseur de Bourbourg. *Popol Vuh: le livre sacré et les mythes de l'antiquité américaine*. Paris: Arthus Bertrand, 1861.

Burgos, Elizabeth. *Me llamo Rigoberta Menchú y así me nació la conciencia*. Barcelona: Seix Barral, 1983.

Cabeza de Vaca, Álvar Núñez. *His Account, His Life, and the Expedition of Pánfilo de Narváez*. Vol. 1, edited by Rolena Adorno and Patrick Charles Pautz. Lincoln: University of Nebraska Press, 1999.

de Certeau, Michel. *L'invention du quotidien*. Paris: Union Générale, 1980.

Chávez, Adrián Inés. *Pop Wuj (Libro del Tiempo o de Acontecimientos)*. Edición Guatemalteca. Quetzaltenango, Guatemala: Centro Editorial "Vile," 1978.

———. *Pop Wuj: Poema Mito-histórico Ki-ché*. Quetzaltenango, Guatemala: Centro de Estudios Mayas, TIMACH, 2001.

Chinchilla Aguilar, Ernesto. "Principales datos biográficos del licenciado Adrián Recinos." *Laureles a la memoria del licenciado en derecho Don Adrián Recinos*, edited by José Luis Reyes M., 45–47. Guatemala City: Tip. Nacional, 1969.

Christenson, Allen J. *Popol Vuh: The Sacred Book of the Maya*. Norman: University of Oklahoma Press, 2007.

Clerc, Charles. *Mason & Dixon & Pynchon*. Lanham, Md.: University Press of America, 2000.

[Columbus, Christopher]. *The Diario of Christopher Columbus's First Voyage to*

America 1492–1493, edited by Bartolomé de las Casas, transcribed and translated by Oliver Dunn and James E. Kelley, Jr. Norman: University of Oklahoma Press, 1989.

Conrad, Bryce. *Refiguring America: A Study of William Carlos Williams's* In the American Grain. Urbana: University of Illinois Press, 1990.

Cowart, David. "The Luddite Vision: *Mason & Dixon.*" *American Literature* 71, no. 2 (June 1999): 341–63.

Crosby, Alfred W., Jr. *The Columbian Exchange: Biological and Cultural Consequences of 1492.* [30th anniversary edition]. Westport, Conn.: Praeger, 2003.

Davies, J. M. "A Rafael Evita." Unpublished poem.

Defoe, Daniel. *Robinson Crusoe.* Harmondsworth, England: Penguin, 1965.

Derrida, Jacques. *Spectres de Marx: l'état de la dette, le travail du deuil et la nouvelle Internationale.* Paris: Galilée, 1993.

"Dixie." *The Barnhart Dictionary of Etymology,* edited by Robert K. Barnhart, 292. New York: H.W. Wilson, 1988.

Dosal, Paul J. *Power in Transition: The Rise of Guatemala's Industrial Oligarchy, 1871–1994.* Westport, Conn.: Praeger, 1995.

Evita, Leoncio. *Cuando los Combes luchaban.* Madrid: Consejo Superior de Investigaciones Científicas, 1953.

Fricke, David. "Top Ten 2000." *Rolling Stone* 858–859 (December 28, 2000—January 4, 2001): 106–8, 110, 113–14, 116–18.

Fryer, T. Bruce. "Aspectos políticos de Guinea Ecuatorial: Raíces hispánicas en África." *Afro-Hispanic Review* 19, no. 1 (Spring 2000): 3–10.

García Márquez, Gabriel. *El amor en los tiempos del cólera.* New York: Penguin, 1985.

———. *Conversaciones con Plinio Apuleyo Mendoza: el olor de la guayaba.* Bogotá: Oveja Negra, 1982.

Gilroy, Paul. *The Black Atlantic: Modernity and Double Consciousness.* Cambridge: Harvard University Press, 1993.

González Echegaray, Carlos. "[untitled prologue]." In Leoncio Evita, *Cuando los Combes luchaban,* 5–6. Madrid: Consejo Superior de Investigaciones Científicas, 1953.

———. "Prólogo a la 2ª edición." *Cuando los Combes luchaban* by Leoncio Evita, 2nd ed., 13–18. Madrid: Agencia Española de Cooperación Internacional, 1996.

Gordon, Avery F. *Ghostly Matters: Haunting and the Sociological Imagination.* Minneapolis: University of Minnesota Press, 1997.

Gruesz, Kirsten Silva. *Ambassadors of Culture: The Transamerican Origins of Latino Writing.* Princeton: Princeton University Press, 2002.

Guthrie, Woody. "This Land Is Your Land." *This Land Is Your Land: The Asch Recordings Vol. 1.* Smithsonian Folkways Records, 1997, version on track 14.

Herbert, Jean Loup. "Prólogo de la última edición a mimeógrafo." In *Kí-chè Zib: Escritura Kí-chè y otros temas* by Adrián I. Chávez, 2nd ed. [Guatemala?]: Alfil[?].

Herrera C., Adalberto. "Adrián Recinos." In "Poema a la memoria de don Adrián Recinos." *Laureles a la memoria del licenciado en derecho Don Adrián Recinos*, edited by José Luis Reyes M., 40–42. Guatemala City: Tip. Nacional, 1969.

Howard, Richard, translator of *The Conquest of America: The Question of the Other* by Tzvetan Todorov. New York: Harper & Row, 1984.

Hulme, Peter. *Colonial Encounters: Europe and the Native Caribbean, 1492–1797*. London: Methuen, 1986.

Knopfler, Mark. "Sailing to Philadelphia." In *Sailing to Philadelphia*. London: Mercury Records, 2000.

Kutzinski, Vera M. *Against the American Grain: Myth and History in William Carlos Williams, Jay Wright, and Nicolás Guillén*. Baltimore: Johns Hopkins University Press, 1987.

Las Casas, Bartolomé de. *Brevísima relación de la destruición de las Indias*. Madrid: Cátedra, 1996.

Latrobe, John H. B. "The History of Mason and Dixon's Line; Contained in an Address." Oakland, Del.: Historical Society of Pennsylvania, 1882.

Lepore, Jill. *The Name of War: King Philip's War and the Origins of American Identity*. New York: Alfred A. Knopf, 1998.

Lionnet, Françoise and Shu-mei Shih, editors of *Minor Transnationalism*. Durham, N.C.: Duke University Press, 2005.

Lomas, Laura. *Translating Empire: José Martí, Migrant Latino Subjects, and American Modernities*. Durham, N.C.: Duke University Press, 2008.

Maass, Peter. "A Touch of Crude." *Mother Jones* 30, no. 1 (January–February 2005): 48–53, 86, 88–89.

Maddox, James H., Jr. "Interpreter Crusoe." *English Literary History*, 51 no. 1 (Spring 1984): 33–52.

Martí, José. "Nuestra América." In *Nuestra América*, 26–33. Venezuela: Biblioteca Ayacucho, 1977.

Marzán, Julio. *The Spanish American Roots of William Carlos Williams*. Austin: University of Texas Press, 1994.

Mbomio Bacheng, Joaquín. "Leoncio Evita o *Cuando los Combes luchaban*: Una obra trascendental." *Afro-Hispanic Review* 19, no. 1 (Spring 2000): 72–78.

McHale, Brian. "Mason & Dixon in the Zone, or, A Brief Poetics of Pynchon-Space." *Pynchon and Mason & Dixon*, edited by Brooke Horvath and Irving Malin, 43–62. Newark: University of Delaware Press, 2000.

Menchú, Rigoberta. *See Burgos, Elizabeth*.

Metherd, Molly. "The Americanization of Christopher Columbus in the Works of William Carlos Williams and Alejo Carpentier." In *A Twice-Told Tale: Reinventing the Encounter in Iberian/Iberian American Literature and Film*, edited by Santiago Juan-Navarro and Theodore Robert Young, 227–49. Newark: University of Delaware Press, 2001.

Miampika, Landry-Wilfrid. "Plaidoirie équato-guinéenne: chronique d'une littérature émergente." *Notre Librairie: Revue des littératures du Sud*. 138–139 (Septembre 1999–Mars 2000): 14–17.

Moreiras, Alberto. "The Aura of Testimonio." In *The Real Thing: Testimonial Discourse and Latin America*, edited by Georg M. Gugelberger, 192–224. Durham, N.C.: Duke University Press, 1996:

Ndongo-Bidyogo, Donato. *Historia y tragedia de Guinea Ecuatorial*. Madrid: Cambio 16, 1977.

———. "Leoncio Evita, o el nacimiento de la literatura guineana." In *Cuando los Combes luchaban* by Leoncio Evita, 2nd ed., 23–32. Madrid: Agencia Española de Cooperación Internacional, 1996.

———. "La literatura moderna hispanófona en Guinea Ecuatorial." *Afro-Hispanic Review*. 19, no. 1 (Spring 2000): 39–44.

Ngom, Mbare. "Leoncio Evita Enoy." In *Diálogos con Guinea: panorama de la literatura guineoecuatoriana de expresión castellana a través de sus protagonistas*, 31–36. Madrid: Labrys 54, 1996.

———. "La literatura africana de expresión castellana: la creación literaria en Guinea Ecuatorial." *Hispania* 76 (September 1993): 410–18.

———. "Postcolonial Hispanic African Children's Literature." In *Critical Perspectives on Postcolonial African Children's and Young Adult Literature*, edited by Meena Khorana, 57–67. Westport, Conn.: Greenwood, 1998.

Nkogo Ondó, Eugenio. "La Guinea Ecuatorial: Reminiscencia histórica, experiencia de las luces y de las sombras de un proyecto político." http://www.hofstra.edu/pdf/Community/culctr/culctr_guinea040209_IXAondo.pdf

———. *Personal communication*: email of 9 April 2009.

Novak, Maximillian E. *Defoe and the Nature of Man*. London: Oxford University Press, 1963.

Olson, Julius E. and Edward Gaylord Bourne, editors of *The Northmen Columbus and Cabot: 985–1503*. New York: Charles Scribner's Sons, 1906.

Onomo-Abena, S. "Sujeto cultural colonial y producción literaria en Guinea Ecuatorial. Lectura sociocrítica del prólogo de *Cuando los Combes luchaban* (1953) de Leoncio Evita." *EPOS* 18 (2002): 215–29.

Ortega, Julio. *Transatlantic Translations: Dialogues in Latin American Literature*, translated by Philip Derbyshire. London: Reaktion, 2006.

Pendi, Augusto Iyanga. "Breve presentación." In Leoncio Evita. *Cuando los Combes luchaban*. 2nd ed., 19–22. Madrid: Agencia Española de Cooperación Internacional, 1996.

Popol Wuj: pa K'iche' Chi' ch'ab'al. Q'axel Tizj: Gaspar Tambriz Gómez. Guatemala, Guatemala: Academia de las Lenguas Mayas de Guatemala, 1998.

Pratt, Mary Louise. *Imperial Eyes: Travel Writing and Transculturation*, 2nd ed. New York: Routledge, 2008.

Pynchon, Thomas. "The Heart's Eternal Vow." *New York Times*. April 10, 1988, late city final edition, section 7: 1+.

———. "Is It O.K. to Be a Luddite?" In *The New Romanticism: A Collection of Critical Essays*, edited by Eberhard Alsen, 41–49. New York: Garland, 2000.

———. *Mason & Dixon*. New York: Henry Holt, 1997.

Raynaud, Georges. *Les dieux, les héros et les hommes de l'ancien Guatémala d'après le Livre du Conseil*. Paris: Ernest Leroux, 1925.

Recinos, Adrián. "Preface." In *Popol Vuh: The Sacred Book of the Ancient Quiché Maya*, translated by Delia Goetz and Sylvanus G. Morley from the translation by Adrián Recinos, xi–xiv. Norman: University of Oklahoma Press, 1950.

———. translator of *El Popol Vuh: las antiguas historias del Quiché*, 4th ed. Costa Rica: Editorial Universitaria Centroamericana, 1975.

Rendall, Steven F., translator of *The Practice of Everyday Life* by Michel de Certeau. Berkeley: University of California Press, 1984.

Rodríguez Beteta, Virgilio. "Adrián Recinos (Una pequeña biografía)." In *Laureles a la memoria del licenciado en derecho Don Adrián Recinos*, edited by José Luis Reyes M., 102–14. Guatemala City: Tip. Nacional, 1969.

Rummell, Kathryn. "Defoe and the Black Legend: The Spanish Stereotype in *A New Voyage Round the World*." *Rocky Mountain Review of Language and Literature* 52, no. 2 (1998): 13–28.

Sarmiento, Domingo F. *Viajes por Europa, Africa i América, 1845–1847*, 2nd ed, edited by Javier Fernández. Nanterre, France: ALLCA XX; Madrid: Fondo de Cultura Económica, 1996.

Schmidt-Nowara, Chris. "'This Rotting Corpse': Spain between the Black Atlantic and the Black Legend." *Arizona Journal of Hispanic Cultural Studies* 5 (2001): 149–60.

Seed, David. "Mapping the Course of Empire in the New World." In *Pynchon and Mason & Dixon*, edited by Brooke Horvath and Irving Malin, 84–99. Newark: University of Delaware Press, 2000.

Shakespeare, William. *Hamlet*. New York: New American Library, 1963.

Shelley, Mary. *Frankenstein*. New York: Dover, 1994.

Sommer, Doris. "No secrets." In *The Real Thing: Testimonial Discourse and Latin America*, edited by Georg M. Gugelberger, 130–57. Durham, N.C.: Duke University Press, 1996.

Sundiata, Ibrahim K. *Equatorial Guinea: Colonialism, State Terror and the Search for Stability*. Boulder, Colo.: Westview Press, 1990.

Taylor, Diana. *The Archive and the Repertoire: Performing Cultural Memory in the Americas*. Durham, N.C.: Duke University Press, 2003.

Tedlock, Dennis, translator of *Popol Vuh: The Definitive Edition of the Mayan Book of the Dawn of Life and the Glories of Gods and Kings*. New York: Simon & Schuster, 1985.

———. translator of *Popol Vuh: The Definitive Edition of the Mayan Book of the*

Dawn of Life and the Glories of Gods and Kings, revised ed. New York: Simon & Schuster, 1996.

Todorov, Tzvetan. *La conquête de l'Amérique: la question de l'autre*. Paris: Seuil, 1982.

Tofiño-Quesada, Ignacio. "Spanish Orientalism: Uses of the Past in Spain's Colonization in Africa." *Comparative Studies of South Asia, Africa and the Middle East* 23, no. 1–2 (2003): 141–48.

Weaver-Hightower, Rebecca. *Empire Islands: Castaways, Cannibals, and Fantasies of Conquest*. Minneapolis: University of Minnesota Press, 2007.

Wenner, Jann S. "Mark Knopfler: Sailing to Philadelphia." *Rolling Stone* 858–59 (December 28, 2000—January 4, 2001): 110.

Wheeler, Roxann. "'My Savage,' 'My Man': Racial Multiplicity in *Robinson Crusoe*." *ELH* 62, no. 4 (Winter 1995): 821–61.

Whitman, Walt. "Starting from Paumanok." In *Leaves of Grass*, 18–29. Philadelphia: Rees Welsh, 1882.

Williams, William Carlos. *In the American Grain*. New York: New Directions, 1933.

———. *The Autobiography of William Carlos Williams*. New York: Random House, 1951.

Zamora, Margaret. *Reading Columbus*. Berkeley: University of California Press, 1993.

Zelnick, Stephen. "Ideology as Narrative: Critical Approaches to *Robinson Crusoe*." *Bucknell Review*. 27, no. 1 (1982): 79–101.

Index

1492, 3, 7–8, 16, 19, 22–25, 29, 32, 37, 65, 91, 114, 133; (January), 24; (October 12), 16, 25, 32–33, 37, 93; (October 14), 25; (October 15), 28; (October 21), 28; (October 28), 29; (October 29), 29; (November 1), 29; (November 15), 29; (November 17), 29; (November 27), 30; (November 28), 29; (November 29), 29; (November 30), 29; (December 3), 30; (December 6), 31; (December 7), 31; (December 12), 31; (December 13), 31; (December 15), 31; (December 16), 37; (December 26), 32, 38

1493, 22–23, 31, 38, 135; (January 12), 31; (January 13), 38–39, 135; (January 14), 39; (January 15), 39; (January 16), 39; (February), 22

1898, 17, 90–92, 94, 100–101, 105, 108, 111, 114–16

aborigine/aboriginal(ity), 5, 8, 16–17, 20–21, 23, 28–33, 37–39, 42, 52, 57, 59, 61, 72, 78–79, 96, 98–99, 109, 122, 124–25, 130–35, 141–44; lands(cape), 91, 133. *See also* indigene/indigenous

absence(s), 1–9, 14–18, 20, 116; aboriginal, 17, 57, 59, 144; and *In the American Grain*, 33–35; contestatory, 21, 60, 67; and the diary of Columbus, 16, 23–25, 28, 30, 37, 40; and *Frankenstein*, 141,

144; indigenous, 20, 30, 33–35, 39, 42, 52, 61, 134, 142–43; and *Love in the Time of Cholera*, 133; and *Mason & Dixon*, 121–22, 124, 131, 133–34; and Menchú, 57–60; and *Metamora*, 142–43; (re)production of, 1–2, 5, 83, 131; as resistance, 5, 15; and *Robinson Crusoe*, 62–71, 73–75, 77–79, 83; and the *Popol Vuh*, 5, 17, 41–43, 47, 51, 54–56; scriptural, 56; and "Starting from Paumanok," 20; and *A Very Short Account of the Destruction of the Indies*, 31; and *When the Combes Fought*, 17, 90, 92, 105, 115–16

absent presence(s), 6–8, 10–11, 14, 20–21, 56, 61, 75, 83, 97, 118, 123, 131–32, 139, 145

absented, 6, 16, 52, 64, 74, 130, 144; absenting, 2, 4, 19, 23, 27–31, 37–38, 42–43, 50, 52, 54, 56, 59–60, 80, 83, 130, 134, 136, 142–43, 145

Academy of the Mayan Languages of Guatemala, 45

Account (of Cabeza de Vaca), 17–18, 79–81. *See also* Cabeza de Vaca, Álvar Núñez

actor(s), 4, 15, 26, 30, 50, 59, 77, 98, 123

Adam, 70–71, 74, 79, 87, 143

Africa, 13, 17, 19, 62, 64–65, 69, 72, 75, 77, 85, 87–88, 90, 92–95, 98–101, 104–5, 108, 113, 115–17, 128; West Africa, 14, 17, 65, 102, 111, 115–16, 132

Union (during the United States Civil
War), 119
United Kingdom, 102. *See also* Britain
United Nations, 105
United States (of America), 10–11, 13–14,
17, 19–20, 36, 48–49, 57, 63, 90–92, 94,
98–99, 102, 108, 111–13, 115–16, 118–20,
123, 126, 139–42
Utatlan, 54

vanish(ed/ing), 1, 8, 23–25, 27, 29, 31, 37,
39, 42–44, 80–81, 87, 130, 134, 141–42
*A Very Short Account of the Destruction of
the Indies*, 31–32, 82–83. *See also* Las
Casas, Bartolomé de
Villa, Pancho, 11
Virtual Americas, 12
visible, 3–5, 9, 26, 30, 45, 54–55, 59, 61,
75, 81, 116, 134, 147; continent, 70–71;
invisibility, 39, 43, 83

Washington, George, 10
Washington (capital), 48, 92, 103
Waterloo, 140
Weaver-Hightower, Rebecca, 68
Wenner, Jann, 121
Western Sahara, 93, 158n4
Wheeler, Roxann, 66, 81, 88

When the Combes Fought, 5, 11, 14, 17, 64,
90, 92, 94–116, 118, 122, 124, 128; Adonis,
101; Carlos, 100–1, 105–8, 112, 122, 134;
Garrido, Martín, 100–1, 105–8, 111–12,
122, 126–27, 134, 136; Miss Leona, 98,
106–8, 113; Penda, 106, 112–14, 162n87;
Roku (king), 98–101, 105, 112, 115;
Stephen, John, 98–100, 105–8, 111–12,
124, 127, 136; Vilangua, 99–100, 106–8,
112–16, 128. *See also* Evita, Leoncio
Whitman, Walt, 10, 19–20, 36, 61, 102,
120, 131
Williams, William Carlos, 10, 16–17,
33–37, 128; autobiography, 37; family,
37. *See also In the American Grain*;
"The Discovery of the Indies"
Williamsburg, 130
witness(es/ed), 6–7, 16, 24, 29–30, 37, 76,
102, 116, 141
The Woman Warrior, 9
World War II, 48

Xela, 46
Ximénez, Francisco, 41–42, 44–51, 56,
58–59, 62, 136. *See also Popol Vuh*

Zamora, Margaret, 22, 24
Zelnick, Stephen, 78